PENGUIN BOOKS
SELF-CONSCIOUSNESS

John Updike was born in 1932 in Shillington, Pennsylvania. He attended Shillington High School, Harvard College and the Ruskin School of Drawing and Fine Art at Oxford, where he spent a year on a Knox Fellowship. From 1955 to 1957 he was a member of the staff of the *New Yorker*, to which he has contributed short stories, essays and poems. Since 1957 he has lived in Massachusetts as a freelance writer. His novels include *The Poorhouse Fair*, *Rabbit, Run*, *The Centaur*, *Of the Farm*, *Couples*, *Rabbit Redux*, *A Month of Sundays*, *Marry Me*, *The Coup*, *Rabbit Is Rich*, winner of the 1982 Pulitzer Prize for Fiction, *The Witches of Eastwick*, recently made into a major feature film, *Roger's Version* and *S*. He has also published many volumes of short stories: *The Same Door*, *Pigeon Feathers*, *The Music School*, *Museums and Women*, *Bech: A Book*, *Bech Is Back*, *Your Lover Just Called* (published in America as *Too Far to Go*), *Problems* and *Trust Me*; books of poetry including *Hoping for Hoopoe*, *Telephone Poles*, *Tossing and Turning* and the Penguin selection of his poetry entitled *Seventy Poems*; as well as three collections of essays and criticism, *Picked-up Pieces*, *Hugging the Shore* and *Assorted Prose*.

JOHN UPDIKE

SELF-CONSCIOUSNESS

Memoirs

PENGUIN BOOKS

PENGUIN BOOKS

Published by the Penguin Group
27 Wrights Lane, London W8 5TZ, England
Viking Penguin Inc., 40 West 23rd Street, New York, New York 10010, USA
Penguin Books Australia Ltd, Ringwood, Victoria, Australia
Penguin Books Canada Ltd, 2801 John Street, Markham, Ontario, Canada L3R 1B4
Penguin Books (NZ) Ltd, 182–190 Wairau Road, Auckland 10, New Zealand

Penguin Books Ltd, Registered Offices: Harmondsworth, Middlesex, England

First published in Great Britain by André Deutsch 1989
Published in Penguin Books 1990
1 3 5 7 9 10 8 6 4 2

Grateful acknowledgment is made to the following for permission to reprint previously published material: *Ched Music Corporation*, *Shapiro Bernstein & Company Inc.*, and *The Welk Music Group*: Excerpt from "The Old Lamplighter" by Charles Tobias and Nat Simon. Copyright 1946 by Shapiro, Bernstein & Company Inc. Copyright renewed and assigned to Harry von Tilzer Music Publishing Company (c/o The Welk Music Group, Santa Monica, CA 90401) and Ched Music Corporation. International copyright secured. All rights reserved. Used by permission. *Marlong Music Corporation* and *Bourne Company*: Excerpt from "All of Me", words and music by Seymour Simons and Gerald Marks. Copyright by Marlong Music Corporation, New York City; Copyright 1931 by Bourne Company. International copyright secured. All rights reserved. Used by permission. *Warner/Chappel Music Inc.*: Excerpt from "Bidin' My Time" by George and Ira Gershwin. Copyright 1930 by WB Music Corporation. (Renewed.) All rights reserved. Used by permission. "Getting the Words Out" first appeared in *Granta*, and a small section in *Boston Review*. Much of "On Not Being a Dove" appeared in *Commentary*.

Printed and bound in Great Britain by
Cox and Wyman Ltd, Reading, Berks

To my grandsons
John Anoff Cobblah *and*
Michael Kwame Ntiri Cobblah

We are persuaded that a thread runs through all things: all worlds are strung on it, as beads: and men, and events, and life, come to us, only because of that thread.

Emerson, "Montaigne; or, The Skeptic"

I find myself saying briefly and prosaically that it is much more important to be oneself than anything else.

Virginia Woolf, "A Room of One's Own"

Of all that might be omitted in thinking, the worst was to omit your own being.

Saul Bellow, "What Kind of Day Did You Have?"

Gratia Dei sum quod sum.

Epitaph of Bishop West of Ely, in Ely Cathedral

Contents

Foreword

Shortly before the first of these personal essays was composed (but several years after the soft spring night in Shillington that it describes) I was told, perhaps in jest, of someone wanting to write my biography – to take my life, my lode of ore and heap of memories, from me! The idea seemed so repulsive that I was stimulated to put down, always with some natural hesitation and distaste, these elements of an autobiography. They record what seems to me important about my own life, and try to treat this life, this massive datum which happens to be mine, as a specimen life, representative in its odd uniqueness of all the oddly unique lives in this world. A mode of impersonal egoism was my aim: an attempt to touch honestly upon the central veins, with a scientific dispassion and curiosity. The veins had been tapped, of course – the lode mined – in over thirty years' worth of prose and poetry; and where an especially striking or naked parallel in my other work occurred to me, I have quoted it, as a footnote. But merciful forgetfulness has no doubt hidden many other echoes from me, as well as eroded the raw material of autobiography into shapes scarcely less imaginary, though less final, than those of fiction. Were I to make this attempt five or ten years from now, it would be different; the medical history of the second chapter, for instance, changed after this account appeared in *The New Yorker* in September of 1985, and has accordingly been adjusted. A life-view by the living can only be provisional. Perspectives are altered by the fact of being drawn; description solidifies the past and creates a gravitational body that wasn't there before. A background of dark matter – all that is not said – remains, buzzing.

I am grateful to numerous Shillingtonians especially my S.H.S. classmate Barry Nelson, for corrections and additions of detail, and to the daughter of "Spooky" Adams for sending me a fragile old pale-green pass to the Shillington Movie Theatre, circa 1942. My mother and my first cousins Jean Kramer-Updike and Virginia Updike Herndon have generously supplied facts and letters pertaining to Hartley Updike and his family. Nan Bright and her reference department at the Free Public Library in Trenton, New Jersey, were kind and helpful beyond the call of duty. To all the people, living and dead, who figure in these memoirs, I tender my affection and, where needed, apologies.

J.U.

I

A Soft Spring Night
in Shillington

Had not my twenty-five-year-old daughter undertipped the airline porter in Boston, our luggage might have shown upon the carrousel in Allentown that April afternoon in 1980, and I would not have spent an evening walking the sidewalks of Shillington, Pennsylvania, searching for the meaning of my existence, as once I had scanned those same sidewalks for lost pennies.

The idea of lost luggage has been flavored for me with the terrible, the void, ever since William Maxwell gently said to me on our first acquaintance, in 1954, when I, newly a Harvard graduate and *New Yorker* contributor, was about to embark for England with my slightly pregnant wife: "People think lost luggage is just like death. It isn't." The words were meant to be comforting, perhaps in response to some nervously expressed worry of my own; but they had an opposite, disquieting effect. From early adolescence on, I had longed to get where now, for a brief interview, I was: inside *The New Yorker*'s offices. And almost the first words spoken to me, with a certain stoic gaiety that made clear I had definitely left behind me the Christian precincts of Berks County, concerned death. I was to lose my luggage a number of times in the peripatetic future ahead: in 1978 my folding suit bag vanished between Rome and Dubrovnik and I was obliged to parade through Yugoslavia, Greece, and Israel in the rumpled denim leisure suit meant to be my airplane pajamas, and was ridiculed for my sartorial gaucherie in the Jerusalem *Post*; in 1980, my big yellow suitcase was mistakenly grabbed by somebody from Long Island (I know because his similar suitcase then became, uselessly and infuriatingly, mine) in

Kennedy Airport and so I had to visit the Yanomamö Indians in southern Venezuela wearing ill-fitting safari clothes borrowed from the American Ambassador. In Allentown, our two bags just weren't on the carrousel, though it went round and round, and at last there seemed nothing to do but turn away, with my daughter and my widowed mother, and drive the forty miles south to where my mother lived and, indeed, still lives, in a rural area called – embarrassingly, at least to me – Plowville.

How circumstantial reality is! Facts are like the individual letters, with their spikes and loops and thorns, that make up words: eventually they hurt our eyes, and we long to take a bath, to rake the lawn, to look at the sea. Where was my wife? Also on a family trip, in Florida, with her nine-year-old son by a former marriage. Why did I leave it to my daughter by a former marriage, the matured fruit of that slight pregnancy twenty-six years before, to check in at the airport? I was parking the car; we were in a rush, because we were late, in turn because since childhood I have been a late sleeper, preferring to let others get the world in order before I descend to it – a mode of efficiency, actually, that seems the opposite. Why (if she did) did my daughter botch this small assignment? Because my first wife and I had raised our children to be innocents, being innocents ourselves and thinking it a nice aristocratic thing to be. Guilt at having left, after twenty-one years of marriage, this other innocent tinges my relations with my four children and makes for a lot of bumbling, of the lost-luggage sort.

In my mother's house – an old sandstone farmhouse, the very one in which she was born in 1904, and which had been reacquired four decades later, in 1945, when the war had put a little money into our pockets and boldness into our hearts – the telephone rang, at six-thirty. A voice from Allentown, brightly female, with that flirtatious-seeming drag of a Pennsylvania accent which after all these years away still strikes me as exactly the right note, announced that the bags were at the airport; they had come in on the next flight.

We were just walking out the door. We had eaten an early supper and planned to see *Being There*, starring Peter Sellers as Chance, at the movie theatre in Shillington, eleven miles away. Rather than disappoint my two female companions and, furthermore, frustrate this third female, on whom our luggage weighed as heavily as a bad conscience and who was offering to bring it to us personally, I improvised this scheme: I, who had already seen *Being There*, would take my mother and daughter to the movie as planned, and then I would be there, under the movie marquee, waiting for the girl from the Allentown airport, with the two suitcases. Her boyfriend lived in the Reading area, she said, and would be driving her.

The plan was agreed to on all sides. The theatre location was described over the phone. The girl thought her boyfriend knew where it was anyway. Then the eleven miles to Shillington were navigated and my two kin were tucked into the movie theatre, which, on this drizzly Thursday night, had attracted no line. The last latecomer bought the last tardy ticket, and I stood alone beneath the marquee. The thinnest of mists drifted across the sulphurous streetlights of Lancaster Avenue and gave the passing tires an adhesive, plaintive sound. The girl from Allentown couldn't be here for another hour at best. I had nothing to do, here at the center of my earthly being.

Dasein. The first mystery that confronts us is "Why me?" The next is "Why here?" Shillington was my *here*. I had been born here, or, rather, been brought back to it from the Reading Hospital, which was located in West Reading. For thirteen years I had lived in the same house on Philadelphia Avenue, number 117. After moving eleven miles away, with my family's quixotic recapture of my mother's birthplace, I still returned to the town for school and social life. Shillington, I can see now, is a typical town of the region, of a piece with Kenhorst and Grille and West Reading and Mount

3

Penn, which had once seemed remote and wildly different places. (An oddity of the area is that the towns call themselves boroughs; in my childhood the chief elected official bore the ancient title of burgess, where now there seems to be both a "mayor" and a "borough manager.") The towns are snug, and red and green in tint. They began as "string-towns" – a few farmhouses, with perhaps a tavern and a feed mill, strung along the road from, in Shillington's case, Reading to Lancaster. The houses were built first of sandstone or limestone and then of brick. The gaps between them gradually filled in (and are still filling in) and then tracts of open acreage back from the road succumbed to development, to rectilinear streets and close-packed rows of semi-detached brick dwellings on thin strips of land that back onto an alley. Garages line the alleys; porches and retaining walls line the streets. The streets are high-crowned and drain well. My grandfather, when his fortunes took a disagreeable turn after his moving to Shillington in the Twenties, joined the town work crews that laid out much of the tidy section north of Lancaster Avenue called Speedway, on the site of an old race track.

I stood facing south. Across the street from the Shillington Movie Theatre stood a yellow brick building with square brick pillars, a second-story porch, and an odd double dormer on top, a kind of cupola; the first story's left side once held Stephens' Luncheonette, where I had smoked and posed and day-dreamed for hours after school, and the right side had been the Shillington Post Office, where as a child I had solemnly traded pennies for war stamps, amid a cacophony of anti-Axis posters. Now the left half of this building was a florist's shop, the right a firm mysteriously called Admixtures, Inc. The post office had moved to a building of its own, on Liberty Street next to Grace Lutheran Church; the Stephenses had moved away while I was in college. They had been kind to me and I, I felt when they were no longer there, not kind to them. I tried to be funny at their expense, calling Mrs Stephens "Gert" when her nickname was "Boo" (for Beulah), and I once stole a candy bar from the counter, or at least watched another boy do it without crying "Thief!" Half the high school, it seemed, came there at twenty past three, when the last class was let out; but then within an hour the teen-agers who lived in Shillington would have walked home and those who lived in Adamstown climbed into their cars and driven home, leaving me with Walt Stephens and the pinball machine.

I waited hours, sometimes, for my father, who taught at the high school and never went back to the farm before he had to. He was the only adult except Walt and Boo I ever noticed in Stephens', and he came in only to take me away, and he never penetrated past the region of the soda fountain, into the booth area, where the cigarette smoke and adolescent intrigue were thickest. Walt was totally bald and had a way of doing hot dogs – cutting them the long way and putting the butterfly shape flat-side-down on the griddle and then serving it in a hamburger roll with the ends sticking out – that was peculiar to him and delicious. But then to teen-age hunger many things are delicious. Cigarettes, for example, were delicious: the sleek cellophane-wrapped rectitude of the pack, the suave tapping out of a single "weed," the chalky, rasping initial inhale, the little crumbs to be picked from the lower lip without breaking conversational stride, the airy pluming gesturingness of it all. Time itself – the time spent idling in Stephens', the time spent anywhere in Shillington – was delicious.

The center of town lay a block to my right, and I walked there. The night was drier now, and warm, with a heedless overflowing pre-summer warmth not felt in New England until May. Where the movie house now stood there had been a long vacant lot, strangely vacant in the center of town; here traveling fairs had set up their stalls and rides, in the days when the Shillington Theatre, under the proprietorship of tall, bald (like Walt Stephens, but with a different, less tapered dome to his skull), mild-mannered Mr Shverha, had been situated a half-block up New Holland Avenue. Nothing was very far from the central, five-sided corner where New Holland Avenue, Philadelphia Avenue, East Lancaster Avenue, Liberty Street, and West Lancaster Avenue met and still meet. On the five corners, beginning with the one where I stood, had been Kindt's Funeral Home, the Shillington Town Hall and its prettily planted grounds, Ibach & Bixler's Restaurant, Ibach's (no relation) Drug Store, and, across Lancaster Avenue from Ibach's – at this crossing I had once been struck by a car on the way to Sunday school and dragged some feet on the bumper while stubbornly clutching my nickel contribution – a curious little stone hut where grown-ups paid their electric bills. This quaint structure, long since replaced by a drive-in bank, was intertwined in my childish mind with German fairy tales, with spidery illustrations in books that beckoned me to look deep into the past, into mankind's communal memory, abysmally deeper than my own. Illustrations affected me more strongly than reality; a picture of falling snow, for example, whether in black-and-white line drawing or blurry four-color reproduction, moves me more than any actual storm. An ideal world was projected by my childish yearning onto commercial Christmas art, and it lies forever embedded there. Real Christmases, in that part of the world, were usually bare of snow – bleak, brown days, such as are depicted in the paintings of Andrew Wyeth.

The lights above Lancaster Avenue had since my childhood become harder, higher, and yellower in tint. The towering horse-chestnut trees shading this corner as I remembered it had been years ago cut down. I crossed Liberty Street, a block up from the Lutheran church whose Sunday school I had been heading toward on the storied day when I was hit by the car. The woman driving had felt terrible, and visited me at home, where I languished for a week with a lapful of candy bars and a bandage around my head. In the police car on the way to the doctor, I pleaded that I would not do it again and should not be put in jail. In one of those birdlike panics of childhood I had ignored Carl Leh's clear signals at the crossing and darted into the traffic. Carl belonged to the three-man Shillington police force, of which the chief was a short gloomy man called "Spooky" (pronounced "Spoogy" in the local accent; his real name was Clifford) Adams and the third member Sam Reich, who seemed to us children fabulously fat. Carl was the only one of the three who seemed capable of violence in our defense; he had been very brave, the children's network had it, once upon a time, in a shootout. Shootouts in Shillington were rare, though gunshops were not. There was a sadness to Carl, however; he seemed to live alone in the back of the building that held the old post office, where fire escapes showed, and I associate the purplish glistening cinders of that bumpy little alley there with his authority. He paid no attention to my sobs and pleas. Only years later could I see the incident from his standpoint: I was a five-year-old child, irresponsible, and his concern was not with my guilt but with my physical condition purely.

Now I walked west, feeling tall, on the north side of Lancaster Avenue. Though for seven years I had walked this route to elementary school, there were houses in this block I knew nothing about – for example, a row of three, indentical, of orange brick, with white-painted porches and trim. It was common, in pre-air-conditioning days, to intensify the cool of the deep porches of Shillington with awnings, usually green; these houses still wore on their pillars and fasciae the attached hardware needed to hook up an awning, but painted over, disused, like some religious custom whose significance has been forgotten. Abbott's Printing and Copycenter, one of them now was. Farther on, there had been an ice-cream parlor – a luncheonette quite lacking, because of its location near the elementary school, the high-school sexiness of Stephens'. Now it was a bar, called in the fashion of our times a pub. Across North Miller Street had stood LaRue's Hardware

Store; its spiky ranks of large gardening tools and its musty agricultural scents of seed and feed had given way, I could see, to an interior of carpeting samples, marketed under some name sadly other than LaRue.

A few housefronts farther on, what had been Henry's Variety Store in the 1940s was still a variety store, with the same narrow flight of cement steps going up to the door beside a big display window. Did children still marvel within as the holidays wheeled past in a slow pinwheel galaxy of altering candies, cards, and artifacts, of back-to-school tablets, footballs, Halloween masks,* pumpkins, turkeys, pine trees, tinsel, wrappings, reindeer, Santas, and stars, and then the noisemakers and conical hats of New Year's celebration, and Valentines and cherries as the days of short February brightened, and then shamrocks, painted eggs, baseballs, flags, and firecrackers? There were cases of such bygone candy as coconut strips striped like bacon and belts of licorice with punch-out animals and imitation watermelon slices and chewy gumdrop sombreros. I loved the orderliness with which these things for sale were all arranged. Stacked squarish things excited me – magazines, and Big Little Books tucked in, fat spines up, beneath the skinny paper-doll coloring books, and box-shaped art erasers with a faint silky powder on them almost like Turkish delight. I was a devotee of packaging, and bought for the four grown-ups of my family (my parents, my

---

* "On the way to school, walking down Lancaster Avenue, we passed Henry's, a variety store where we bought punch-out licorice belts and tablets with Edward G. Robinson and Hedy Lamarr smiling on the cover. In October, Halloween masks appeared, hung on wire clotheslines. Hanging limp, these faces of Chinamen and pirates and witches were distorted, and, thickly clustered and rustling against each other, they seemed more frightening masking empty air than they did mounted on the heads of my friends – which was frightening enough. It is strange how fear resists the attacks of reason, how you can know with absolute certainty that it is only Mark Wenrich or Jimmy Trexler whose eyes are moving so weirdly in those almond-shaped holes, and yet still be frightened. I abhorred that effect of double eyes a mask gives; it was as bad as seeing a person's mouth move upside down." – "The Dogwood Tree" (1960)

mother's parents) one Depression or wartime Christmas a little squarish silver-papered book of Life Savers, ten flavors packaged in two thick pages of cylinders labelled Butter Rum, Wild Cherry, Wint-O-Green . . . a book you could suck and eat! A fat book for all to share, like the Bible. In Henry's Variety Store life's full promise and extent were indicated: a single omnipresent manufacturer-God seemed to be showing us a fraction of His face, His plenty, and leading us with our little purchases up the spiral staircase of years. Department stores, with their escalators and clouds of perfume and ranks of nylon lingerie, were like Heaven itself. I retain from earliest childhood a vision of my mother, young and slim, against a background of swagged fabrics like a glamorized movie star, from the days when she worked as a salegirl in the drapes department of Reading's great emporium, Pomeroy's, and I would visit her there, in that tall cave of stuffs. In Pomeroy's my mother appeared as I very much wanted her to appear – at one with the thriving world. Tapping away in the front bedroom at her unpublished stories, tending our hedged-in yard and garden, she seemed to me to be hiding from the global bustle led by Uncle Sam and Santa Claus.

Next to Henry's had been Gerhard's camera shop, where my mother, with-it enough in this respect, would bring a roll of the film she had laboriously exposed, pacing off the distances, gazing down into the prism-shaped viewer, guessing at the light. Without those accumulating photographs my past would have vanished, year after year. Instead, it accumulated, loose in a set of shoeboxes, in no order, and because of its randomness ever fresh, ever stunning: shuffled windows into a sunlit abyss. Though this block of Lancaster Avenue was mostly businesses, the buildings were irregularly set back from the sidewalk, and there was a shagginess, a confusion of weeds and shrubs, that slightly disturbed me. The one story I ever managed to write about elementary school ended here, as I imagined it, in this overgrown area around Henry's, where a recognition of sex pounced out upon the naïve fifth-grade hero and the less naïve children slid by like the tail of an alligator.

Beyond Gerhard's, in the war, a "rec hall" had been established where Artie Shaw's "Begin the Beguine" soared up out of the jukebox and Betty Zimmerman tried to teach me how to dance. I felt wooden, holding her; how to manage the double consciousness, of my own body and feet and of my willing partner's, is a problem I never completely solved. Lacking brothers and sisters, I was shy and clumsy in the give and take and push and pull of human interchange. That slight roughness, that certainty of contact we ask for from others, was hard for me to administer; I either fled, or was cruel. Taking a body entrusted to my arms and moving it across the floor amid a feverish welter of stimulations – the big-band music, the lights, the hand in mine, the other person's back sweating under my other palm, the voice in my ear, the scrape of my feet such a great distance below my chin – thrilled me too much; my muscles locked. But the music, like the far-off war it accompanied and lent its jiviness to, pumped on, and Betty and I haltingly revolved with it.

Across Lancaster Avenue stood the Shillington Elementary School, a stately edifice built seamlessly in two stages, in 1901 and 1912, as the Shillington School, with many tall windows and a rather Byzantine recessed front entrance. In the 1970s it was converted to a business block rented, room by room, to dentists and realtors and to therapists of the many sorts that flourish in this allergy-plagued, diet-uncon-scious region. And during the renovation I had sneaked into the building and crept down past stacks of wallboard and insulating wool to the basement where I had gone to kinder-garten. It had been a lively place then, full of skittish four- and five-year olds and painted wooden toys. I remember especially a big blocky shoe on which we were supposed to learn how to tie laces. I'm told, nearly fifty years later, that I learned wrong; my wife says I put an extra step into the forming of the bow. And it is true, my laces are always coming undone. But I can still, ever so dimly, retaste the triumph of my first apparently successful attempt, and the praise that showered down from our teacher, raven-haired Miss Becker, whom I once invited, on behalf of a delegation of make-believe dwarves, to be Snow White. My sneaking visit showed the large old room to be empty, a barren basement, with a concrete floor. It couldn't, I felt, be the same place where so much magic had taken place – the glittering bottom, alive with frogs and phosphorescence, of my educational well.

The school building had six classrooms on each of its two main floors. Like silkworms munching mulberry leaves, we consumed it, we little Shillingtonians. Divided into A and B classes of about thirty each, we moved to the front of the building for the first grade, back to the middle for the second, and to the rear for the third, then straight upstairs to the fourth grade, forward to the fifth, and forward again to the sixth, the A section of which was taught by the immaculate, stern, gray-haired elementary-school principal, Mr Dickinson; after this grade, there was nothing left to do but fly through the windows onto Lancaster Avenue and head eastward up the street, past the five-sided corner, to the orange brick high school, which held six more grades, seventh through twelfth. As a structure, the high school lacked the compactness and logic of the elementary school; the adamant distinction between the As and the Bs broke down into diversified "courses" (college prep, business), and long rows of anonymous lockers in the halls symbolized anarchic new stretches of possibility and freedom.

The A/B distinction, like the sheep/goats cleavage anticipated in the Bible, was a hard one, and was especially hard on those on the borderline: a pair of twins, as their marks fluctuated, were in and out of the A section via a kind of revolving door, now one and now the other and now neither. And another boy, who became a friend of mine in high school, felt the onus of being a grade-school B with such force that he eventually compensated by becoming a vice-president of the New York Stock Exchange and, presently, a Washington lawyer. The As had the same side of the building as the girls' playground; the playground encircled the building like an asphalt moat, and the boys' and girls' sides were demarcated by the broad cement walks that led up to the front and back portals. Even to chase a soccer ball into the girls' side was against the rules, occasioning a flurry of shrieks.

So, male and female, A and B, we were divided up, and forbidden trespass; on the other hand, we all came from Shillington, a unique square mile of global surface, and thus we were united against the world: against Mohnton on the one side and Kenhorst on the other, against the grade ahead of us (in which a number of our girls later found boyfriends) and the grade behind (which was to supply some of us boys with girlfriends), and, from the third grade on, against Japan and Germany. The week after Pearl Harbor, Jimmy Trexler described to us, on unimpeachable authority, how our Navy men were holding the little Japanese by the heels and dropping them one by one into the battleship propellers. Jimmy rapidly became a general in our imitation army of scrap-collectors. Mountains of flattened tin cans and salvaged rubber filled a corner of the boys' playground, and a new order of war-effort prizes and mock-military rankings was superimposed upon the preëxistent order of bells and birthdays and field days and those class photographs late in May, on the back school steps, that came to join the treasure of lost time in my mother's shoeboxes.

I was an obedient student, if anything a little oversold on the possibilities of this bounteous institution called school. I could not understand how anybody could rebel against a system so clearly benign. One classmate would raise his hand to go to the bathroom and would then instead run home, up an alley, called Catherine Street, behind the school, all the way to New Holland Avenue. The teacher, Miss Tate (wonderfully tall, and wonderfully comical when, one Hal-lowe'en, she dressed up as a little girl with dabbed-on freckles and a giant Band-Aid on her knee), took then to assigning another boy to accompany the rebel down to the lavatory in the basement. Once when this was my duty, he tricked me, by lying and promising to be good. Halfway down the back stairs was the door to the outside; we had an earnest discussion in which, in a rapid whispering voice, he assured me I could wait for him at the head of the stairs. While I trustfully did so, he vanished from the basement lavatory. I heard the door slam and raced to the edge of the playground in just enough time to see his figure flying up the alley. Now party to his guilt, I had to go back to the classroom breathless and red-faced and report his astounding escape. Miss Tate (or was it Mrs Fritz?) took this outrageous and premeditated criminal act more philosophically than I had expected, with a wry shrug. There was more "give" in the system than obedient souls like me dreamed. I didn't realize this about the teachers: they were stuck with us, just as we were stuck with them. A classmate we acquired, because he flunked a year, was even more confrontational in his disobedience, and once butted a teacher in her stomach; repeatedly he had to be sent into Mr Dickinson's office. Even this scandalously bad boy did not strain the system to breaking; somehow it kept him in. In later life – not altogether surprisingly, from a stucturalist point of view – he became a schoolteacher, as the school's other notorious discipline problem became a policeman.

The older we got, the more we could move around. In the upper grades, the A and B sections would switch teachers and rooms for some classes, filing across the hall with much happy twitter at even so small a breach of routine. It was in the 6B room, the homeroom of young Miss Huntzinger, that one evening I stayed after school to stencil the cover of the school's mimeographed monthly, *The Little Shilling*. The soft blue stencil was cut with stylii of different shapes on a tilted frame holding a plate of glass with a light bulb under it. There was

13

a certain art to not tearing the wax-coated paper as you squintingly traced the drawing underneath, and I concentrated, but not so intently as to be unaware that Mr Dickinson had, with a silent tread, come into the room. The only male teacher in the school, he was, I suppose, a handsome man – erect, always neat, with hooded eyes and hawkish profile, and not so ancient as he seemed to an eleven-year-old. His iron-gray hair was combed straight back from a fine sloping forehead. He spoke very distinctly, with a slightly menacing "Dutch" accent, and was a calm and frightening disciplinarian, conveying in every economical directive a persuasive desire that standards be met and order be maintained. Miss Huntzinger and Mr Dickinson softly talked over by the windows, their words lost in the swish of Lancaster Avenue traffic but a peculiar impression being borne in upon me of informal intimacy. My face was hot from the light bulb underneath the stencil. Dusk was gathering in the tall windows that needed a window pole to close, here in this emptied school building, where the overhead lights floated like deflated moons and my cartoon turkey or Santa Claus was building, slow line by line, white cut into soft warm blue. I realized that these two adults did not live solely to keep me and others like me in the assigned seat and room until the bell rang. This day's last bell had rung, and my being in my small way "artistic" had given me access to an after-hours world, where voices were kept low and indistinct. To this quiet but indelible memory attaches a sensation that one of these two teachers came over and ruffled my hair, as if we had become a tiny family; but it may be simply that one of them stood close, to see how far along I was, because when I was finished we could all go to our separate homes.

Though the girls' and boys' playgrounds were segregated areas during school hours, when the last bell released us for the day we were free to mingle and run where we would, and those who lived in my direction raced diagonally across the forbidden asphalt and jumped down the little wall at the corner onto the sidewalk. This side of Lancaster Avenue – retaining walls, cement steps, iron railings, double porches, business placards – felt to be part of my father's territory, adult territory, though I walked it every day. Here, up a number of steps, was a tailor's shop run by a hunchbacked dwarf, Shorty Wartluft, who like my father was active in the Lutheran church and with whom he always had things to say. The narrow place smelled of steam, and scorch, and the counter was extraordinarily low, for Shorty's convenience; now it was still a tailor's shop, though some of the adjacent businesses – hair styling, television repair – were unheard of when I daily walked along here. Denny's Hair Styling, here at the corner of South Miller Street, had been Bohn's Oyster House, called "Boonie's"; one entered by a side door, and there were round oilcloth-covered tables in a long dim room muskily smelling of seashells and cigar smoke, with a kind of fish store at the back where on Sundays of exceptional festivity we used to buy a pint of shucked Chesapeake oysters and carry them home in a cardboard carton cleverly fitted with a handle of bent wire. Across Miller, beyond stout cement walls and the only deep front lawn in the vicinity, Doc Rothermel had received patients in the front rooms of an impressive house whose stucco was full of sharp small stones like the salt grains stuck into pretzels.* The doctor, who had supervised my birth, was a heavy, slow, pink-lidded man, with a slippery lower lip; he carried with him on his dark

* "On either side of the steps up to the lawn there were two stone posts topped by large concrete balls, a device of exterior decoration common in Olinger but rare, I have since discovered, elsewhere. . . . In the vestibule of his house there was a cocoa mat and an immense stucco umbrella stand ornamented, higgledypiggledy, with chips of colored glass. . . . [In his waiting room] old oak furniture padded in cracked black leather lined the walls and encircled a central table laden with battered copies of *Liberty* and *The Saturday Evening Post*."

– *The Centaur* (1963)

clothes the medicinal smell of his office, where the black-cushioned waiting-room furniture produced, sat on, a sound like his own weary sighs. When he came to pay me the bedside visits that my fragility or fever sometimes warranted, he unlatched a black five-sided bag and revealed phials of colored pills aligned in tiers like little cork-headed people in a grandstand. A sweetness had rubbed off onto him from his medications; his round, short-fingered hands had the healing touch, and the triangular rubber hammer with which he tapped my knees seemed a kind of candy. Now his stout retaining walls had been knocked down and his house had been transformed into a restaurant of wild architectural inappropriateness: a protruding addition with fake Tudor timbering had swallowed his old waiting room.

The next block, to New Holland Avenue, had been crammed with commercial excitements: the A&P, and Artie Hoyer's barber shop (where Artie for a joke would do a shuffle-one, shuffle-two, tap-tap-tap on the hairy linoleum floor), and a bicycle shop, and Mr Boyer's jewelry shop, and, of course, Ibach's, whose rack of magazines called out to me with the slick voice of New York, and where I once mildly astonished the Ibach son manning the soda fountain by having him leaf through a *Collier's* on the marble counter while I rapidly identified every cartoonist, cartoon by cartoon, glimpsed upside down. In front of Ibach's, one waited for the trolley car to Reading; it came every twenty minutes, just infrequently enough for a missed trolley to be a minor tragedy. New Holland Avenue climbed the hill, past the movie theatre and the Reformed church straight up to the town cemetery and the wooded hill called Cedar Top. Across New Holland, at the corner, by the curb, all the water from the ice plant up behind Philadelphia Avenue disappeared down a grating with a twisting, golden tumult that in my tame landscape had a Wordsworthian resonance. The ice plant was no more, the water no longer flowed, the trolley cars had ceased, and the tracks, whose parallel silver gave a kind of abstract arrowing look to Lancaster Avenue, had been torn up and paved over.

The soft warm air had turned humid again, and I craved rain, remembering how one could walk and stay dry under trees that no longer existed. I was on the even-numbered side of Philadelphia Avenue, the side across from my own house and hence slightly foreign. Near the corner, the Gehrets' house of gray fieldstone was the oldest house in Shillington, built in 1742 and, for a time, the home of Samuel Shilling, who in 1860 laid out lots along Philadelphia Avenue and called the development Shillingsville – a name upgraded in 1884, when a post office was established. A series of men had married into this land. Samuel's father, Jacob, in 1816 had married the daughter of Valentine Straub, who in 1777 had married the daughter of George Riehm, who had brought two hundred eighty acres from Jacob Weiss and Thomas Jones; they, in 1733 and 1734 respectively, had purchased their holdings directly from William Penn. In 1761 Riehm had built the Three-Mile House, an inn three miles from Reading on the Lancaster Pike. Horse racing near the Three-Mile house became common after 1850, and in 1868 one Aaron Einstein built a half-mile dirt racetrack called the Reading Driving Park or Speedway, of which a remembrance lingered in our high-school cheers, where the Shillington teams were called "the Speedboys" – "Come on, Speeders, skin 'em alive!" As a child, I had known little of this, despite a frequent rumble of local history from my grandfather's direction, and the fact that Samuel Shilling's aged son Howard "Pappy" Shilling lived a few houses up the street.* But a sense of ghosts had made me always walk quickly past the Gehrets'. There was a sense, too, that Fred Gehret in his handsome old

---

* "All through those years Pappy Shilling, the surviving son of the landowner after whom the town was named, walked up and down Philadelphia Avenue with his thin black cane and his snow-white bangs; a vibrating chain of perfect-Sunday-School-attendance pins dangled from his lapel."   – "The Dogwood Tree" (1960)

stone manse – a *wide*-faced building, on a street of narrow lots and façades – was a cut above the neighborhood, which consisted, in my eyes, of peaky plain houses with terraced front lawns, gray milk-bottle receptacles on the porches, and a variety of those speckled composition sidings popular in the Thirties. Who lived in them? I hardly knew, though the steps going up to the different porches felt different – some you dared step on in passing, and some you would never dare. This side of the street, involving safer street crossings than the odd-numbered side, was the way to grade school and the movies, and I was usually running.

I crossed Franklin Street, and the territory warmed, for I was drawing opposite our old house. Up above a wall topped with spiky stones, Clint Shilling had lived with his white-haired wife and long-haired collies. Clint (who lived to be nearly a hundred) was not only a Shilling, the grandson of Samuel, but the town's most prominent artist, a painter and sculptor both, and a restorer at the Reading Museum. When I was quite young my mother had persuaded him to give me painting lessons, on our side porch beneath the grape arbor.* Next door to the Shillings', the Lutzes had become famous

* "Clint Shilling's drawing lessons: in
   the sun he posed an egg on paper, and said
   a rainbow ran along the shadow's rim –

   the rainbow at the edge of the shadow of the egg.
   My kindergarten eyes were sorely strained
   to see it there. My still-soft head

   began to ache, but docilely I feigned
   the purple ghosts of green in clumsy wax:
   thus was I early trained

   and wonder, now, if Clint were orthodox.
   He lived above a spikestone-studded wall
   and honed his mustache like a tiny ax

   and walked a brace of collies down our alley
   in Pennsylvania dusk
   beside his melodic wife, white-haired and tall."
                                    – "Midpoint" (1968)

during the war, for supplying five sons to the armed forces and having a five-star flag in their window; Mrs Lutz's picture was in the Reading papers, as a kind of war heroine, more than once. The Lutz family shared a semidetached house with the Van Derherchens, who baked and sold "sticky buns." Next door lived Charlie Marx; he always wore dark clothes and, fifteen years after we had moved away, was found murdered in his feed store in Reading. Did he really always wear dark clothes, or has my memory, knowing of his grisly end, dressed him appropriately? Spying from our front windows, I would watch him descend his long cement steps with an odd sideways bias, favoring one leg, looking like a dark monkey on a string. Next to the Marxes' was the Yoders', where Wilma Yoder with tireless good cheer tried to teach me to play the piano, while her very slender mother moved back and forth semi-visibly and a fascinating circular grate in their front room poured out heat and a cokey smell. Remembering this smell, I seem to hear old Mrs Yoder speaking in her high-pitched, humorous, worried Pennsylvania voice, a kind of sigh crossed with a whimper, plaint blending into resignation.

From the Yoders' front porch I could admire my own home, the grandest in this little stretch of neighborhood. My grandfather, John Hoyer, had bought this house in 1922. Before I was born, and when Wilma herself must have been quite young, she had taken from an upstairs window a snapshot of the house as it was in the first decade after my grandparents had moved in. The windows and trim a dark color, and the surrounding hedge sculpted with rounded humps at the corners and at measured intervals, and the whole well-kept property prettily soaked in one of those moist little two- or three-inch snowfalls that affect me nostalgically as no New England blizzard can, the house sits proud on its half-acre of Shillington, the vast flat fields of the high-school and poorhouse properties white and dim beyond, and Reading's Mount Penn barely seen beyond them. The old color scheme – dark-green trim, pale-yellow bricks – persisted into my childhood; that yellow somehow "goes with" green was my first aesthetic perception. But several coats of white had overlaid this primal harmony by the time we sold the house.

Early in his ownership my grandfather had had built at the foot of his yard a chicken house, with colorless large asbestos shingles, set diagonally; and in all that area only this structure, fifty years later, looks quite unchanged. The house has been expanded and modified by the owner who bought it in 1945 and has now lived in it longer than the Hoyers and Updikes did. In the yard, the cherry and walnut trees I climbed are gone. The privet hedge is gone and replaced by a tall and forbidding one of arborvitae; little Shilling Alley, on whose loose gray stones I used to skin my knees, has been paved and straightened and renamed Shilling Street. The vacant lot across the alley where we used to play fungo and kick-the-can holds a ranch house. And the horse chestnuts have vanished that used to shade the curb in front of our house. My mother tells a story: I was sitting on this curb as a little fellow, watching the traffic, and when she suggested I come into the house I replied, "No, I want to be where the people are."

I was like my father in this, and walking the streets of Shillington this misty spring night was his act as much as mine; a set of cracked steps, or the worn look of a porch, or an angle of vista unchanged in forty years would bring him close, his diffuse and confused hunger to be "out," searching for something, with his wonderful free walk – long straight-ahead strides and head held high. Six feet two, rather narrow-shouldered for his height, he never slouched. On blackout nights during the war, he would be out in his air-raid warden's helmet. On Sunday mornings, while the three other adults hung inside the house with their chores and the Sunday *Eagle*, he was out teaching Sunday school. Every weekday morning he was out, striding down along the narrow path between the yard and our asparagus patch, along the grape trellis with its traps for Japanese beetles, across the alley to the high school, to fend for the dollar. On summer evenings, when the scissoring sound of lawn mowers and the fragrance of fresh-cut grass permeated the back yards of Philadelphia Avenue, and the Tiffany lampshade over the dining-room table cast a brownish light down upon my mother's solitaire game, and my grandparents muttered and cleared their throats in their bedroom, my father would be out on inscrutable errands, "rubbing elbows," "mixing it up." He had coated these slow-changing streets with his presence, though the town had fallen to him by accident, his in-laws' town; he had come from Trenton, New Jersey. "Trenton Makes, the World Takes," he often quoted proudly, himself one of its exports.

I crossed over and stood near the spot where as a child I had sat with my feet in the gutter, wanting to be where the people were. I had met few people during my walk, and none I knew. The sidewalks were less used nowadays than when I was a child, though the streets – streets I had often heard resound with the lonely clop-clop of a horse-drawn wagon – held much more auto traffic. I stood there waiting, self-consciously, to feel something, and felt less than I had hoped. The street, the house where I had lived, seemed blunt, modest in scale, simple; this deceptive simplicity composed their precious, mystical secret, the conviction of whose existence I had parlayed into a career, a message to sustain a writer book after book. I had often enough described my old house, its yard, the emotional nuances that hid beneath its details like so many dust mice and cobwebs; its familiar face and I had little to say to one another this evening.

A writer's self-consciousness, for which he is much scorned, is really a mode of interestedness, that inevitably turns outward. The furtive magic of Philadelphia Avenue most powerfully adhered to the view away from the corner of our yard (where there had stood a flagpole on which my grandmother, on patriotic holidays, would run up a faded flag with a frayed rope as tenuous, it seemed to me, as the connection between my closeted, elderly, somehow faded family and the active, aggressive nation boasted of in the wartime newspapers) – the view up the street, where the tall row houses of the Kegerises and the Kendalls and the Olingers and four or five others stood behind their retaining walls so loftily as to seem airborne. There was a dove grayness to their united mass in my memory and the reality, however often revisited, never failed to improve upon memory with a fresh enchantment. Mr Kegerise, who moved with a cane and sat for long hours on the porch, as high above what he surveyed as any enthroned sultan, was gone; but the benevolence of the greetings he would call out to even such neighborhood small fry as myself still lingered in the air. Before he had had his disabling stroke, when my mother was young in the neighborhood, he played the cornet, and its sound from up the street would lull her, she once told me, to sleep. This patch of tall, knobby housing, with its spindly porches and narrow cemented passageways between the house walls through which people passed into their back yards, gave a hivelike impression of intense and contented population. Farther in the same direction as these houses there was Second Street, where in solid small brick rows lived the sexy girls, the buoyant, sassy, handsome daughters of factory workers and skilled tradesmen. Bright life, indeed, lay about me in all directions in Shillington, while there was something of a musty stillness, of balked and abandoned tendencies, in the long white house where I ate and slept and soaked up strength and love.

Though I had been walking not more than twenty minutes, the luggage from Allentown was drawing nearer, like a comet, and I must be present under the marquee. I headed down Philadelphia Avenue on the odd-numbered side. The dusk had deepened, and the humidity thickened into a palpable, prickly drizzle that lent my walk a heightened feeling of sheltered stealth. I knew *this* side of the street from the dawn of my consciousness; our neighbors the Matzes and the

Pritchards, and Hen Kieffer's grocery store, and the Krings' and the Pottses' houses, where my first playmates, all girls, lived. These houses down the street, though not every inhabitant was known by name to me, had each been as distinct to my childish awareness as the little troughs in the cement which led rain from their roof gutters out through the sidewalk to the street, and which punctuated my progress on roller skates or on my scooter. As the street sloped downward, there was a just-perceptible descent in the social scale as well: the porches got lower to the ground, and the front yards became exiguous. Over the years, there had been changes: wooden porch banisters and pillars had been replaced by wrought iron, in a vaguely Southern or Spanish style. Throughout Shillington, not only had houses I remembered as homes become stores but, stranger still, stores – Pep Conrad's up on Franklin and Second, Hen Kieffer's here – had reverted to being homes. How had the new residents divided up those open, shelved spaces? How did they live with all those ghostly aromas of merchandise? How did they utilize the man-high meat locker out of which Pep Conrad, his body spilling vapor like a Popsicle, would haul a gory side of beef? In Hen Kieffer's store one bought "fastnachts," squarish holeless doughnuts drenched in powdered sugar, six to the bag, and traded red cardboard tokens for meat during the war. In the Krings' front parlor, one admired their Christmas tree, as piney in smell as a forest and tucked full of old-fashioned, brittle ornaments of glass and tin – two stamped pieces of tin fastened together with little tabs to make a semi-rounded clown, or a milkmaid with a red spot on each cheek. At the Pottses', I felt most welcome, though not so welcome as to escape a gentle rebuke from Mrs Potts when I pressed my face to a crack in the door to see Mary Jane being given a washcloth bath while standing naked on a kitchen chair.

These houses, on the "safe," on "our," side of the street, however little or much I knew them from the inside, knew me – Wes and Linda Updike's boy, John and Katie Hoyer's grandson. Where now I made my way down the pavement on Proust's dizzying stilts of time, virtually floating, a phantom who had not set foot on these very squares of cement for perhaps thirty years, I had once hastened low to the ground, day after day, secure as a mole in the belief that I was known, watched, placed.

What *was* our standing in Shillington? Social position in America is not easy to be precise about. My grandfather bought our big white house to retire in; but he then lost his money in the Crash, and took a job, old as he was, on the town highway crew, spreading oil and shovelling crushed stone. My grandmother never seemed to change her dress and ate standing up, while the rest of us sat at the table; but she was Aunt Katie to the Kachel sisters, who were, all three, beautiful, competent, and well thought of in Shillington. It was thanks to Elsie Kachel Becker's husband, Orville, who owned the local landmark Becker's Garage and who was on the school board, that my father got his teaching job, when millions were out of work. My father was a high-school teacher, known (I imagined) to everyone; but teachers were thought of in Berks County as rather ineffectual figures, well below machinists and full-fashioned knitters in the scale of prestige. My mother had been a belle of sorts, flashily dressed by her father in his palmy period, and the possessor of a master's degree from Cornell; but she had walked out of the classroom after a few hours of teaching seventh grade, and blamed herself for this refusal, and seemed to me to be hiding from the town, in our house and yard. Updike was an unusual name, savoring of high expectations and good self-regard; it was also something of a joke, used more than once in Hollywood movies for comic minor characters, winning howls of local laughter in the movie house on New Holland Avenue. My family sold asparagus and pansies for odd money, embarrassing me; but agricultural enterprise – the most depressing activity, I felt, in the world – was not really déclassé in a town where cornfields marched up to the back yards, and almost every garden grew vegetables, and every woman put up preserves.

On the finely graded social scale within Shillington homogeneity, I seemed to myself a cut above the children who came to school from the west end of Lancaster Avenue and the tough areas toward Pennwyn or behind the hosiery mill, and a cut below those who came from the newly built section toward Slate Hill, with curved, sycamore-shaded, Wyomissing-style streets. Wyomissing was Reading's nicest suburb; when my grandparents moved here, Shillington had been. There *had* been money, our property and some of our furniture and even our way of talking and behaving declared. My mother, herself raised in expensive clothing, took me to buy my clothes at Croll & Keck and my shoes at Wetherhold & Metzger. I was given a weekly allowance of thirty-five cents, which enabled me to go to the movies three times a week and still have a nickel for the little slotted wooden barrel that was passed around at Sunday school. There was no stinting on paper and pencils and cardboard to feed my "creativity." If our Christmas tree was not as sumptuously furnished as the Krings', what I had asked for was usually under it, and a plucky little blue Lionel train that went round and round its miniature countryside of cotton snow and sponge-and-stick trees and lead cows and a lake that was a mirror and gave you back your giant face, the face of a God looking down. Magazines plopped through the letter slot and coal slid with a torrential noise down the chute from a truck backed up on the sidewalk. I had an aunt who lived in Greenwich, Connecticut, and an uncle, evidently even richer, who lived in Florida. We had no car, but then when we rented one I got carsick anyway. It seemed to me I possessed whatever a reasonable boy needed – an Elgin bike, a Flexible Flyer sled, a Jimmy Foxx fielder's glove. When, many years later, I was recalling some of these happy circumstances in the company of my father, he interrupted me with an exclamation almost agonized; "Oh, no, Johnny – we were *poor!*"

His cry came from the heart. He earned twelve hundred dollars a year, teaching, with no raises or job security; the entire faculty was fired in May, to be rehired or not for September. His summer vacations he spent working on construction crews or doing manual labor for Carpenter Steel. When his hernia got too bad to allow lifting, he got a job as a timekeeper on a road gang. I once dreamed of his being cast out by society, of his being harried, white-faced and clad in a barrel like a cartoon bankrupt, down the town hall steps. One of his extracurricular school duties was to manage the money for the athletic department, and I had an impression, from troubled nocturnal discussions I overheard, of informal loans from these school funds to make ours reach. Our family banking was quite informal: a little metal Recipes box, with floral decorations and a red lid, sat on top of the icebox, and those with expenses took from it the bills and coins they required. Every day after lunch, I was allowed to take six cents from it, so I could buy a Tastykake at Kieffer's on the way back to grade school. When the money ran out, the Recipes box stood empty until my father's next pay envelope.

But it was a world where a dime bought a sandwich and a hobo would come to the door for a meal and get it. The Berks County rich, the mill owners, kept behind their tall hedges and iron fences, and there were only Hollywood movies to remind us that a condition existed above respectable scrounging. However pinched my guardians felt, they did not pinch me; what was available I shared, and there were touches, in that Shillington life, even of elegance – our flower beds and the birdbath, our cherry trees in blossom, the piano in the parlor with the little brass tiger from China on top, the oil painting of the Provincetown sand dunes that had cost thirty-five dollars and that hung like a votive image above the living-room bookcase, which was full of books my mother had accumulated at college. I didn't read them, but in the walls of my life the bookcase stood like the door to a secret passage.

Toward the end of Philadelphia Avenue, beside the park that surrounds the town hall, I turned and looked back up the straight sidewalk in the soft evening gloom, looking for what the superstitious old people of the county used to call a "sign." The pavement squares, the housefronts, the remaining trees receded in silence and shadow. I loved this plain street, where for thirteen years no great harm had been allowed to befall me. I loved Shillington not as one loves Capri or New York, because they are special, but as one loves one's own body and consciousness, because they are synonymous with being. It was exciting for me to be in Shillington, as if my life, like the expanding universe, when projected backwards gained heat and intensity. If there was a meaning to existence, I was closest to it here. Also, there was something in my excitement of having "showed" the town: more people had heard of me now than had ever heard of Philadelphia Avenue.

Though the community was a borough, the words SHIL-LINGTON TOWN HALL identified a stately red brick building with a Greek-temple façade. Inside, there were offices and stairs down to the little lock-up and the grated windows where one could pay bills; but I went inside only once a year, at Christmas, when the movie house and the civil authorities united to reinforce the religious holiday: after a free hour of cartoons and carols, in the middle of the morning, and a Hershey bar presented personally by Mr Shverha, we children of Shillington trooped down New Holland Avenue and into the town hall to receive our free box of candy from fat Sam Reich, dressed as Santa Claus. Then I would walk back home, back up into the very perspective I was now gazing into, with my favorite chocolates (the ones with corners, which had caramel centers) melting in my mouth and my childish awe at this long-anticipated day's being at last *here* dissolving in my heart. There was a round, after lunch, of visiting other children and admiring their presents, and perhaps, if December had been unusually cold, an attempt at ice skating; but the holiday was rarely white or very crisp, winter manifest mostly as an ebb in the color of things. Yet the day did have a taste, an excited buzz in the lining of the brain, a nearness of tears in the eyes and the tickle of a shout in the back of the throat, that used to merge, it seemed to me now as I headed down the south side of East Lancaster Avenue toward the movie-house marquee, with the Christmas scenes in books, the curvaceous heaps of blue-shadowed snow and the golden windows lighted by the warmth and blessed plenty within.

I stood under the marquee a long while, sheltered from the gentle rain, my back against the glass-protected posters. The ticket booth had closed, and the movie going on inside was felt out here as a faint leakage of mood music and muffled outbursts of laughter. Cars licked by on the asphalt, the streetlights overhead burned sulphurously, silhouettes in slickers and parkas once in a while walked by, and one of them even recognized me and stopped to talk, mostly about my father, who was still more vivid in the town than I could ever be. My father has posthumously acquired a saintly reputation, but he did, it has occurred to me, strive to establish everywhere a margin of special treatment for himself. Once, for instance, on the basis of an acquaintance with the absent foreman, he led me into a pretzel factory in Reading and began to eat pretzels right off the travelling belt; the foreman who was on the job rushed over, bawled us out with good German hysteria, and ordered us to leave. I was humiliated, but not, to any point of repentance, my father; he saw the episode as a study in human nature, and the lesson he wanted to impart to me that day – the art of pretzel manufacture, as demonstrated by the experts, who were mostly women with fat white arms and dimpled elbows sitting in chairs and plucking up snakes of dough as they crawled past and giving them a flip in mid-air to make that knotted shape – has never been forgotten. With Mr Shverha my father seemed to have reached an understanding that he could wander into the movie house at random and watch some minutes of the show while standing in the back, free. Even when he attended with my mother and me and paid for his ticket, he took the seat on the end of the aisle and, if the picture failed to hold his attention (and most did fail), would leave it abruptly and stand at the rear, chatting audibly with the usher. If I had been my father, I would have gone into the movie house and watched some minutes of Peter Sellers, since it looked as if the suitcases from Allentown would never arrive. But true to my docile, good-child nature I stood outside, enjoying the rain and the passing traffic and the sensation that all this would be happening whether or not I was here. Life breeds punchers and counterpunchers, venturers like my father and ambushers like me: the venturer risks rebuff and defeat; the ambusher risks, like Kafka's hunger artist, fading away to nothing while his moment never arrives. "What a fellow you are!" the circus overseer exclaims, discovering the hunger artist still alive in the dirty straw of his cage. He wanted to be admired for his fasting, even though no food had ever appealed to him. All those years in Shillington, I had waited to be admired, waited patiently, for there was considerable pleasure in the waiting, the lying low, the keeping (in one of my grandfather's favorite phrases) "out of harm's way" – pleasure in the shyness, the malicious slyness, the burrowing in New York magazines and English mystery novels for the secret passageway out, the path of avoidance and vindication. I hid a certain determined defiance. I would not teach, I would not farm, I would not (deep down) conform. I would "show" them, I would avenge all the slights and abasements visited upon my father – the miserly salary, the subtle tyranny of his overlords at the high school, the disrespect of his students, the laughter in the movie house at the name of Updike. He was, in this snug world into which I

had been born, an outsider. He had, it seemed, been hurt by
the failure of the local Lions' Club (or was it the Masons?) to
elect him to membership. I therefore have relished every
election to membership I have received, especially those I
declined. Leaving Pennsylvania, where my father had been
pinned by necessity, was another such reversal on my part, a
spurning on his behalf. Life had given my father a beating,
beginning with his hard childhood peddling papers in Trenton; his own father's failures and sorrow and early death had
poured through him like rain through a broken window. And
his, in turn, through me: the beating showed on his face, in
the battered nose repeatedly broken by playing college football, in his sunken triangular eyes; it showed in the gallows
humor of his talk, in his pathetic sweat-stained truss and
repeatedly aggravated hernia, in the varicose veins on his
milk-white legs. Shillington, in a sense, was where I waited
in ambush to take my revenge. Never since leaving it have I
enjoyed such thrilling idleness; the long hours hanging out in
Stephens', the long summers hanging out at the dusty playground playing box hockey and roof ball, the long afternoons
spent upstairs with a book or in bed sick and listening to the
radio. Now I enjoyed the idleness of waiting in front of the
movie house, gazing at where the trolley tracks and Stephens'
Luncheonette and the post office used to be.

A small mustard-colored Japanese car came down Lancaster
Avenue hesitantly. I went to the curb, the car stopped, a
pretty young face in the window established that I was indeed
the man who had lost his luggage. She and her boyfriend
handed over the bags in an atmosphere of jollity: we had
pulled off an amusing logistical feat. I gave expert directions
on the best route out of Shillington, and they went on their
way, like logs over a waterfall.

Two sensations stood out as peculiarly blissful in my
childhood, before I discovered (at the same time as leaving
Shillington) masturbation. The first has been alluded to: the

awareness of things going by, impinging on my consciousness, and then, all beyond my control, sliding away toward
their own destination and destiny. The traffic on Philadelphia
Avenue was such; the sound of an engine and tires would
swell like a gust of wind, the headlight beam would paraboli-
cally wheel about the papered walls of my little room, and
then the lights and the sound would die, and that dangerous
creature of combustion and momentum would be out of my
life. To put myself to sleep, I would picture logs floating
down a river and then over a waterfall, out of sight. Mailing
letters, flushing a toilet, reading the last set of proofs – all
have this sweetness of riddance. The second intimation of
deep, cosmic joy, also already hinted at, is really a variation
of the first: the sensation of shelter, of being out of the rain,
but *just* out. I would lean close to the chill windowpane to
hear the raindrops ticking on the other side; I would huddle
under bushes until the rain penetrated; I loved doorways in a
shower. On our side porch, it was my humble job, when it
rained, to turn the wicker furniture with its seats to the wall,
and in these porous woven caves I would crouch, happy
almost to tears, as the rain drummed on the porch rail and
rattled the grape leaves of the arbor and touched my wicker
shelter with a mist like the vain assault of an atomic army. In
both species of delightful experience, the reader may notice,
the experiencer is motionless, holding his breath as it were,
and the things experienced are morally detached from him:
there is nothing he can do, or ought to do, about the flow, the
tumult. He is irresponsible, safe, and witnessing: the entire
body, for these rapt moments, mimics the position of the
essential self within its jungle of physiology and its moulder-
ing tangle of inheritance and circumstance. Early in his life
the child I once was sensed the guilt in things, inseparable
from the pain, the competition: the sparrow dead on the
lawn, the flies swatted on the porch, the impervious leer of
the bully on the school playground. The burden of activity,
of participation, must plainly be shouldered, and has its

pleasures. But they are cruel pleasures. There was nothing cruel about crouching in a shelter and letting phenomena slide by: it was ecstasy. The essential self is innocent, and when it tastes its own innocence knows that it lives forever. If we keep utterly still, we can suffer no wear and tear, and will never die.

I put the lost luggage into the trunk of my mother's car. The parking lot was beside the movie house, and cars entered not off Lancaster Avenue but from an alley that ran parallel. It was still a good half-hour until *Being There* would end, with that inspired addendum of outtakes, under the credit roll, wherein Peter Sellers tries again and again to relay in his impeccably put-on American accent, the obscene message from the menacing black boy, and breaks up laughing, again and again: Sellers, so incredibly clever, so lively in his impersonations, so quick, and now dead. I walked down the alley, east toward Brobst Street. In this direction, too, memories welcomed me. Just the texture of the fine-pebbled Shillington alleys put me back into sneakers, slouching toward a basketball scuffle around a telephone pole. Along this alley, past Brobst, there had been the Speedway Greenhouse. Here one bought corsages for one's dates at formal dances; such erotic expenditure belonged to a later time, when I lived eleven miles from Shillington but still attended the high school.

Girls wore strapless gowns of shiny taffeta then, and in the darkened gym, under the drooping twisted streamers of crêpe paper, bathed in spotlights tinted by colored cellophane, one seemed to be swimming among naked shoulders. The corsages wilted and the rented tuxedos rumpled in the heat, the sweat, the twirling exertions called forth by the wah-wah of the muted trumpets and the heart-lifting runs of the clarinet. After a slow dance, you and your partner separated stickily, and a red blotch marked where your cheek had been pressed against hers. Your hand shifted uneasily on her damp, tightly bound back, moving up from the waist to the hard ridge of the bra strap. The tops of her breasts were plumped up in a way that was not the least of her mysteries: we thought girls came naturally in such dramatically rounded shapes, their waists cinched and their hips widened by crinoline petticoats. Their arms were glossy long extensions of their shoulders' nakedness, lightly swirling with forearm hair and tipped with scarlet fingernails that matched their lips. Looking at my old high-school yearbook, I am struck by the darkness, the blackness, of my female classmates' smiling lips; these seventeen- and eighteen-year-olds look flashlit and starchy, with their white blouses and Ginger Rogersish hair brushed to a shine. But what heats, what shadowy, intense glandular incubations came packaged with that five-dollar purchase of a baby orchid in a transparent plastic box! It surprised me, as an adolescent, how at each stage of our outward venture merchants stand ready, equipped to sell us what we think we need – cap guns, cigarettes, and so on. One imagines, when young, that everything desirable must be obtained in spite of the adult world, against its grain. But society knows us better than we know ourselves, and Mr and Mrs Lloyd Miller,*

---

* Mr Miller, also, was our mailman, a stocky short man leaning doggedly away from the pull of his leather pouch. As a small child I would look up Philadelphia Avenue for his coming and, when his footsteps scraped our front brick walk, would lie down in the foyer against the front door, hold my breath, and let his clacking shower of mail fall all over me.

From "Confessions of a Wild Bore" (1959): "I am oppressed by a peculiar vague emotion, or circular set of propositions, about my home town that, boiled down to its essence, might go as follows: 'It seems extraordinary to me that the town where I was born, and spent all my formative years, had nothing extraordinary about it. Yet is not this, in a sense, extraordinary?' Not that I ever state it so baldly. My effort to unburden myself of this strange message usually takes the form of a sentence beginning, 'In the town where I grew up,' and going on to describe some innocuous condition like the way the mailman walked up one side of the street and then down the other."

That mailman was Mr Miller.

who ran the greenhouse, knew down to their apron pockets the erotic value of their fragrant, fragile merchandise.

I was often in love but didn't have a *real*, as they say, girlfriend until my senior year. She was a junior, called Nora. Though my only girlfriend, she was enough – sensitive, nicely formed, and fond of me. It was courtesy of Nora that I discovered breasts are not glazed bouffant orbs pushing up out of a prom dress but soft poignant inflections, subtle additions to the female rib cage, which is distinctly yet not radically different from that of the male. She was as fragrant and tactful and giving as one could wish; in the relative scale of our youth and virginity, she did for me all that a woman does for a man, and I regretted that my nagging specialness harried almost every date and shared hour with awareness of our imminent and necessary parting. I was never allowed to relax into her; the perfect girl for me would take me away from Shillington, not pull me down into it. My avenging mission beckoned. Shillington in my mother's vision was small-town – small minds, small concerns, small hopes. We were above all that, though my father drew our living from it. My love for the town, once we had moved from it, had to be furtive, and my dates with Nora also; I was not allowed to be a normal boyfriend but had always to be sneaking and breaking up and saying goodbye.

Now the goodbyes had all been endured, though in this half-hour I was still sneaking. I continued walking east, toward Nora's old house. Emerging from the alley, I crossed Brobst Street and walked down the half-block to Walnut, past Mary Ann Stanley's house. Mary Ann had been a tall, calm, handsome girl; she and I had played the mother and father in both our junior and senior class plays, and I have felt, ever since, slightly married to her. For one of our performances, she had been quite ill with food poisoning, and threw up when she could, between the acts, backstage. On stage, I shouted at her with the perennial exasperation of fathers in high-school class plays. My mother afterwards said her malaise, evident in the footlights, made me look cruel; but at the time I admired, as I still do, Mary Ann's brave determination to go on with the show. That is one of the things school is supposed to teach us: to go on with the show. My father, earaches and fevers and unruly adolescents notwithstanding, went on with his show every school day, and I did not let Nora's satiny skin and powdered warmth and soft forgiving voice prevent me from going on with my show.

This Speedway section of Shillington, when newly filled with brick semidetached houses, had been planted with Norway maples – a dull, thickly leafed tree, which branches low to the ground. The freshly unpacked leaves of spring made a comforting roof over my head as I walked along. The rain had become a real rain, gentle but insistent. The houses here, uniform and solid unlike the variegated houses of Philadelphia Avenue, always made me feel safe; the something anonymous and interchangeable about the streets took me in. Nora lived a block up, at the corner of Walnut and State Streets, in a house with a big living-room window and a retaining wall decorated, like Doc Rothermel's, with concrete balls. The high school, on East Lancaster Avenue, was a block away. On its two symmetrical wings was fixed in metal letters its symmetrical motto: "LEARN TO LIVE / LIVE TO LEARN." This school, its quaint enveloping world of mottos and trophies and class colors and penetrating cheers ("*Come* on, Speeders, skin 'em a*live!*"), seemed suddenly close. I remembered the smell of wax in its halls and the sound of locker doors slamming. One night I had been obliged to say a word, a very few words, in introduction of some classmates at an evening ceremony in the auditorium, and had stuttered. I had a stammer that came and went, pouncing upon me when I least expected it – not, say, during the lengthy speeches of a class play, but in some trivial performance like placing a phone call or saying a few obligatory words from the stage. I left the stage and the school building and, my cheeks burning, walked along Lancaster to State and down a block to Nora's house. It was close to nine o'clock. My status with her parents was not such that I could ring the bell; instead, I hung around on the curb opposite, hoping she would accidentally look out the window or intuitively sense my presence, and come out to comfort me. And she did. Nora did come out, and we talked.

On this corner across the street had been in those days an old-fashioned grocery store, with one of those entrances you see in Pennsylvania: a tall door set diagonally at the corner of the building, with the second floor forming a triangular overhang. This store, too, was no longer a store; gone were the tin signs and decals for 7 Up and Maier's Bread. The display windows were painted white on the inside, so no one could look in, and all the windows were dark. I sat on the porch, to get out of the rain, and waited for Nora to come out of her house. But she was not there: the whole family had moved, decamped; perhaps her father like mine was dead, perhaps like me she had married and remarried. Her old house showed one dim light, a night-light or the glow of a radio dial, on in an upstairs room. Otherwise, it was dark. She did not come out. But the rain continued, hard enough to make a close pattern of dots on the asphalt under the streetlight, here among the Norway maples and brick houses of Shillington.

Dasein. Nothing I have described here has importance except to me, and to those few thousands who thanks to chance also live or have lived in Shillington; they will see that I haven't described it very well, for I haven't described *their* town – only mine, lost luggage by and large, a few scraps preserved by memory and used more than once, used to the point of vanishing like the wishing hide in the fairy tale, used up and wished away in the self-serving corruptions of fiction. Yet isn't it a miracle, the oddity of consciousness being placed in one body rather than another, in one place and not somewhere else, in one handful of decades rather than in ancient Egypt, or ninth-century Wessex, or Samoa before the missionaries came, or Bulgaria under the Turkish yoke, or the Ob River Valley in the days of the woolly mammoths? Billions of consciousnesses silt history full, and every one of them the center of the universe. What can we do in the face of this unthinkable truth but scream or take refuge in God? Perhaps what I loved most about Shillington is that here time had moved slowest, had all but stood still in reference to a child's future that would never come, and even now, even in its alteration of remembered landmarks, moved cautiously, as if subdued by the Hebraic promises that had come to me via the stolid church that was called and is still called Grace Lutheran.

There had been much self-consciousness about my walk this night, a deliberate indulgence of a nostalgia long since made formal in many words. I had propelled my body through the tenderest parts of a town that was also somewhat my body. Yet my pleasure was innocent and my hope was primitive. I had expected to be told who I was, and why, and had not been entirely disapppointed. The raindrops made a pattern on the street like television snow, or like the scrambled letters with which a word processor fills the screen before a completed electric spark clears it all into perfect sense. I studied the drops, feeling fulfilled and suspended. Rain is grace; rain is the sky condescending to the earth; without rain, there would be no life. The triangular shelter of the porch gave just enough shelter, like the upturned wicker chairs on the old side porch. Now and then a car passed, the slanting colorless lines of rain showing in the headlights. I was "where the people are." I was "out of harm's way." I was "by myself" – a phrase whose meaning could not be deduced by a stranger to the language even though he knew the meanings of "by" and "myself". A passing car slowed suspiciously, diluting my intense happiness. Perhaps by sitting on this porch – no longer, after all, the porch of a grocery store – I was doing something illegal. I, a child of the town, arrested, with my gray head, for trespassing! This head became distinctly wet as I walked back to the movie theatre, to join my mother and daughter, to resume my life. A fortunate life, of course – college, children, women, enough money, minor fame. But it had all, from the age of thirteen on, felt like not quite my idea. Shillington, its idle alleys and darkened foursquare houses, had been my idea.

II

At War with My Skin

My mother tells me that up to the age of six I had no psoriasis; it came on strong after an attack of measles in February of 1938, when I was in kindergarten. The disease – "disease" seems strong, for a condition that is not contagious, painful, or debilitating; yet psoriasis has the volatility of a disease, the sense of another presence coöccupying your body and singling you out from the happy herds of healthy, normal mankind – first attached itself to my memory while I was lying on the upstairs side porch of the Shillington house, amid the sickly, oleaginous smell of Siroil, on fuzzy sun-warmed towels, with my mother, sunbathing. We are both, in my mental picture, not quite naked. She would have been still a youngish woman at the time, and I remember being embarrassed by something, but whether by our being together this way or simply by my skin is not clear in this mottled recollection. She, too, had psoriasis; I had inherited it from her. Siroil and sunshine and not eating chocolate were our only weapons in our war against the red spots, ripening into silvery scabs, that invaded our skins in the winter. Siroil was the foremost medication available in the Thirties and Forties: a bottled preparation the consistency of pus, tar its effective ingredient and its drippy texture and bilious color and insinuating odor deeply involved with my embarrassment. Yet, as with our own private odors, those of sweat and earwax and even of excrement, there was also something satisfying about this scent, an intimate rankness that told me who I was.

One dabbed Siroil on; it softened the silvery scales but otherwise did very little good. Nor did abstaining from chocolate and "greasy" foods like potato chips and French fries do much visible good, though as with many palliations there was no knowing how much worse things would be otherwise. Only the sun, that living god, had real power over psoriasis; a few weeks of summer erased the spots from all of my responsive young skin that could be exposed – chest, legs, and face. Inspecting the many photographs taken of me as a child, including a set of me cavorting in a bathing suit in the back yard, I can see no trace of psoriasis. And I remember, when it rained, going out in a bathing suit with friends to play in the downpour and its warm puddles. Yet I didn't learn to swim, because of my appearance; I stayed away from "the Porgy," the dammed pond beyond the poorhouse, and from the public pool in West Reading, and the indoor pool at the Reading "Y," where my father in winter coached the high-school swimming team. To the travails of my freshman year at Harvard was added the humiliation of learning at last to swim, with my spots and my hydrophobia, in a class of quite naked boys. Recently the chunky, mild-spoken man who taught that class over thirty years ago came up to me at a party and pleasantly identified himself; I could scarcely manage politeness, his face so sharply brought back that old suppressed rich mix of chlorine and fear and brave gasping and naked, naked shame.

Psoriasis is a metabolic disorder that causes the epidermis, which normally replaces itself at a gradual, unnoticeable rate, to speed up the process markedly and to produce excess skin cells. The tiny mechanisms gone awry are beyond the precise reach of internally taken medicine; a derivative of vitamin A, etretinate, and an anti-cancer drug, methotrexate, are effective but at the price of potential side-effects to the kidneys and liver more serious than the disease, which is, after all, superficial – too much, simply, of a good thing (skin). In the 1970s, dermatologists at Massachusetts General Hospital developed PUVA, a controlled light treatment: fluorescent tubes radiate long-wave ultraviolet (UV-A) onto skin sensitized by an internal dose of methoxsalen, a psoralen (the "P" of the acronym) derived from a weed, *ammi majus*, which grows along the river Nile and whose sun-sensitizing qualities were known to the ancient Egyptians. So a curious primitivity, a savor of folk-medicine, clings to this new cure, a refinement of the old sun-cure. It is pleasant, once or twice a week, to stand nearly naked in a kind of glowing telephone booth. It was pleasant to lie on the upstairs porch, hidden behind the jigsawed wooden balusters, and to feel the slanting sun warm the fuzzy towel while an occasional car or pack of children crackled by on Shilling Alley. One became conscious, lying there trying to read, of birdsong, of distant shouts, of a whistle calling men back to work at the local textile factory, which was rather enchantingly called the Fairy Silk Mill.

My condition forged a hidden link with things elemental – with the seasons, with the sun, and with my mother. A tendency to psoriasis is inherited – only through the maternal line, it used to be thought. My mother's mother had had it, I was told, though I never noticed anything wrong with my grandmother's skin – just her false teeth, which slipped down while she was napping in her rocking chair. Far in the future, I would marry a young brunette with calm, smooth, deep-tanning skin and was to imagine that thus I had put an end to at least my particular avenue of genetic error. Alas, our fourth child inherited my complexion and, lightly, in her late teens, psoriasis. The disease favors the fair, the dry-skinned, the pallid progency of cloud-swaddled Holland and Ireland and Germany. Though my father was not red-haired, his brother Arch was, and when I grew a beard, as my contribution to the revolutionary Sixties, it came in reddish. And when I shaved it off, red spots had thrived underneath.

Psoriasis keeps you thinking. Strategies of concealment ramify, and self-examination is endless. You are forced to the mirror, again and again; psoriasis compels narcissism, if we can suppose a Narcissus who did not like what he saw. In certain lights, your face looks passable; in slightly different other lights, not. Shaving mirrors and rearview mirrors in automobiles are merciless, whereas the smoky mirrors in airplane bathrooms are especially flattering and soothing: one's face looks as tawny as a movie star's. Flying back from the Caribbean, I used to admire my improved looks; years went by before I noticed that I looked equally good, in the lavatory glow, on the flight down. I cannot pass a reflecting surface on the street without glancing in, in hopes that I have somehow changed. Nature and the self, the great moieties of earthly existence, are each cloven in two by a fascinated ambivalence. One hates one's abnormal, erupting skin but is led into a brooding, solicitous attention toward it. One hates the Nature that has imposed this affliction, but only this same Nature can be appealed to for erasure, for cure. Only Nature can forgive psoriasis; the sufferer in his self-contempt does not grant to other people this power. Perhaps the unease of my first memory has to do with my mother's presence; I wished to be alone with the sun, the air, the distant noises, the possibility of my hideousness eventually going away.

I recall remarkably few occasions when I was challenged, in the brute world of childhood, about my skin. In the second grade, perhaps it was, the teacher, standing above our obedient rows, rummaged in my hair and said aloud, "Good heavens, child, what's this on your head?" I can hear these words breaking into the air above me and see my mother's face when, that afternoon, I recounted them to her, probably with tears; her eyes took on a fanatic glare and the next morning, like an arrow that had fixed her course, she went to the school to "have it out" with the teacher who had heightened her defective cub's embarrassment. Our doctor, Doc Rothermel in his big grit-and-stucco house, also, eerily, had psoriasis; far from offering a cure out of his magical expanding black bag, he offered us the melancholy confession that he had felt prevented, by his scaly wrists, from rolling back his sleeves and becoming – his true ambition – a surgeon.

"'Physician, heal thyself,' they'd say to me," he said. I don't, really, know how bad I looked, or how many conferences among adults secured a tactful silence from above. My peers (again, as I remember, which is a choosing to remember) either didn't notice anything terrible about my skin or else neglected to comment upon it. Children are frank, as we know from the taunts and nicknames they fling at one another; but also they all feel imperfect and vulnerable, which works for mutual forbearance. In high school, my gym class knew how I looked in the locker room and shower. Once, a boy from a higher class came up to me with an exclamation of cheerful disgust, touched my arm, and asked if I had syphilis. But my classmates held their tongues, and expressed no fear of contagion.

I participated, in gym shorts and tank top, in the annual gym exhibitions. Indeed, as the tallest of the lighter boys, I stood shakily on top of "Fats" Sterner's shoulders to make the apex of our gymnastics pyramid. I braved it through, inwardly cringing, prisoner and victim of my skin. It was not really *me* was the explanation I could not shout out. Like an obese person (like good-natured Fats so sturdy under me, a human rock, his hands gripping my ankles while I fought the sensation that I was about to lurch forward and fly out over the heads of our assembled audience of admiring parents), and unlike someone with a withered arm, say, or a port-wine stain splashed across his neck and cheek, I could change – every summer, I *did* become normal and, as it were, beautiful. An overvaluation of the normal went with my ailment, a certain idealization of everyone who was not, as I felt myself to be, a monster.

Because it came and went, I never settled in with my psoriasis, never adopted it as, inevitably, part of myself. It was temporary and in a way illusionary, like my being poor, and obscure, and (once we moved to the farm) lonely – a spell that had been put upon me, a test, as in a fairy story or one of those divinely imposed ordeals in the Bible. "Where's my public?" I used to ask my mother, coming back from the empty mailbox, by this joke conjuring a public out of the future.

My last public demonstration of my monstrosity, in a formal social setting, occurred the day of my examination for the draft, in the summer of 1955. A year in England, with no sun, had left my skin in bad shape, and the examining doctor took one glance up from his plywood table and wrote on my form "4-F: Psoriasis." At this point in my young life I had a job offer in New York, a wife, and an infant daughter, and was far from keen to devote two years to the national defense; I had never gone to summer camp, and pictured the Army as a big summer camp, with extra-rough bullies and extra-cold showers in the morning. My trepidation should be distinguished from political feelings; I had absolutely no doubts about my country's need, from time to time, to fight, and its right to call me to service. So suddenly and emphatically excused, I felt relieved, guilty, and above all ashamed at being singled out; the naked American men around me had looked at my skin with surprise and now were impressed by the exemption it had won me. I had not foreseen this result; psoriasis would handicap no killing skills and, had I reported in another season, might have been nearly invisible. My wife, when I got back to my parents' house with my news, was naturally delighted; but my mother, always independent in her moods, seemed saddened, as if she had laid an egg which, when candled by the government, had been pronounced rotten.

It pains me to write these pages. They are humiliating – "scab-picking," to use a term sometimes levelled at modern autobiographical writers. I have written about psoriasis only twice before: I gave it to Peter Caldwell in *The Centaur* and to an anonymous, bumptious ceramicist in the short story "From the Journal of a Leper." I expose it this third time only in order to proclaim the consoling possibility that whenever in my timid life I have shown some courage and originality it has been because of my skin. Because of my skin, I counted myself out of any of those jobs – salesman, teacher, financier, movie star – that demand being presentable. What did that leave? Becoming a craftsman of some sort, closeted and unseen – perhaps a cartoonist or a writer, a worker in ink who can hide himself and send out a surrogate presence, a signature that multiplies even while it conceals. Why did I marry so young? Because, having once found a comely female who forgave me my skin, I dared not risk losing her and trying to find another. Why did I have children so young? Because I wanted to surround myself with people who did not have psoriasis. Why, in 1957, did I leave New York and my nice employment there? Because my skin was bad in the urban shadows, and nothing, not even screwing a sunlamp bulb into the socket above my bathroom mirror, helped. Why did I move, with my family, all the way to Ipswich, Massachusetts? Because this ancient Puritan town happened to have one of the great beaches of the Northeast, in whose dunes I could, like a sin-soaked anchorite of old repairing to the desert, bake and cure myself.

Even now, over a decade since I left the town, Ipswich excites me to be in. On its familiar streets, greeted by small memories, reminiscent faces, altered façades, and enduring outlines, I feel light-hearted, desirable, healthy. I have presence. If Shillington gave me my life, Ipswich was where I took possession of it, the place where in my own sense of myself I ceased to be a radically defective person. I brought to the town, at the age of twenty-five, a number of tics and inabilities that seventeen years of life there pretty much eased away. In Ipswich, for instance, I stopped choking. My grandmother would sometimes choke on her food, and have to go out on the side porch in Shillington, where one or another member of the family would follow and hammer on her back while she clung, gagging, to the porch rail.* It was one of our observances, marking our familial awkwardness, our shared tension. Whether by inherited tendency or imitated example, I also would choke now and then. My album of sore moments includes a memory of crouching above my tray in the Lowell House dining hall at Harvard, miserably retching at something in my throat that would not go up or down, while half-swallowed milk dribbled from my mouth and the other students at the table silently took up their trays and moved away. On the edge of asphyxia, I sympathized with them, and wished that I, too, could shun me.

I came to Harvard with not only this disgusting, frightening tendency, and an excitable stammer, and my wretched skin, but morbid fear of spiders and insects – specifically, a fear that they would become very large, a frequent theme of the movies and adventure stories of my boyhood.† This phobia was not soothed by the growing power of photographers, as lenses and film improved, to bring us, in such educational

* "My mother's father squeezed his Bible
  sighing, and smoked five-cent cigars
  behind the chickenhouse, exiling the smell.

  His wife, bespectacled Granma,
  beheaded the chickens
  in their gritty wire yard

  and had a style of choking during dinner;
  she'd run to the porch, where one of us
  would pound her on the back until her inner
  conflict had resolved."   – "Midpoint" (1968)

† I need not have worried. Insect size is limited by the fact that mass is cubed when linear dimension is doubled – an elephant-sized flea would have to have legs sturdy as an elephant's and thus would cease to be flealike. Also, insects' method of respiration, by means of spiracles opening directly into the air, limits oxygen intake and oxidization of ingested food and therefore energy conversion and sustainable body dimension. Insect giants – six- or even seven-inch beetles such as *Dynastes herculeanus* and *Titanus giganteus* of South America, *Xixythrus beyrouski* of Fiji, the goliath beetles of Africa, and stick-insects like *Pharnacia serratipes*, which attains a length of thirteen inches – tend to be tropical, and mercifully sluggish.

magazines as *National Geographic*, images of the enlarged anatomies of bees and dragonflies, of sideways-munching mandibles and hairy pronged forelegs, of segmented antennae and many-faceted, hemispherical eyes. A playful roommate put on my desk one such spread of blow-ups – especially vivid, in color, on the big pages of *Life*. Both offended and alarmed, I "acted out" my genuine fright and tried to flush the bristling, staring pages down the toilet. They were too large, and stiff, to go down, and kept sluggishly rising with their complicated, brainless, merciless faces, and I had to keep poking them with a ruler, to encourage them to vanish; I could not bear to touch them with my fingers, and, even now, have a hard time plucking the bodies of dead wasps from the winter windowsills, where they get trapped behind the storm panes. Another roommate, from nearby Winchester, invited me home for a meal: I was served the great New England treat, lobster. I could not believe, seeing this scarlet arthropod proudly set before me, that I was expected to eat it, to take it into my fingers and tear off and suck its many little segmented limbs. My roommate's mother, much as she might have tossed together a vegetable meal for a Hindu friend her son had brought back from cosmopolitan Harvard, kindly fried up a hamburger for me instead.

In Ipswich, I learned to eat lobster. I learned to grapple in the tidal mud for the edgy smooth forms of clams, like rocks except they are alive, and *feel* alive, with an ever-so-subtle imparting of motion to the palm of your hand, even of emotion as in their dark clenched housing they find themselves pulled up out of the safe muck, and tossed into the bucket where, with something like nervousness, they cleanse themselves preparatory to being steamed. I learned to strip a steamed clam (its shell unhinged in death and rather touchingly thin) of the rubbery little sleeve on its neck and to plop the whole slippery loose remainder, with its stringy and problematical anatomy, into my mouth. All sorts of squeamishness were teased and goaded out of me in Ipswich, by women who seemed gorgeous and men who seemed knowledgeable and staunch. I, whose idea of summer contentment had been day after identical day at the Shillington playground, with its drowsy rounds of roof ball and box hockey and Chinese checkers, learned to play the rich child's games of tennis and golf, and to ski. Above all, I learned, in the buoyant salt water of the beach and the tidal creeks, to swim, without fear – though the thought of sharks did now and then cross my mind and nibble my toes, and, submerged in a friend's swimming pool, I would for fun torment myself with the fantasy that I was caught below-decks in a sinking ship, and must twist my way through narrow, darkening hatchways to the surface before my lungs exploded.

My wife and I found ourselves in a kind of "swim" of equally young married couples, an hour north of Boston and dependent upon each other for entertainment. There was a surge of belonging – we joined committees and societies, belonged to a recorder group and a poker group, played volleyball and touch football in season, read plays aloud and went Greek-dancing and gave dinner parties and attended clambakes and concerts and costume balls, all within a rather narrow society, so that everything resonated. The sisters and brothers I had never had were now on the phone or at the back door; the "gang" I had seen slide by like an alligator was, at last, all here. As a group, we had lovely times being young adults in Ipswich, while raising our children more or less absent-mindedly and holding down our jobs in much the same style.

My profession of free-lance writer was strange here, but not so strange as it would have been in Shillington. John Marquand sometimes came down from Newburyport to appear at an Ipswich cocktail party. Lovell Thompson, one of the genial grandees of Argilla Road, had been a distinguished figure in Boston publishing, and on his retirement established a small, choice publishing house – Gambit – right on Meetinghouse Green. Of the cultivated older generation that had us frisky young folks in for drinks, a number had produced books: Homer White wrote about Spain; his wife, Annie, for children; and Isadore Smith (under the pen name of Ann Leighton) on gardening. Further back, John Wise's independent-minded pamphlets and Nathaniel Ward's *Simple Cobler of Aggawam* had been penned in colonial Ipswich, and Anne Bradstreet had written some of the New World's first poems on High Street, a short walk from where I lived, for twelve years, on East Street. The town, which billed itself (because of John Wise) as "The Birthplace of American Independence," had long been a maverick kind of place; alone among the major settlements of Essex County, it stood aloof from the witch-hunt of 1692, and turned back the delegation from Salem – the legend went – at the Choate Bridge. For witches and writers, Ipswich was "out of harm's way."

I loved it all – its authentic depth of history, its great changing marshes and winding odd-named roads (Heartbreak, Turkey Shore, Labor-in-Vain), its social and ethnic variety, its homely hodgepodge downtown, its casual acceptingness of me. I remember coming back to the town, early in our years there, from several days in New York, to which I still travelled, laboriously, by train; tired from the seven-hour trip, I walked from the station with my suitcase, on a winter night, up to the high school, where the annual town meeting was in progress. I gave my name, was checked off and admitted, and stood there in the doorway of the gymnasium-auditorium in my city suit, looking in at the brightly illuminated faces of my fellow citizens. They were agitated by some thoroughly local issue on the floor; my wife and the friends we had made were somewhere in this solemn, colorful, warm civic mass, and I felt a rush of wonder that I had come to be part of this, this lively town meeting sequestered within the tall winter night, below the basketball nets. It occurs to me now that this was the same crowd that had come to the Shillington gym exhibition, seen from a different angle.

I turned thirty, then forty. My four children went to

private nursery schools, then the public schools, and then one by one, for all my secret hopes of their becoming cheerleaders and quarterbacks as I had never been, they drifted into private education, into the orbit of the North Shore upper class. This class was of no interest to me; I saw myself as a literary spy within average, public-school, supermarket America. It was there I felt comfortable; it was there that I felt the real news was. I wrote short stories for *The New Yorker* all those years like an explorer sending bulletins from the bush, and they published most of them, and my prosperity slowly drove me upwards in the social scale to a stratum that I thought was already well enough covered, by Marquand, Cheever, and others. Children are what welds a family to a town – its meetings and elections, its circles and cliques – and my children came to sense earlier than I that we were not poor. And our friends, it has turned out, were not poor either: with some exceptions, they would come into inheritances, and were en route from privileged childhood to well-padded middle age while I was scribbling for my life.

Like my father, I had left my native state and moved to my wife's region. Acquiring more financial ease than he ever had, I took perhaps even more pleasure than he in the transactions of a middle-class man with his society, from a joking relation with the brothers who ran the liquor store to a Christian camaraderie with the stalwarts of the local Congregational church. Though I had sneered at the deacons' meetings that got him out of the house, I myself now served on church committees and the Ipswich Historical Commission; I got along well, I like to think, with the "nice" people, the venerable, civic-minded Ipswichians who ran for selectman and organized civic observances and acted as caretakers for the town's historical edifices, and who lived in immaculately kept houses full of knickknacks and chintz. They knew things – how things run and what once happened – and a writer always needs to know people who know things. Further, they reminded me of Shillington people, those Shillington residents who stood a step or two higher on the stairs of fulfillment than our somehow blighted, quixotic household, and they, perhaps, responded to the conscientious Shillington boy in me. In Ipswich my impersonation of a normal person became as good as I could make it. I choked only when attempting an especially hearty vitamin pill, and a stammer rarely impeded my incessant sociability.

The tunnels – tending to pass through the throat – between my self and the world were open to traffic. My phobias eased, though I was still not charmed when, say, a daddy longlegs came to assist me as I painted storm windows in the cellar and in his survey gruesomely lost one leg after another to the wet paint. The existential terrors that had driven me, after college, in Oxford and New York, to Chesterton and Aquinas, Kierkegaard and Barth, were eased aside by the coöperative nature, now, of growing older. The couples we knew were also aging, and also had given ever more demanding and uncontrollable hostages to fortune, and paid rising taxes and suffered automobile accidents and midnight illnesses and marital discontent; but under the tireless supervision of gossip all misfortunes were compared, and confessed, and revealed as relative. Egoistic dread faded within the shared life. We celebrated each other's birthdays and break-ups in a boozy, jaunty muddle of mutually invaded privacies. Somewhere in my reading, an old Bostonian claims he doesn't care where he goes after death, Heaven or Hell, as long as his fellow club-members are there. An illusion of eternal comfort reposes in clubbiness – an assurance that members of tribes and villages have extended to one another for millennia, the assurance that no earthly adventure, from puberty to death, is unprecedented or incapable of being shared and that one's life is thoroughly witnessed and therefore not wasted. It was potentially terrifying, to advance into time – every day, a new newspaper on the porch! – toward death, but like an army taking comfort in its own massed song and smell we pressed forward. The weekend get-togethers supplied courage to last the week.

And there was, in those Ipswich years, for me at least, a raw educational component; though I used to score well in academic tests, I seemed to know very little of how the world worked and was truly grateful for instruction, whether it was how to stroke a backhand, mix a martini, use a wallpaper steamer, or do the Twist. My wife, too, seemed willing to learn. Old as we must have looked to our children, we were still taking lessons, in how to be grown-up.

From April to November, my life was structured around giving my skin a dose of sun. In the spring, at Crane's Beach though the wind off the sea was cold, the sun was bright and the hollows in the dunes were hot. I would go there alone, with a radio and book, and without benefit of lotion inflict upon myself two hours of mid-day ultraviolet. I wanted to burn; my skin was my enemy, and the pain of sunburn meant that I had given it a blow. Overnight, the psoriasis would turn from raised pink spots on white skin to whitish spots on red skin; this signalled its retreat, and by June I could prance back and forth on the beach in a bathing suit without shame. To add to my exposure in those sunny years, I bought convertibles, and would drive back up Argilla Road admiring my red, stinging nose and forehead in the rearview mirror and singing in happiness, because normality was on the way; I had packed in a day's worth of radiation.

In the meantime, my pariahlike solitude in the dunes felt somewhat majestic, amid the sandy immensities back from the beach, before summer had begun, when there were no other persons to be seen but a few bundled dog-walkers and perhaps a pair of riders galloping their horses along the ocean's sliding, foaming edge – Ipswich Bay, with a broad sandbar a half-mile out, rarely admitted surf of any real thump. Once down in my chosen hollow and stripped to the bathing suit that I had worn beneath my trousers, I was out of sight, and out of the human world. The world of the dunes, in summer too hot to inhabit, in spring still held puddles of snow-melt. The chill wind whipped a white haze from the rippled surfaces of the dunes and, when I laid my head on the towel, tried to fill my ears with sand. As the minutes went by, silent but for the concussion of the waves on the distant beach and the cry of a gull like a sudden bubble in the smooth blue glass of the sky, the meagre details within my hollow were magnified by boredom almost into omens. The rusted cans and charred driftwood left by a bonfire last autumn; the circles and half-circles that the sharp bent wands of beach grass scribed about themselves; the tenacious gnarled beach-plum bush that gestured at me from a sandy ridge; the sand itself, so minutely sparkling and faceted, spilling warmly through my fingers as, lying there sun-stunned, I idly dug down through the dry top layer to the cooler, more stable and secretive moist darkness beneath. Nature in its starkness and intricacy and uncomplaining monotony enclosed me in my wide trough of sand while masses of mauve and gray spring clouds rode the wind overhead, blotting out the sun for minutes I impatiently outwaited. At first, it seemed that natural appearances, the glinting grains and dried leaves and sticks and stubborn exerophytic worts, would speak to me, like the shapes of letters or at least like the intelligible tracks the gulls and deer and rabbits left on the dampish floor of the hollow. Lying there in the service of my skin, I had plenty of time to learn a language; but my communion, for those many seasons of scorching self-cure, was with an inflexible, if benign, speaker of an alien tongue: Nature pronounced a round, firm word, over and over, but no translation was ever offered as to what the word might mean.

It was least stupefying in the dunes if a Red Sox game were on the radio. I had moved to New England, in part, to be closer to Ted Williams. But by two o'clock, when the afternoon games started, the healing rays had tipped too far from the zenith. Before two, there was music on the radio, with news on the half-hour. The early-rock overture to the coming counterculture sounded, to me, merely noisy; I wanted to hear the mellow saxophones and lilting clarinets and muted trumpets of late-Forties high-school dance music, which had faded forever from the air waves. There were games one could play, patterns both tactile and visual one could fiddle at while the sun flattened the brain to a rosy blankness. I would spit, and watch the little blots and balls of mud fade back into pale, crystalline sand. I would put a stick in the sand to make a sundial. And of course I tried to write and read – but always with a sense of mental effort and optic abuse that led to faint headaches and nausea. Ultraviolet light, that breaks down the DNA in overexposed skins, also attacks consecutive thought. Writing is a thoroughly shady affair.

The first year in Ipswich, I wrote in a marble-floored room at the back of the little lavender house we rented on Essex Road; one winter night, a storm blew the door open and filled my boxes of *Poorhouse Fair* manuscript with snow. In the roomier seventeenth-century house that we then bought, I worked in a small corner aerie upstairs; there, looking out upon the intersection of East and Spring Streets, my eyes level with the limbs of a great old elm and the crossbars of an especially complicated telephone pole,* I tried to imagine the Pennsylvania scenes of *Rabbit, Run*. By late 1960, our fourth child was born, and the house was full of commotion and small emergencies that seemed to invite my participation; I was surprised when my wife suggested that she was tired of making lunch for me every day and that my presence was not

---

* "Our eyes, washed clean of belief,
   Lift incredulous to their fearsome crowns of bolts, trusses, struts,
      nuts, insulators, and such
   Barnacles as compose
   These weathered encrustations of electrical debris –
   Each a Gorgon's head, which, seized right,
   Could stun us to stone."

– "Telephone Poles" (1960)

really indispensable. And so I rented a room downtown, four blocks away. The beginning rent was eight dollars a week, and my frugal landlord, courtly old Mr Lampropoulos, observing that I didn't sleep there, would turn off the radiator every night, so on winter mornings I would face a room cooled to a temperature suitable less for writing than for running in place, wearing gloves and a hat. The room and I would slowly warm up together.

In summer, though, what fullness of life it seemed, to put in a few hours at the typewriter and then race downstairs (the room was above a restaurant) and leap into a station wagon or convertible containing my wife and quartet of children, all of them plump and brown in their bathing suits! They would have brought my bathing suit and I would change in the car as my wife drove the five miles to the beach. Then, there, to be waved past the ticket booth by its pith-helmeted guardians, who knew us by sight and name, and to proceed to the town lot to which our taxes and beach sticker entitled us, and to park, and unload our lunch-basket, our toys, our towels and mats and paperbacks, and to walk down the boardwalk in procession, myself the leader and evident support of so much healthy flesh – what pagan, bourgeois bliss! In New York City, sallow and spotty, I had gone to the Forty-second Street library's nation-wide collection of telephone books and looked down the column of names under "Ipswich" and imagined myself among them; now I was here, a citizen in good standing, partaking of the splendid local summer as if entitled since birth. We would settle on the hard cool flat stretch of beach between the icy blue sea, which invited only the fanatically hardy in for more than a dip, and the loose white sand beyond the high-tide mark, which burned your feet if you did not step quickly. This stretch, beside the water's edge, held a promenading of friends and strangers, of caramel-colored teen-agers and middle-aged men with shrunken legs and grizzled barrel chests, of wasp-waisted homosexuals from Boston and pregnant young brides here for a week of vacation.

It was, for me, a matter of pride, a willed achievement, to be among these nearly naked strollers, to be an inconspicuous part of this herd, to be in this humble sense human.

One went visiting at the beach as if up and down a village street carved from these magnitudes of light and salt air and glittering ocean. Women of our acquaintance were strung, with their blankets and books and tubes of Bain de Soleil, as far as the point where Crane's Beach became Castle Neck Beach. Bearing four children in less than six years had given my wife some varicose veins but otherwise her body was still a young woman's; in those years before bikinis took hold, she wore a series of one-piece black bathing suits in which she looked strikingly graceful and ripe. Her body, with its well-tanned skin, lent mine, I felt, beauty by association as, on the excuse of looking for sand dollars with the children, we went calling. This book is about my self-consciousness and not hers, but I think she had her own reasons for adolescent insecurity and for gratitude at belonging to this glorious, informal, amusing, accepting, not quite surburban town. We both loved the beach, though it tended to bore the children, once they were past the age of sand castles; they didn't, after all, have psoriasis or need a beauty tan.

A kind of fly called the greenhead arose from the extensive marshes of Ipswich and Rowley in late July, in unstoppable numbers; this obtuse pest bit, with a curiously hot and malevolent chewing action, and rendered the outdoors uninhabitable for the first weeks of August. We began to rent for a month on Martha's Vineyard, to escape the greenheads and to return, obliquely, to New York, whose literary circles supplied a significant portion of the Vineyard's summer people. It was a life in another sort of sun, an all-day sun, enjoyed while reading proofs on the porch overlooking Menemsha Bight, or playing tennis on the glaring clay courts at the Chilmark Community Center, or sailing across warm salt ponds to South Beach, where heavy waves towered and (a pale celery-green light shining through at the moment of cresting) crashed in a sportive, challenging manner not seen in Ipswich Bay. One dived straight into them or underwent a terrifying tumble. One took showers in wooden outdoor stalls and walked naked across the prickly, sandy lawn. The Vineyard was soaked through and through with summer, like an old pine picnic table left outside beside the rusty barbecue grill. There were clay cliffs, and Indians with legal grievances, and plain stores with fancy prices, and softball games. The air was moist and bright, a kind of robe we all wore. Without the incentive of my skin, I would never have pushed myself into this paradise, among Cambridge professors and Manhattan word-merchants – many of whom, having had desert-dwelling ancestors, took a much better tan than I did.

A bit of psoriasis, erased, seems to steal a little melanin away with it; my skin, always freckled, had developed small freckles of pallor, across the shoulders and upper arms especially, so that, examined closely, it showed the chromatic complexity of mottled linoleum or a Pollock masterpiece. Also, in August, when the summer's harvest of swarthiness and glow should have been at its fullest, small hard raised spots would appear: the psoriasis was fighting back. My skin, once so thirsty and grateful for solar rays, and so sensitive to them, had grown toughened and blasé over the years. By November, however many October noons I had gone to the beach and forced myself into the bitter blue water and lain there glistening and shivering on the depopulated sand, my skin would have become again a cause for self-consciousness; by January, it was time for my trip to the Caribbean. My search for superficial perfection had additionally goaded me all the way to the tropics, where an old-fashioned Shillington boy would never have thought to go, where the air, the music, the vegetation, the houses, the accents of the people and their color were all entirely different, where even the clouds and the stars presented different formations.

For the first Caribbean trip, in the winter of 1960, we all went – my wife and I and our then three children. The third, a seven-month-old boy, was diagnosed just before we left to have feet that needed straightening. Daisy and Selma, the two servants who came with the house we had rented on the island of Anguilla, used to pack his squarish, toed-in feet in the sand, an act of magic not much different from the plaster corrective casts he eventually wore. We had thought to spend the entire winter in the sun, to heal me, and a friend of a friend knew Anguilla to be remote and seldom visited and therefore cheap. We established communication, via fragile blue air-letter forms that arrived in Ipswich wrinkled and bleached as if by the salt spray and sunshine at their source, with a Mr Gumbs, who rented us what turned out to be "the Captain's House," in the part of Anguilla called Sandy Ground. The geographical divisions of the island were simplicity itself – Valley, Road, East End, West End – and the Captain's House turned out to be the mansion of its modest neighborhood: a solid two-story structure of which we occupied the second story only. The lower, of stone and permanently shadowed by our veranda, was occupied by a short dark woman who could be seen busily spreading her clothes to dry on the oleander bushes around the house and who otherwise broke into our consciousness rarely, but for two occasions I remembered in one stanza of a poem:

> The night Rebecca's –
> she lived beneath us –
> sailor lover returned from sea
> and beat her for hours,
> it was as hard to sleep as the time
> she tied a rooster
> inside an oil drum.

From the front veranda one looked straight down a kind of grassy roadway at the beryl-colored sea and a blunt cement-and-wood structure that served as a quay; there was no more elaborate dock on the island, and supplies were rafted in to the beaches. We ate vegetables canned in England and balls of fried dough that Daisy called "bakes" and, for protein, freshly caught fish or some poor scrawny chicken brought alive to us for inspection and then clumsily killed with a machete in the yard. A five-year-old boy, Hilton, the same age as my daughter, was handed the machete one time by the squeamish Daisy and he and the chicken had a prolonged time achieving the latter's death, as it raced squawking around the threadbare yard with its half-severed head at an angle. A small population had mysteriously arisen from Sandy Ground to serve us; in addition to Daisy, the cook, and Selma, the babysitter, there was a handsome boy, fifteen or so, who every morning pumped up water out of our cistern into the holding tank, and Eliot Carty, called "Mr Eliot," who had white blood and a Jeep and who would give us rides to "town" – to the Factory in Valley. This Factory did not make things but sold them; it was a general store, English-colonial style, and designated in the old sense of "factor" as "one who makes transactions." Though at night Sandy Ground became as dark as the jungle, with clacking black insects hurling themselves against our hissing tilly lamps and centipedes the size of mice pulsing in the shadowy corners, and though it more than once occurred to me that our mass murder would take a week to make the North American newspapers, we were, I can appreciate now, well looked after and sustained by the invisible network of this primitive place. The Third World takes better care of its guests than the First.

We were rare white visitors on an almost entirely black, undeveloped island, an extreme backwater in the fast-fading British Empire. Once a day or so, a policeman on a bicycle, wearing a helmet and shorts, would whizz down the road. Small children in blue school uniforms would walk their way to and from a school where they learned the British counties and the monarchs of England. Young women would come to the faucet in front of the Captain's House and fill buckets of water they would carry away on their heads. At night, a boy down the road would practice on his steel drums. For large stretches of the day, nothing at all seemed to be happening; but then the Shillington of the Thirties might have looked as dormant and secretive to an Anguillan. The little houses around us, with slat sides and hipped roofs of corrugated iron, generally had their shutters closed. Here and there a man might be hoeing or a woman hanging up wash while hymns out of Antigua blew from the radio on her windowsill. Across the road, in a large house surrounded by a low fence and with a yard shaded by dusty trees dripping clusters of brown pods, lived the other white people in Sandy Ground, an old island family that owned vast stretches of cliff and several expensive wooden schooners at anchor in the bay. But they themselves resembled the underfed, squinting people in Dorothea Lange's Depression photographs. One of the brothers was always absent; the other, who was present, was usually drunk; of the sisters, one was either crippled or mad and never emerged from the house, and the other sat in her yard, surrounded by fallen palm fronds, and made conversation in a melancholy sing-song. Only the tiny family matriarch had a certain dignity and zest to her style; years later, when Princess Margaret visited Anguilla, the old lady went through the receiving line and affronted protocol, we heard, by giving the Princess a kiss. All the family had that curious complexion of tropical whites – a dingy, mat color, the color of sun-avoidance in a climate rife with photons.

And there also seemed to be another elderly white woman, who tended the little library up the road, where I borrowed the works of Ian Fleming and where the handsomest black girl in Sandy Ground worked as an assistant. This girl had a mischievous Caucasian touch to her features and, passing the Captain's House, would give me a glance as I sat on the veranda reading. Married and young and further inhibited by my diseased skin, I could explore the possible meaning of that glance only in my imagination, at night, lying under the ghostly canopy of the mosquito netting.

I had never been among black people before. The "colored people" of Berks were ghettoized in south Reading and given the benefit of German views on race. My grandmother's hair, a story of our family went, had turned white when she saw a "boogie" peeking in at the window of the Plowville house. A single Negro family, the Johnsons, attended Shillington High, and were admired for their singing (the girl) and athletic skill (the boys). When one Johnson boy, however, took a white bride, his house somehow burned down. There seemed to be, in this southeast corner of Pennsylvania, including Philadelphia, a certain Southern illusion of a mutally enjoyed *apartheid* – though in doctrine Penn and the Quakers were radically egalitarian, and in Frederick Douglass's autobiography the thrilling escape into freedom takes the form of the short train ride from Baltimore to Philadelphia. Our household gathered by the radio to cheer Joe Louis on, my mother and I were low-level jazz buffs, and my father brought home from his summer employments tales of his camaraderie with his Negro fellow-workers. When I worked as a copyboy for the Reading *Eagle*, I was shocked to hear an editor bawl out one of the photographers for bringing back from the city playgrounds too many shots containing "them." It was my belief, as of 1950, that the United States' black tenth had contributed much more than their proportionate share to what is distinctive and universally eloquent in American culture, and I believed that realizing full equality for blacks was our foremost domestic priority. Nevertheless, however liberal my views, I had no dealings with blacks either as equals or as servants and was shy and nervous with them. At Harvard, there were two blacks in my freshman dorm; friendly as we whites all wanted to be and felt we were, after freshman year we lost touch, and I heard that by our junior years both these members of Harvard's minuscule, pre-affirmative-action black minority had left the college. And I met no blacks in Oxford, nor at *The New Yorker*, nor in Ipswich. So, as Isak Dinesen grandly puts it in *Out of Africa*, "The discovery of the dark races was to me a magnificent enlargement of all my world."

Anguilla had been too poor and small to attract many whites or to hold those who did come there. On the East End, an old shipwreck had deposited some Scandinavian sailors whose descendants, though still pale enough to shelter their faces with straw hats, seemed otherwise to have forgotten that they were not black like everybody else. An Irish airline pilot, Captain Martineau, and his wife were the only white tourists besides ourselves; frequent visitors, they eventually bought land and built on Anguilla. They showed us coves and beaches away from Sandy Ground; self-consciously, early in our stay, I explained my psoriasis to Mrs Martineau, who had not seemed to notice it. She noticed it now, and exclaimed dryly, "You poor thing." That seemed the right comment; I was always in danger, with my skin, of forgetting that I was its victim and not its author. Within a few weeks of Caribbean sun and salt water I had no more cause for self-consciousness, and even when my skin was at its worst I had the sensation of being overlooked and forgiven as, each noon, with my book and sunglasses and towel, I plodded up the arc of dazzling white coral beach, past the patchy wooden houses half-hidden behind the bushes of sea grape, to sock my spots with sun.

One was as alone here as in the Ipswich dunes. The soft, pale-green ocean, a few steps away, kept up a lulling slap and hiss of advance and withdrawal, and, in front of the high cliff to the left, pelicans dived, collapsing themselves like umbrellas for their long twisting drop to the sea and then struggling back into the air with a flash of silver in their pouched beaks. A few hand-hewn sailing vessels rocked in the bay, and an occasional native walked up the beach, which was, for the population of Sandy Ground, a thoroughfare to their homes. We would exchange a syllable of greeting, and I would try not to cringe in shame. White people were so unusual and odd here, I told myself, that my personal unusualness and epidermal oddity might go unnoticed. Small transparent crabs lived in the pure white coral sand, and their cautious scuttlings formed another sort of traffic, once I persuaded myself that, unlike the spiders of evil fantasy, they would not attack me. To them, after all, I was huge, and my arrangement of limbs bizarre. I swam merely to wet my skin to speed the therapy, for a vivid island story told of a woman on the cliff who saw children playing on this beach while a huge shark cruised a few yards from shore, in the very shallow water; she shouted, and the mother plucked them back just in time, as if from the tracks of an onrushing locomotive. No such titanic predator made a pass at me, but, between the sea grape and the sea, the only sunbather on a mile of beach, while the pelicans monotonously threw themselves toward their glinting prey, I was aware of a possible cliff-high vantage from which my self-solicitous life was negligible, and my imperfect skin a less than immense matter.

I would return to the house around two and wait for the sunburn to well up at drink-time, at the hour when Daisy and Selma, having set dinner on the table, would start out toward their own homes along a path that a dike carried right across the big salt pond behind Sandy Ground, so the two girls seemed to be walking on water. In less than a month, my skin had cleared and become as brown as it ever could be. I relaxed, and went to the beach only when my wife and thin-skinned children did. As a family we would stroll down toward the dock in the late afternoon and swim as the shadows lengthened and the black children in their blue uniforms, holding their shoes in their hands, walked home along the beach and the fishermen hauled their dories up on the yielding coral sand, so soft and porous that it took a footprint two inches deep. Mornings, I lay on a musty red Victorian sofa with hard springs and wrote short stories with a ballpoint pen – "Pigeon Feathers," "Home," "Archangel," "The Sea's

Green Sameness." At night, I read Kafka and Ian Fleming. We began to get bored, and came home earlier than planned.

To be forgiven, by God: this notion, so commonly mouthed in shadowy churches, was for me a tactile actuality as I lay in my loathed hide under that high hard pellet, that suspended white explosion, of a tropical sun. And the sun's weight on my skin always meant this to me; I was being redeemed, hauled back into mankind, back from deformity and shame. The sun was like God not only in His power but also in the way He allowed Himself to be shut out, to be evaded. Yet if one were receptive, He could find you even at the bottom of a well; one could board a plane in a blizzard, bounce for a few hours in the fuselage's pastel tunnel, slide far down the lines of longitude, and get out, and He would be there, waiting. The sun-softened humid air would hit your face like an angel's kiss at the airplane's exit door, at the top of the stairs. There would be puddles from a momentary tropical shower drying on the runway. Inside the terminal the black customs officials in their shorts were indolently waiting, and the air was full of black greetings, black languor and laughter, black aromas. Waiting for my baggage to come down the belt, I would unbutton one shirtsleeve and take a peek at my arm. Already my skin would look better.

After Anguilla, I returned to the Caribbean every year. St Thomas and Antigua, Aruba and Sint Maarten/St Martin, St Croix and Puerto Rico – all were visited, sometimes with my wife and once (Tortola) with our four children as well, but more often alone, in trips of a week or less, to give my skin a hit to tide me over till April and my furtive return to the Ipswich dunes. San Juan was easiest to get to, but urban, with a drab, broad, rather dirty beach and populated not by blacks but by irritable speakers of Spanish. The little islands had the black magic, and the sweet curved coral beaches one could hide on.

St Thomas was the most Americanized and accessible. In those days there were no direct flights; you flew over from San Juan in little prop planes whose aisle tilted upward and whose black stewardesses gave you a piece of hard candy to ease the pain in your eustacian tubes. From the air, the islands were outlined in white and the turquoise water was spotted with submerged islands, purplish coral reefs. I arrived at Harry S. Truman Aiport, the first time, without a hotel reservation. The taxi took me to The Gate, a small hotel up a steep street near the center of Charlotte Amalie, in an old stone building with a big iron gate, curved brick stairs, and thick shutters. At night, downstairs, a steel band played and there was no sleeping until one o'clock. But then I never slept well in the Caribbean anyway, what with sunburn and my raw excitement at being there, at having reached the sun. The steel drums unleashed their belling, momentous music beneath my bed and a car with a broken muffler revved under my louvered window and I was roasting in a kind of heaven, happily hurting in every square inch of skin save the bathing-suit area and the soles of my feet. I got the treatment down to a science, after a few trips in which I had burned myself so badly as to lose the next day entirely, spent in my hotel room while I shivered and stroked Noxzema onto my scorched thighs and belly and upper arms. Skin remembers, and, once burned, remains sun-shy. Blisters, I noticed, would well up at the edge of the psoriatic lesions, as if the transitional skin here were least defended against ultraviolet. It hurt, but it meant I had taken the offensive, and the spots were in retreat.

On St Thomas, I would hire a taxi or drive my rented VW bug to Morningside Beach or Magens Bay and walk, fully clothed, to the far end, stake out with my towel a spot near some sea grape or a shelter made of palm thatch, strip down to my bathing suit, and begin to pass the hours. Two hours was about the maximum, unless clouds muddled the exposure. If I had been there a few days and my skin was half-cured, I might be bold enough to walk in my bathing suit down to the beach restaurant and have a hamburger and milk. I almost never talked to anyone, except to ask for food. The island, and especially Morningside Beach, did not lack for vacationing North American males. They were kind of a local industry. A young black cab driver, driving me across the island's ridge to Magens Bay, drove slower and slower, waiting for my homosexual proposition, and my embarrassment became as intense as my desire to press on the accelerator and get me to the beach and started on my cure. On another trip, after about five days on the island long enough for me to feel normal and a normal need for human conversation – I was invited by another single gentleman on the beach to have dinner with him that evening. I accepted; he had recognized me from a dust-jacket photograph, perhaps that on *Couples*, so I felt there could be no basic misapprehension. We had a very pleasant boozy meal and found a subject we could both talk enthusiastically about: our mothers.

But generally my solitude was part of the charm of those pilgrimages to the sun, part of the relief from my constant temperate-zone performances as father, partygoer, committee-man. Down here, my minor role as a leper became predominant, and I didn't want to be touched. My daily stint on the beach behind me, I would wander through the tax-free shops and the local forts with their torpid displays of old muskets and leg-irons. I would walk along the waterfront and marvel at the boats, evidences of that whole other life, dependent on many ropes and cunning brass fittings, that men live at sea. I would wait for that quick tropical dusk, violet and lemon in color, to descend, so I could go to a bar – my favorite was Trader Dan's, an open four-sided bar under a pavilion roof on the Charlotte Amalie harbor – and cool my insides with a daiquiri or two. My chest and legs by now would be aching under my clothes, and it was as if with the rum I were rewarding myself for a good day's work.

Dinner was awkward, alone; on St Thomas, I found a cafeteria a few blocks off the tourist track where the locals and I could eat meatloaf and peas off a tray. Then back to The Gate, to wait with a book in my room for the steel band to arrive, its clangorous unpacking and jocular jabber and the tentative peals of tuning up.* I would go down and sit at the bar alone and drink beers and watch the dancing. In those days The Gate offered the only in-town entertainment; all the rest, the limbo dancers and calypso singers, was at the posh beach hotels, out of bounds to the natives who came and paid their dollar at the old iron gate, along with the white college kids and the more adventurous, louder middle-aged tourist couples. It was a black-and-white crowd, blacker as the night wore on, and the black girls were mesmerizing, doing the mambo with their understated, utterly certain little motions, the feet shuffling back and forth a few inches, the hips swaying no more than necessary, the torso and head softly, steadily bobbing in a solemn chickenish kind of urging onward of the music, which did roll on and on, the soprano pan brighter and quicker than a marimba and the bass – two whole oil drums, usually played by the band's fattest man – shaking the floor like an organ's "Amen."

I suppose I desired them, those stately rapt black girls, but, whatever my yearnings, the touching fact remains that I never had a sexual adventure in all those solitary trips to the Caribbean. *At last*, I can hear the reader sighing, *we're getting*

---

* "Five Negroes, uncostumed, in motley clothes and as various in size as their instruments, had assembled on the shadowy platform, kidding and giggling back and forth and teasing the air with rapid, stop-and-start gusts of tuning up. Abruptly they began to play. The ping-pong, the highest pan, announced itself with four harsh solo notes, and on the fifth stroke the slightly deeper guitar pans, the yet deeper cello pans, and the bass boom, which was two entire forty-four-gallon oil drums, all at once fell into the tune, and everything – cut and peened drums, rubber-tipped sticks, tattered shirtsleeves, bobbing heads, munching jaws, a frightened-looking little black child whipping a triangle as fast as he could – was in motion, in flight. The band became a great loose-jointed bird feathered in clashing, rippling bells. It played 'My Basket,' and then, with hardly a break, 'Marengo Jenny,' 'How You Come to Get Wet?' and 'Madame Dracula.'"

– "At a Bar in Charlotte Amalie" (1969)

down to it. For of course my concern with my skin was ultimately sexual, the skin being a sexual organ and the moment of undressing the supreme personal revelation and confiding. Yet women, in my limited experience, were not put off by my troubled epidermis; they take, I came to be persuaded, a rather haptic, holistic view of men in which the voice, the style, the aura, and the three-dimensional effect matter more than surface blemishes. Oddly enough, sexual contentment, whether that of the happily married or the illicitly adored, has never reconciled me to psoriasis or relaxed my wish to combat it; my war with my skin had to do with self-love, with finding myself acceptable, whether others did or not.

In the Caribbean, my need to make contact found release in minor cross-cultural trespasses – the purchase of a pair of scissors, for instance, at a downtown sundries store where tourists rarely ventured (on a trip wherein my own scissors, carried in my briefcase for some self-editing I wanted to do, were confiscated on the airplane as an anti-hijack measure and not returned), or afternoon walks up into the slopes of Charlotte Amalie, where roosters crowed and tobacco-brown old ladies with toothless mouths lifted their hands in surprised greeting of this wrong-colored pedestrian. In St Thomas one Sunday, I discovered the Lutheran church not too many blocks up from The Gate, all polished wood and black faces inside, with plaques in Danish up near the rafters and in the pulpit a pale Englishman, a Greeneish-looking tropical cleric, gnawed by an inner worm. The old walls and pews still smelled of cedar, and the singing, like the steel band, like the sun, enfolded you entirely.

The trips gradually became less effective; some winters there had to be two, one in December and one in March. In the fall of 1974, I left my wife and Ipswich. The next fall, perhaps because there had been no summer on the beach, perhaps because guilt had triggered a metabolic riot, my skin attacked me – my face broke out, my shoulders and neck became so encrusted

I couldn't turn my head without pain. In the emergency I flew to St Thomas and, though I arrived too late for the high sun, parked my rented car by a little beach near the airport and lay there, as a Catholic in crisis might nip into a cathedral. The good old sensations – the moist tropical air, the yielding abrasion of the sand, the slap and hiss of the water, the rustle of the palms, the soft pressure of the solar rays, the illusion when the eyelids closed, of being absolved within a blind red universe – were the same, but my skin failed to react as it once did, with the sunburn that put all the cells, somehow, back to Go. Perhaps I had grown too soft on my skin, using too much Coppertone; or perhaps my skin had grown stubborn. In the next days, the sleepy long curve of Magens Bay was as Edenic as ever, and the translucent water as alive with silver fish, and the sands of Morningside Beach (a big new hotel had been erected since I had first gone there) still held well-oiled male couples wearing European-skimpy trunks, and the smells of rum and charbroiled burgers still drifted out from the bar, and the black taxi drivers still cracked jokes in the dusty parking lot; but my scabs balked at fading away, though the skin between them got freckled and tan. I had used up the Caribbean. At forty-two, I had worn out the sun.

Providentially (let's say), at this very time, a few blocks from where I was living in Boston, dermatologists at the Massachusetts General Hospital were developing the PUVA program, still in the experimental stage. My future wife's psychiatrist passed on word of it, and I quickly applied. It turned out that my son David had once taken guitar lessons from the chief dermatologist's son. The doctor directly in charge of PUVA was an Australian, and his letter offering me an appointment had the clipped, minimal elegance, centered on a large sheet of paper, of advisements from the British revenue service. Those admitted to the program had to be severe cases; from the startled expression on the Australian's face when I took off my shirt, I knew that I had passed. I would not flunk this enlistment. I stripped and, fussily clucking and clicking, he photographed my lesions with a Nikon. It was draft exam and swimming lessons and gym exhibition all over again; but I was nearing the end, I felt, of a long line of humiliating exposures. And in a few months pills and artificial light had done what salt water and sun could no longer do. I was, in the language of the therapy, "clear" – the clearest I had been since kindergarten.

On Anguilla, Daisy's young cousin, who was intellectual and hoped to study abroad at an English university, had once been speaking to me and cause had arisen to refer to some third party who was white. "He is – clear?" had been his delicate way of putting it. White is right, clear is dear; cured, I could now abandon all imagined solidarity with the unclear of the world, those whose skin gives them difficulty. And yet, I self-consciously wondered, was not my sly strength, my insistent specialness, somehow linked to my psoriasis? Might it not be the horrible badge of whatever in me was worth honoring: the price, high but not impossibly so, I must pay for being me? Only psoriasis could have taken a very average little boy, and furthermore a boy who loved the average, the daily, the safely hidden, and made him into a prolific, adaptable, ruthless-enough writer. What was my creativity, my relentless need to produce, but a parody of my skin's embarrassing overproduction? Was not my thick literary skin, which shrugged off rejection slips and patronizing reviews by the sheaf, a superior version of my poor vulnerable own, and my shamelessness on the page a distraction from my real shame? I have never cared, in print, about niceness or modesty, but agonize over typos and factual errors – "spots" on the ideally unflecked text. Having so long carried a secret behind my clothes, I had no trouble with the duplicity that generates plots and surprises and symbolism and layers of meaning; dualism, indeed, such as existed between my skin and myself, appeared to me the very engine of the human. And with my changeable epiderm came a certain transcendent optimism; like a snake, I shed many skins: I had emerged relatively spotless from many a summer and holiday, and the possibility of a "new life," in this world or the next, has been ever present to my mind.

A psychiatrist, I happen to know, would be bored by these linkages; by Freudian lights my mother's failings (if any) matter far more than my skin's. In certain moods even I could put my affliction in perspective. My eyes saw keenly, my legs moved briskly, my genital equipment worked well enough; I was in no serious way handicapped. Indeed, psoriasis is so customarily associated with general good health that the Italians call it *morbus fortiorum* – "the disease of the strong." So wrapped up in my skin, so watchful of its day-to-day permutations, I have, it might be, too little concern to spare for the homeless, the disenfranchised, and the unfortunate who figure so largely in the inner passions of smooth-pelted liberals like my first wife. *I* am unfortunate, is my prime thought: Nature played a quite unnecessary trick on me. Other disfigured or handicapped people annoy me, in reminding me of myself. How much hard-heartedness is normal? I sometimes worry that my self-obsession on the epidermal level has deadened those feelers that sentimentally interact with the rest of mankind. Away from the mirror, I am hard to distress, and uncannily equable. I have been since early childhood caged with my fierce ugly skin and all struggles outside the cage* – that is to say, the general run of human

---

* "Last night's dreams. I am skiing on a white slope, beneath a white sky. I look down at my feet and they are also white, and my skis are engulfed by the powder. I am exhilarated. Then the dream transfers me to an interior, a ski hut where the white walls merge into the domed ceiling indistinguishably. There is an Eskimo maiden, muscular, brown, naked. I am dressed like a doctor, but more stiffly, in large white cards. I awaken, immensely ashamed.

"In the negative print of this dream I am sitting on a white bowl and my excrement overflows, unstoppably, unwipably, engulfing my feet, my

travails – are relatively a relief. Family life – the hurled pot, the sick child, the burst water pipe, the midnight dash for the hospital – had a joyous undercurrent for me of being more or less standard. When, playing touch football, I broke my leg and had to have it operated upon, I chiefly remember amid my pain and helplessness being pleased that my shins, at that time, were clear and I would not offend the surgeon.

With my admission to the PUVA program, I was no longer alone with my skin. The world's dermatological wisdom had come into the cage with me. In the years since, I have watched my skin fight back. The psoriasis irrepressibly strains against the treatment, breaking out in odd areas like the tops of the feet, the backs of the hands. To my body, which has no aesthetic criteria, psoriasis is normal, and its suppression abnormal. Psoriasis is my health. Its suppression constitutes a poisoning of the system, of my personal ecology. Not only is my skin, after decades of being battered by sunlight and artificially supplied UV-A, full of keratotic and potentially cancerous cells but there is such a thing, it turns out, as phototoxicity, which builds up over the years of PUVA and when it strikes feels like sunburn of the muscles, and chews the skin beneath the epidermis so that it flakes off in little chunks. In my case the flanks were worst hit; I walked like a Japanese woman, with little toed-in steps, and found getting in and out of cars a curious agony. The remedy, slow, was cortisone ointment smeared under a sarong of Saran Wrap. After several episodes of deep burn, I was taken off photo-therapy and put on a small weekly dose of methotrexate, which suppresses mitosis, or cell division; it inhibits DNA synthesis by competing as a substrata for dihydrofolate reduc-tase. Science is getting closer to the internal biochemical

---

thighs in patches I try to scrape. I awaken and am relieved to be in bed, between clean sheets. Then I look at my arms in the half-light of dawn and an ineluctable horror sweeps over me. This is real. This skin is me, I can't get out."   – "From the Journal of a Leper" (1975)

riddle, the simple curative pill I have always longed for. My skin cleared once more, and furthermore lost its artificial tan; my basic, unPUVAed, unpsoriatic skin was returned to me, weathered and wrinkled but my own, out of the mists of infancy. Miraculous methotrexate, however, is hazardous to your liver, and I have had to stop drinking alcohol lest cirrhosis occur. My father's favorite saying was "You don't get something for nothing."

I endure these developments with a certain detachment, at the remove of shared responsibility. My psoriasis no longer seems quite the self-generated scandal it did in Shillington when only my mother and Doc Rothermel knew what it was, and there was nowhere to take it but the sun porch overlooking Shilling Alley. Fifty years have demythologized the disease, to an extent; it is mentioned on television commercials, and its "heartbreak" is publicly joked about, by Bette Midler (or is it Erica Jong?). Ironically, even as I, at the cost of an incessant sobriety, am successfully keeping my skin clear, my life provides almost no occasions to display it – no locker rooms, no swimming parties, no gym exhibitions, no sudden seductions. Eventually, I suspect, my old friend *morbus fortiorum* will wear out the methotrexate, but perhaps by then another clever chemical will have been developed. I also foresee that when I weaken, when I am at last too ill for all these demanding and perilous palliatives, the psoriasis like a fire smoldering in damp peat will break out and spread triumphantly; in my dying I will become hideous, I will become what I am.

The psoriatic struggles for philosophy, for thoughts that are more than skin deep. What could matter less than the integument a skeleton once wore? Despite my skin I have had my fun, my children and women and volleyball games. What concupiscent vanity it used to be, playing midsummer volleyball bare-chested, leaping high to spike the ball down into a pretty housewife's upturned face, and wearing tomato-red bicycle shorts that as if casually slid down to expose an inch more of tanned, normal-appearing derrière, even to the sexy dent where the cleavage of the buttocks begins! I have preened, I have lived. Between now and the grave lies a long slide of forestallment, a slew of dutiful, dutifully paid-for maintenance routines in which dermatological makeshift joins periodontal work and prostate examinations on the crowded appointment calendar of dwindling days. For the first time in my life I own a house within walking distance of a beach, and I walk there scarcely three times a summer. Life suddenly seems too short to waste time lying in the sun.

III

Getting the Words Out

The Jerusalem *Post* of November 10, 1978, having attacked my rumpled attire after I'd lost my luggage,* went on to expose my stutter: "Updike has the slight slurp of a speech impediment, the sort of thing once affected by cavalry subalterns." I liked to imagine, all evidence to the contrary, that it, like my deplorable skin, was unnoticeable – that only I was conscious of it. Conscious, that is, of a kind of windowpane suddenly inserted in front of my face while I was talking, or of an obdurate barrier thrust into my throat. My first memory of the sensation is associated with our Shillington neighbor Eddie Pritchard, a somewhat larger boy than I whom I was trying, on the sidewalk in front of our houses, to reason into submission. I think he was calling me "Ostrich," a nickname I did not think I deserved, and a fear of being misunderstood or mistaken for somebody else has accompanied the impediment ever since. There seems so much about me to explain – all of it subsumable under the heading of "I am not an ostrich" – that when freshly encountering, say, a bored and hurried electrician over the telephone, my voice tends to seize up. If the electrician has already been to the house, the seizing up is less dramatic, and if I encounter not his voice but that of his maternal-sounding secretary, I become quite vocal – indeed, something of a minor virtuoso

---

* "Updike is rumpled. Really rumpled. Not the studied casual wrinkles of the well-tenured professor, but crimped-necktie, creased-shirt, battered-jacket, accordion-trousers *rumpled!* Despite the elegant speech, the cocktail cool, the 20 years of New York slick and chic, this man is ragged-assed *rumpled!* Even his *eyes* are rumpled!"

– byline: Matthew Nesvisky

of the spoken language. For there is no doubt that I have lots of words inside me; but at moments, like rush-hour traffic at the mouth of a tunnel, they jam.

It happens when I feel myself in a false position. My worst recent public collapse, that I can bear to remember, came at a May meeting of the august American Academy and Institute of Arts and Letters, when I tried to read a number of award citations – hedgy and bloated, as citations tend to be – that I had not written. I could scarcely push and batter my way through the politic words, and a woman in the audience loudly laughed, as if I were doing an "act." Similarly, many years before, one spring evening, on the stage of the Shillington High School auditorium, I (I, who played the father in our class plays, who was on the debating team, who gave droll "chalk talks" with aplomb even in other county high schools) could barely get out a few formal words in my capacity as class president. I did not, at heart, feel I deserved to be class president (whereas I did somehow deserve to give the chalk talks), and in protest at my false position my vocal apparatus betrayed me. In most people there is a settled place they speak from; in me it remains unsettled, unfinished, provisional. Viewing myself on taped television, I see the repulsive symptoms of an approaching stammer take possession of my face – an electronically rapid flutter of the eyelashes, a distortion of the mouth as of a leather purse being cinched, a terrified hardening of the upper lip, a fatal tensing and lifting of the voice. And through it all a detestable coyness and craven willingness to please, to assure my talk-show host and his millions of viewers that I am not, appearances to the contrary, an ostrich.

As with my psoriasis, the affliction is perhaps not entirely unfortunate. It makes me think twice about going on stage and appearing in classrooms and at conferences – all that socially approved yet spiritually corrupting public talking that writers of even modest note are asked to do. Being obliging by nature and anxious for social approval, I would never say no if I weren't afraid of stuttering. Also, as I judge from my own reactions, people who talk too easily and comfortably, with too much happy rolling of the vowels and satisfied curling of the lips around the grammatical rhythms, rouse distrust in some atavistic, pre-speech part of ourselves; we turn off. Whereas those who stutter win, in the painful pauses of their demonstration that speech isn't entirely natural, a respectful attention, a tender alertness. Words are, we are reassured, precious. The senior Henry James evidently had some trouble enunciating, for after meeting him in 1843 Carlyle wrote to Emerson, "He confirms an observation of mine, which indeed I find is hundreds of years old, that a stammering man is never a worthless one. Physiology can tell you why. It is an excess of delicacy, excess of sensibility to the presence of his fellow-creature, that makes him stammer."

Stuttering* is disarming, and may subconsciously be meant to be. Popular culture associates it with fear and overexcitement – "Th-th-there's a t-t-t-tiger in there!" – and of course I was afraid of big blank-faced Eddie Pritchard, afraid of being miscast by him into a role, perhaps for life, that I did not wish to play. I am afraid of the audiences I discomfit and embarrass, to my own embarrassment and discomfiture. I am afraid of New York audiences, especially; they are too smart and left-wing for me. And yet some audiences can be as comforting, with their giant collective sighs and embracing laughter, as an ideal mother – Southern

---

* Dictionaries treat "stuttering" and "stammering" as synonymous, with "stammering" the older, British usage; yet I had imagined stuttering had more to do with consonants, and stammering with vowels. No two cases of dysphemia that I have known are quite alike. *A.* gets stuck on certain consonants and explodes through them with a hiss and an angry stare; *B.* keeps up a curious prolonging murmur in his hesitations like a swarm of bees; *C.* Tries to shake the word loose with a spastic and quite disconcerting snapping of his head; *D.* blushes and casts his gaze down rather girlishly while a dainty little silence builds; *E.* under nervous stress keeps interrupting himself with a scraping little bray, like the boys-into-donkeys of *Pinocchio*; and so on.

college audiences, particularly; unlike audiences recruited from the tough old Northeast, they hold nary a wiseguy or doubting Thomas or mocking cackle in a thousand, just hosts of attentive and kindly faces shining at the sight of "an author," lightly sweating in their congregation, and drawing forth from my chest my best and true music, the effortless cello throb of eloquence. One could babble on forever, there at the lectern with its little warm lamp, and its pitcher of assuaging water, and its microphone cowled in black sponge and uptilted like the screened face of a miniature fencer. Reading words I have written, giving my own impromptu answers, I have no fear of any basic misapprehension; the audience has voluntarily assembled to view and audit a persona within which I am comfortable. The larger the audience, the better, the larger it is, the simpler its range of responses, and the more teddy-bear-like and unthreatening it grows. But an electrician brusquely answering the phone, or a uniformed guard bristling at the entrance to a building, or a pert stranger at a cocktail party, does not know who I am, and I apparently doubt that my body and manner and voice will explain it. Who I am seems impossibly complicated and unobvious. Some falsity of impersonation, some burden of disguise or deceit forms part of my self, an untrustworthy part that can collapse at awkward or anxious moments into a stutter. The burden was present even in Shillington, perhaps as my strong desire, even as I strove to blend in and recognized each day spent there as a kind of Paradise, eventually to get out.

If fear – fear, that is, of an unpredictable or complex response that might wrench aside my rather delicately constructed disguise – activates the defect in my speech, then anger, nature's adrenal answer to fear, tends to cancel it. A frontal attack clarifies the mind and stiffens the tongue. Testifying once on my own behalf in a lawsuit, I never thought to stutter; I spoke loudly and carefully, my tone observing no distinction between falsehood and truth. I laid on words as one lays on paint. And I remember with pleasure a reading given long ago, in the fraught and seething Sixties, at some newly founded two-year community college in Dallas, where the audience, instead of presenting the respectful white faces I was accustomed to, consisted of a few young blacks sprinkled in bored postures throughout the arc of plush, mostly empty auditorium seats. It was the Sixties, and black hostility was expectable and even to be approved of, and my studiously composed souvenirs of small-town, monoracial life, whether rhymed or unrhymed, did seem rather off the point here; nevertheless, I had contracted to make this appearance, my gorge rose to the challenge, and I gave (in my own ears) one of the better, firmer readings of my negligible public career.

No, it is not confrontation but some wish to avoid it, some hasty wish to please, that betrays my flow of speech. The impediment comes on amid people of whom I am fond, and wish very much to amuse – perhaps to distract them from some fundamental misapprehension that I suspect exists within even our fond relationship. My stuttering feels like an acknowledgment, in conversation, of the framework of unacknowledged complexity that surrounds the simplest exchange of words. This tongue-tripping sense of complexity must go back to my original family, the family of four harried and (except for my grandmother) highly verbal adults into which I was born. As I remember the Shillington house, I was usually down on the floor, drawing or reading, or even under the dining-room table, trying to stay out of harm's way – to disassociate myself from the patterns of conflict, emanating from my mother, that filled the air above my head. Darts of anger rayed from her head like that crown of spikes on the Statue of Liberty; a red "V," during those war years, would appear, with eerie appositeness, in the middle of her forehead. Her anger was aimed rarely at me. I was chastised for coming home late – not so much for being careless or wilful about time but for allowing myself to be the weak-minded victim of my retentive playmates. She seemed to fear that I was subject to homosexual seduction, and once scolded me for wrestling with some other boy in the vacant lot across Shilling Alley. On another fraught occasion, her wrath fell heavily on me for cutting my own hair; a forehead lock had kept getting in my way as I bent to a complicated, mirrored tracing toy, and with my paper-cutting scissors I resourcefully snipped it off.

My mother was fanatic about haircuts; the full weight of her underutilized intelligence and sensitivity fell on my head when I returned from the barber's, where each chair was manned, to her fine eye, by a different scissoring style, a different proclivity to error. The prevalent theory about stuttering ties it to parental overcorrection of the three-to-five-year-old child's flawed and fledgling speech. I don't recall ever having my speech corrected, but certainly the haircuts with which I returned from Artie Hoyer's barber shop were subject to an overwhelming critique – in detail, behind the ears and at the back of the neck, as well as in regard to overall effect and balance. My mother and I had both been difficult births: a forceps had been used on her, leaving the "V," and my reluctant exit from her womb had left my skull slightly lopsided. Part of the barber's job seemed to be to compensate for this latter irregularity. As my mother looked me over, a hothouse perfectionism enclosed my head and I would hold my breath. My stuttering feels related to the vulnerability of the human head, that odd knob of hair and rubbery moist sensory organs, that tender bud our twig puts out to interact with the air and the psychic waves of others. Other people – their eyes, their desires, their voiced and unvoiced opinions, their harbored secrets – make an atmosphere too oppressively rich, too busy; my sensation, when I stutter, is that I am trying, with the machete of my face, to hack my way through a jungle of other minds' thrusting vines and tendrils. Or, sometimes, it is as if I have, hurrying to the end of my spoken sentence, carefully picked and plotted my way out of a room full of obstacles, and, having almost attained (stealthily, cunningly) the door, I trip, calling painful attention to myself and spilling all the beans.

Where these beans have already been partially spilled, the pressure is less. My speech eases where I feel already somewhat known and forgiven, as, for example, with:

(1) people from Shillington

(2) people from Ipswich

(3) literary people, especially agents and editors

(4) people who want something from me

(5) women – but not children, at least children whom I have harmed. With my own children, after I left them, I developed a sharp and painful stutter that had not been there before. I stutter, then, when I am "in the wrong," as, for example, with:

(1) people of evident refinement or distinction

(2) New Englanders of many generations

(3) law-enforcement officers

(4) Israeli journalists and intellectuals

(5) men

With the second set, my tongue and vocal cords feel caught in some unspoken apology for

(1) my psoriasis

(2) my humble origins

(3) my having nothing, as a memorable early review of one of my books put it, to say

(4) my ponderously growing oeuvre, dragging behind me like an ever-heavier tail

(5) my wish to look and live well while simultaneously maintaining an ironical Christian perspective on all earthly gratifications

(6) my voice itself. The Pennsylvania Germans adapted in various degrees to the dominant English-speaking culture. At one extreme, the Old Order or "house" Amish abjure contemporary dress, the public schools, electricity, and gasoline-powered machinery, and in their church services and social intercourse hold to their dialect of Low German; near the

other extreme, the Hoyers were considered especially "English" in their approach. My maternal grandfather spoke a beautiful, cadenced, elocutionary English, though he also would talk to my grandmother in Pennsylvania Dutch. My mother had inherited his silver tongue, and my father came from New Jersey. Thus I was early estranged from the comfortable regional accent of Shillington and Berks County. On my first day at the Ruskin School of Drawing and Fine Art in Oxford, while standing in the enrolment line, I was asked by a fellow American with a strong Southern accent if I were English. I was startled. Had I so thoroughly betrayed my national and regional origins? The legitimacy of my voice, wherever I am, seems a question. In New York and then New England, I have been surrounded by people who do not talk quite as I do. I tend, like a foreigner, to resist dropping consonants (leaving a trace, say of the "l" in "palm" and elongating "Worcester" as "Wooooster" in acknowledgment of the spurned letters; I pronounce words as they look in print, and hence consistently mispronounce "monk," "sponge," and "Wodehouse." Yet we all, in a world of mingling clans, exist in some form of linguistic exile, and most people don't stutter.

So: what to do? As Gerald Jonas pointed out in *Stuttering: The Disorder of Many Theories* (1977), the foremost experts, to a dismaying extent, are inveterate stutterers who still, for all their expertise, can't get the words out. The defect arises, it would seem, from self-consciousness – a failure to let the intricate muscular events of speech be subconscious. Between the thought and the word falls a shadow, a cleavage; stuttering, like suicide and insomnia and stoicism, demonstrates the duality of our existence, the ability of the body and soul to say no to one another. And yet self-consciousness (which does nothing for psoriasis but make it agonizing) can be something of a cure here: concentrating on not stuttering, we do stutter less. My flattering father would tell me I had too many thoughts in my head, and that I should speak slower. This did help. Keeping my voice in the lower half of its register also helps; other stutterers, I notice, tend to have high, forced voices, riding a thin hysterical edge. When they manage to speak, it is louder or faster than normal. Stuttering, perhaps, is a kind of recoil at the thrust of your own voice, an expression of alarm and shame at sounding like yourself, at *being* yourself, at taking up space and air. A well-known principle of speech therapy is that any mechanism which displaces your customary voice – singing, having a sore throat, affecting a funny accent – eliminates the stoppage; the captive tongue is released into *Maskenfreiheit*, the freedom conferred by masks. The paralysis of stuttering stems from the dead center of one's being, a deep doubt there. Being tired increases the doubt, and – contrary to what one might suppose – so does having had too much to drink; speaking is a physical act and susceptible to the same chemical drags that impair the coördination of other physical acts.

Stuttering, I have come to believe, is a simple matter of breath: we arrive at our ridiculous spasm when in truth we are out of breath, when in our haste and anxiety we have forgotten to breathe. Taking a breath, or concentrating on keeping the breath flowing erases the problem as easily as mist wiped from a windowpane. Could that have been me, a moment ago, hung up on a mere word? Impossible!

But breathing, too, is not necessarily easy. It is one of these physical acts on the edge of thought; it can be conscious or unconscious. These semi-conscious acts are troublesome: start to think about your blinking, and it is hard to stop, and hard not to feel squeamish about your entire optical apparatus; consider your walking, and you tend to stiffen and stumble. Though I was never diagnosed, as a child, as having asthma, I was generally "snuffly," with colds in the winter and hay fever in the warm months. The precariousness of breathing was borne in upon me when, in one unfortunate moment, I leaped toward my father's arms while he was treading water in a swimming pool, and found myself sinking in an unbreathable molten green while my own bubbles rose up in my vision like ornaments on this terrible tree of my strangling.* I was plucked out soon enough, back into the immense and lovely air, and I gasped and coughed the water from my lungs; but the sensation lingered enough to make me dread water – its sting of chlorine, its indifferent coldness, its semi-opacity.

My claustrophobia I date from a radio play that, sometime in the early forties, I heard over the little wooden round-topped Philco that sat on a table next to our red easy chair, its arms stained by many peanut-butter-and-cracker sandwiches I consumed there, in what we called "the side parlor." Here stood the upright piano, with the brass tiger on top, and here we gathered, in a rare family circle, to listen to broadcasts of Joe Louis's fights and, Sunday nights, to the consecutive half-hour shows of Jack Benny, Phil Harris and Alice Faye, and Edgar Bergen and Charlie McCarthy. But I was alone the evening I listened to a radio play that told of two prisoners trying to escape from jail. One was a large man, and one was small. Their plan involved crawling through ducts and pipes; the larger man insisted the smaller go first, and in the end the listener discovers why: the big prisoner gets stuck. The muffled sounds, as he communicates his hopeless immobility there at some turning in the tight and implacable darkness, were conveyed as vividly as only the art of radio could, with no visual distractions to mitigate the illusion of reality. The fat prisoner's gasping, diminishing voice echoed in the pipes, urging his friend on, and the smaller man presumably did crawl and squeeze his way to freedom; but my attention stayed behind, with the stuck man and his living entombment, his slow suffocation and futile struggles, his eventual death and the shrivelling and rotting of his corpse.

* "Then the blue-green water was all around him, dense and churning, and when he tried to take a breath a fist was shoved into his throat. He saw his own bubbles rising in front of his face, a multitude of them, rising as he sank; he sank it seemed for a very long time, until something located him in the darkening element and seized him by the arm." – "Trust Me" (1979)

On the farm to which we moved a few years later, as it happened, a corrugated metal conduit ran diagonally under the dirt road; the pipe, perhaps thirty inches in diameter, was long, but not so long that you could not see the disc of light at the end. Many times I stood at the end nearer to the house daring myself to crawl through. The space was ample, and the destination clear, but I could not bring myself to bend down, and achieve the passage. The idea of it – of being in the middle, equally far from either end – made me breathless.

And then, that first year of sudden rural isolation, we acquired a part-chow, part-collie puppy called Copper; he was my first pet and followed me everywhere as though I, a raw thirteen, had all the answers. New to such power, I would tease him, shying pebbles and crab apples at him; he would take refuge in a six-inch tile drainage pipe that protruded into the yard, down by the barn. One day, Copper had grown just enough so he could not turn around in the pipe and come out as usual. He whimpered, in there beyond my reach; he was stuck. I had caused my nightmare to come true. As in fright and guilt I cried and prayed, the whimpering dog discovered he could back up, inch by inch, and thus he made his way out into the light and my arms. How I hugged him, and begged his forgiveness! Yet afterwards, I often carried or tugged him to the mouth of the pipe, to feel him whimper and wriggle in remembered fear. I needed to rehearse the incident, to show him the hole, to "rub his nose" in it. What is our tremendous human cruelty, after all, but the attempt to discharge our pent-up private nightmares onto the open ground of actuality? Animals, lacking imagination, are never sadistic; the face of the cheetah as he brings down the gazelle and of the cat as it torments the mouse are studies in focused innocence.

The dread of being buried alive is not, of course, in itself peculiar, or unusual. Poe has made the phobia familiar to generations of American schoolchildren, and the unquiet grave standardly figures in horror movies. Cremation owes some of its popularity, no doubt, to its elimination of the possibility of waking in a satin-lined box six feet underground, in an utter darkness smelling of formaldehyde and wilted flowers. Our lives begin with a slither through a tight place, and end, acording to Tolstoy's vision in "The Death of Ivan Ilyich," with being pushed deeper and deeper into a black sack. The cause of natural death is generally one form of constriction or another; we all will be buried alive in those last seconds, lying immobilized like the Frau Consul in *Buddenbrooks*: "Her lips were drawn inward, and opened and closed with a snap at every tortured effort to breathe, while the sunken eyes roved back and forth or rested with an envious look on those who stood about her bed, up and dressed and able to breathe." We move and have our being within a very narrow band of chemical conditions, on a blue-skinned island of a planet from which there is no escape, save for the legendary few who have enjoyed space travel or bodily ascension. Our lives depend upon an interior maze of pumping, oozing tubular flow whose contemplation itself can induce claustrophobia.* The radio play about prison escape dramatized the precarious squirming that, in our constricted carnal circumstances, forms the alternative to death, and it sharpened my awareness of how narrow are those passageways by which the ego communicates with the world.

The throat: how strange, that there is not more erotic emphasis upon it. For here, through this compound pulsing pillar, our life makes its leap into spirit, and in the other direction gulps down what it needs of the material world. I watched my grandmother's choking fits at the kitchen table, and my own throat would feel narrow. Once, at the age of nine or so, I was sledding, high on Chestnut Street, which slanted sharply up to Cedar Top and whose bottom block, after a snowstorm, the town fathers strewed with cinders – a

---

* Though I found the intravenous adventures of *Fantastic Voyage*, with Raquel Welch along, less terrifying than the conventionally submarine *Das Boot*.

thrifty method, amid Depression simplicities, of creating a civic playground. I had put a fresh cough drop in my mouth, and in the excitement of sitting upright on a Flexible Flyer behind a playmate and getting set for the cheek-stinging ride down into the scraping, sparking patch of cinders that halted us short of Philadelphia Avenue, I swallowed it. I swallowed the cough drop. I felt it slide irretrievably into the slippery downhill at the back of my oral cavity and lodge halfway down my throat. The distinction between esophagus and trachea was hazy in my mind, and I thought that if the cough drop stayed long in my throat I would suffocate and die. I ran home – dragging, as I remember these nightmarish moments, the sled behind me and carrying a swelling lump of panic in my chest – down Chestnut Street, the four steep blocks of it, and then along Philadelphia Avenue, gagging watery-eyed at the obstacle in my throat. I arrive at my big white house and here, in memory, the season changes, for it is summer, and I seem to be in shorts, and Al Richards, one of my father's fellow teachers, is visiting the house and standing under the leafed-out grape arbor with him. Al sizes me up, swiftly grabs me by the bare legs, and holds me upside down, while my father pounds my back. My throat convulses once more, and the cough drop lies on the ground inches from my eyes, puddling what has become, again, snow. I can see it exactly – it is a golden oblong honey-flavored Luden's; this brand was made right in Reading, in a huge factory that scented one whole side of the city with menthol. I think, *I will live*. I will live to see many other sights, few of them more welcome than this, the cough drop no longer in my throat but lying there half-melted in the snow. Though it would (I now believe) have dwindled and slipped down of its own, I credited Al Richards – a former semi-pro shortstop with a quaint, centrally parted hairdo and a son my own age – with saving my life, and could never, even in high school when he became my social-studies teacher, look at him without love, as the embodiment of the benign forces in Shillington that protected and preserved me for something beyond.

A parallel incident occured nearly thirty years later, after I had developed, in my ripe maturity, asthma. I and my wife and our four children were visiting my parents, and the eight of us crowded the old stone farmhouse. My parents, when we visited in the summer, betook themselves to the barn, and slept on a mattress on an old haywagon, surrounded by bundled newspapers, pigeon droppings, antique rusted farm tools, and horsefeed bags full of empty catfood cans. This comical hardship – the sort of thing my father, costumed like a Beckett character, seemed to relish – added by way of empathy to the congestion in my mind and chest. At the height of the pollen season, in an overburdened house besieged at the back door by the hordes of stray cats that my mother had taken to feeding, I was playing the triple familial role of son, husband, and father, and the demands from each side sliced my inner freedom thinner and thinner. As my children – seaside New Englanders unaccustomed to the jungly outdoors of rural Pennsylvania, where cornfields receded to the horizon and poison-ivy vines grew to the size of wisteria – bunched around the television set and its fuzzy images from Philadelphia, they were terrorized by an old dog my parents had, a collie with a blind and droopy eye, a crooked inquisitive way of holding his head, and a bad habit of suddenly snapping. Several of my children had already been nipped. Dog hair was on all the furniture and ghosts of the past in every conversation. Furthermore, this particular afternoon, the Houcks were coming to visit, adding yet more presences to my crammed inner theatre.

Karl and Caroline Houck, like my parents, had gone to Ursinus College, courted there, married, settled in Berks County, and been blessed with one cherished child. They figured in our oldest snapshots and in my earliest memories; my very first memory, indeed, is of looking down into a playpen in a city house that must have been theirs in Reading:

I smell the oilcloth mat and see these toys that are not mine but magically and ominously, someone else's, someone not there. As is the way with one's parents' friends, the Houcks' friendliness with me seemed to constitute one more demand – a debt incurred in a world I had never made. As the time of their visit approached, my breathing grew shallower and shallower; repeated gulps of isoproterenol and epinephrine from my constant pocket companion, the Medihaler, failed to bring the hoped-for relief, that opening of the bronchial tree which is to asthmatics an interior sunrise, a rebirth into the normal world. I thought the house and its dust might be the problem and moved outside to the lawn. There, on a little walk of spaced sandstones we had made in those first hard-working years here on this farm (where I had never wanted to be), a few feet from the privet bush my grandmother had transplanted from the Shillington yard when we moved and that she had defended with her life when a bull escaped from our rented meadow and in his bafflement gored the little round green thing with his horns, giving it a splayed shape it still bore – here, I tried one more hit from Medihaler, and felt no space in my lungs.

An asthma attack feels like two walls drawn closer, and closer, until they are pressed together. Your back begins to hurt, between the shoulder blades, and you hunch. I could not stand up straight and looked down at the flourishing grass between the sandstones. I thought, *This is the last thing I'll see. This is death.* The breathless blackness within me was overlaying the visual world, this patch of my mother's grass, with a thin gray film, and the space between the two walls I was struggling to pry apart felt hardly wide enough for a razor blade. My children and parents had come out on the back porch to watch me, and a rictus twitched my face as I thought how comic this performance must look, this wrestle with invisible demons, and here where my brave grandmother had battled the bull on behalf of the privet bush I felt immensely angry at my own body and at everybody. Like a child blind in his tantrum I thought, *Serve them right*, and waited to die, standing bent over and gasping, of suffocation.

It was at this point that the Houcks arrived. Karl was a doctor, a Reading bone surgeon. Like Al Richards long ago, he acted swiftly and calmly. He had me climb into his Mercedes and drove me the eleven or twelve miles to the Reading Hospital, where I had been born. During the drive, I sat hunched in the front seat, studying the fancy dashboard and trying to be droll, with what breath I could muster, about my incapacity. He talked, but not too much. He was a surgeon, not an internist: a wiry, mustached man who loved to play tennis and whose strong hands could force broken thigh bones back into alignment. His manner could be brusque but he belonged to that dying breed that still called me "Johnny," and I thought, as I perched there cupping my strained lungs within me, how pleasant his voice was – a slow, deliberate, self-assured baritone, with a well-combed fringe of Pennsylvania accent, the consonants standing upright. Both the Houcks, for that matter, had stately and elocutionary voices; she had been the class May Queen at Ursinus, and she always called my father, in that indolent caressing tone acclaimed beauties acquire, "Uppie." From on high, as it were – the Houcks lived on Hampden Boulevard, high above Reading's packed brick rows – they shed rays of respectability and continuity upon my parents' struggling lives.

My breathing slightly eased; encapsulated inside Karl's speeding Mercedes, I was relieved of some psychological pressure. The hospital was in a tony, spacious area of West Reading that also, comfortingly, held the local art museum and many expensive homes. I breathe easier, it would seem in an atmosphere of money. We arrived and walked across the parking lot in the milky Pennsylvania sunshine; without much delay I was sat on the edge of a high hospital bed and given a shot of adrenaline and, praise God, was born again. Though cataleptics on the edge of a fit must be allowed the divine ecstasy that Dostoevsky described, something should be said for the rush of bliss that floods an asthmatic whose bronchial muscles have unclenched. Of course: air, in, out: this is how people do it. How simple. As with stuttering, it is difficult to believe there had ever been a problem. I thanked the young doctor who had injected me; I thanked Karl Houck. Full of adrenaline, the asthmatic trembles, as if violently scoured to re-admit the passage of oxygen. As I recall, there was another shot of adrenaline before I was dismissed, and an appointment made for the next day, with a third doctor, who smilingly told me then that Medihalers can be overused, to the point that their condensed mist clogs the bronchial passageways, and that I had made a wise decision in leaving allergen-rich Berks County. Both facts were not unknown to me, but in the beggarly physical condition to which I had been reduced I was grateful for all admonitions and encouragements.

My asthma, or at least my consciousness of it, had begun in this manner: as part of my attempt to lead an adult life in Ipswich, I let myself be persuaded to buy some life insurance, and the routine medical examination found my lungs "slightly emphysematous." The adjective was new to me. I looked up "emphysema" in the dictionary and then in medical reference books, and could only conclude that, young as I was, still in my twenties, I had death in my lungs; the pockets of tissue whereby inhaled air oxygenated my blood were bloated and slack, and could only get worse. These alveoli wink out one by one, like brain cells, irrevocably. "Unfortunately," the encyclopedia said, "treatment is often ineffective when the condition is advanced, and prevention of further injury is all that the physician can hope to accomplish." My friendly family practitioner, sensing my panic, ran me through a battery of tests whose conclusion was that my lungs were, in his considerate phrase, "not significantly emphysematous"; he did, however, hear wheezes through his stethoscope, and I did have the barrel chest – the spread rib cage – of the chronic asthmatic. Though I was judged a good-enough health risk to be allowed to pay insurance premiums, the message had been delivered: I was mortal. I carried within me fatal wounds. My efforts to quit smoking cigarettes became more serious, and my efforts to live what life I had left became slightly more reckless.

In my memory there is a grayness to that period of my life in Ipswich, a certain desperation out of which I struggled to piece together those last, fragmentary stories in *Pigeon Feathers*, which I think of, in retrospect, as my best, perhaps because the words were attained through such an oppressive blanket of funk. The sky was gray. Shortly after the insurance report, I was playing basketball – we husbands and fathers were still young enough to play this game of constant motion – and I looked up at the naked, netless hoop: gray sky outside it, gray sky inside it. And as I waited, on a raw rainy fall day, for the opposing touch-football team to kick off, there would come sailing through the air instead the sullen realization that in a few decades we would all be dead. I remember squatting in our cellar making my daughter a dollhouse, under the close sky of the cobwebby ceiling, and the hammer going numb in my hand as I saw not only my life but hers, so recently begun, as a futile misadventure, a leap out of the dark and back.* The rust and rot of material things, in that town of ancient wooden houses, spoke the same lesson; our house dated from 1687 and its foundation walls were unmortared fieldstones heaped up by men long reduced to bones, and the cellar felt crowded by semi-forgotten objects that rose to my eyes encrusted with time as if with oxide-ruddy earth – the old furnace, the corroded pipes overhead, my dull few

* "Matter has its radiance and its darkness; it lifts and it buries. Things compete; a life demands a life."

    – "Packed Dirt, Churchgoing, a Dying Cat, A Traded Car" (1961)

carpentry tools, the cumbersome and ill-fitting storm windows and screens, and the moldering souvenirs of previous owners, which I somehow lacked the energy to sort and remove.

These remembered gray moments, in which my spirit could scarcely breathe, are scattered over a period of years; to give myself brightness and air I read Karl Barth and fell in love with other men's wives. Kierkegaard had gotten me through the two years in New York. The previous year, in Oxford, I associate with Chesterton and Maritain and C. S. Lewis and with a charmingly technical and donnish pamphlet by Ian T. Ramsey called "Miracles: An Exercise in Logical Mapwork." That year, I would gaze in dumb faith at the fat uniform spines of the collected Aquinas at Blackwell's great book store on Broad Street; surely in all this volume of verbiage there lay the saving seed, the pinhole of light. Ipswich belonged to Barth. The other women – I would see them in bright party dresses, or in bathing suits down at the beach, and in my head they would have their seasons of budding, of flamboyant bloom, and of wilt, all while my aging, emphysematous body remained uxorious and dutiful.

Dreams come true; without that possibility, nature would not incite us to have them. In brief: I tried to break out of my marriage on behalf of another, and failed, and began to have trouble breathing. "I love you" are words that are perhaps too easy to get out; but at least for the time being the dread of eventual death was wholly replaced by immediate distress and emotional violence. The social fracas held for me a personal triumph, a selfish triumph, in terms of self-consciousness: beneath the pain my dubious opinion of myself had been soothed. I had at last ventured into harm's way. I had not only been daring but had inspired daring in another. Her obituary on the affair was the dry comment, "We tried to do too much."

A door had opened, and shut. My timidity and conscience had slammed it shut. My wife and children were my captors, but I could not blame them; they had done nothing, after all, but come when I called. When young I had wanted a wife who would be attractive, and motherly, and artistic, and quiet, and she materialized. We wanted children, and they obediently came, healthy and lovable and two of each sex. Now, through no fault of their own, they composed a household whose walls seemed to be shrinking around me, squeezing my chest. No first attack stands in my memory; the squeezing, the panic crept in and were suddenly there. Like my Barth-reading and my poetry-writing (for I was never more of a poet than in this angst-besmogged period) the breathlessness would tend to come on in the evening. We didn't know what it was – pure inner demons, or an ingenious psychosomatic mechanism to make my wife feel guilty about being still married to me, or what. I remember, from the time before I had been prescribed any medication, sitting on the wild old floorboards in front of one of our many fireplaces, trying to settle my struggling lungs with a cigarette and contemplation of a log fire; my wife observed that my difficulties seemed to be going with the smoke up the chimney. It was her artistic nature to make hopeful, pictorial observations like that. The children watched in scared silence. I tried to suppress my panic, my inner clenching, for their sake. The anxiety surrounding me made breathing yet harder; it reduced my space. On another evening, my wife returned from her Monday-night singing group with a merry clutch of friends, and one of them, a singing doctor (doctors appear to have been as omnipresent in my life as teachers), looked down to where I lay gasping on the floor (since dramatizing my condition seemed the next-best thing to curing it) and observed that this syndrome was usually confined to teen-aged girls. When they fainted, he said, their breathing went back to normal.

I never fainted. But I had many bad nights, my head up on two pillows and my breath, I felt, travelling in and out of me by a very small aperture, a little gap between the cotton skin of the pillow and the dark that filled the room. My own, non-singing doctor, having dismissed the emphysema as less than significant, seemed to regard my new complaint, as, again, exaggerated. But William Maxwell, who had once tried to reassure me about lost luggage, detected over the phone, in one of our editorial conversations, that I needed to see yet another doctor, and sent me to see his own. So it was in New York – New York, where I *really* lived, as an earthbound saint lives in Heaven, piling up merit there – in New York with its towering grid of light and shadow, amid millions of wary but not unbenevolent strangers, that I was given the dignity of a diagnosis and a prescription: bronchial asthma and a Medi-haler, a little plastic gun I fired into my own mouth – *pffft!* – to widen my bronchi.

It was like sucking in freedom, like inhaling the blue sky; I became an addict. I carried my knobbly little plastic lifeline everywhere, bulging my pockets and letting lint and sand work into its crevices, especially into the tiny hole, no bigger than a mustardseed, where the life-giving mist shot out, with that delightful admonitory hiss. Sometimes I inhaled grit and pellets of fluff, but didn't care. Without my Medihaler, I felt lost and naked; once, in the middle of the second fairway of a golf course, I had to walk off and drive home and get the thing. After that, I kept one in my golf bag. I kept another in the glove compartment of my car, and several more in drawers around the house. And so for some years I enjoyed the illusion of chemical-induced security, until that moment in Pennsylvania just before Dr Houck arrived, when in what felt like a terminal paroxysm I stared down at the lawn, each greasy blade of grass distinct and a venomous, smothering green. The Medihaler had its limits. As with the psoriasis, cures wore off, leaving me again alone with my defective, imperilled self.

The final answer turned out to be cats. Cat dander, and to a lesser extent that of our dogs as well, were giving me asthma. When the children were small we had acquired Pansy and Willy, a sister and brother though she was a calico and he taffy-colored. We saw Pansy through a number of litters before getting her "fixed," and welcomed Willy home after a number of bloody fights before performing the same kindness for him. Even so, Willy had suffered eyeball injuries, and there was a long and clumsy series of ministrations, with drops and a purple spray, before his worse eye was at last, in Boston, removed by a team of experts. They rarely had a chance to operate on cats and were grateful to try. How these animals in our midst suffer, for our edification! How poor Willy would wriggle when we tried to hold him still for his dose of purple eye-spray! *Pffft!* It was meant, I believe, for cows, and must have stung fearfully. Nevertheless, both cats lived to a ripe age. They outlived my tenancy with my family, in fact.

They used to sleep on my pillow, and my doctor's advice, when I would go to him with my wheezing lungs and panicky bronchi, was invariably, "Get rid of the cats." But how could we get rid of two such venerable members of our family, who from kittenhood on had enriched our conjoined lives with lessons in birth and murder, flirtatiousness and fortitude, who had endured and tamed a succession of bouncy puppies and brought us gifts of half-chewed field mice many a dewy morning? We tried keeping the cats outdoors and in the cellar, but of course they were too old and stubborn to change habits, and sneaked back in, to their cozy nests on the furniture. As I contemplated the problem, it seemed easier to get rid of me. My children sensed the crisis: I painfully glimpsed my younger son, fifteen years old in those last months when I lived with him, angrily throwing Willy down the cellar stairs; the boy had tears of exasperation in his eyes. In the end, rather than discomfit the cats, I discomfited the human beings of my family and moved to Boston. This was twelve years after my first attempt to break out. In that dozen of years, my children had grown to their full sizes if not quite adulthood, and my wife, that mysterious partner of my life, had developed, my hopeful and self-serving impression was, some resources of her own. Ten years before, in the Soviet Union, a picturesque elderly artist had given us a drawing of two overlapping heads with the third eye shared between them; he said it was of us. It was true, she and I saw many things the same way, and never had much trouble understanding one another. We rarely needed, it seemed, to talk, and under this quietness resentments and secret lives came to flourish. Had we had two eyes each, we might have made a better couple. But she saw, with me, that it was impossible to drown or give away Willy and Pansy, and that it *was* possible, at last, that I go.

Two respiratory developments succeeded my move to Boston: my asthma got better, and I began to stutter with my own children. Their cheerful unblaming voices over the phone, and the apparition of their healthy round pale faces, summoned into my presence now by appointment and invitation, put a stopper in my throat. Stuttering had not been a problem for years. Suddenly I was afraid, again, of being misunderstood, of being mistaken for somebody else. I doubted my worthiness to mar the air with my voice.

Yet I felt at ease, oddly *arrived*, in my bachelor rooms; twenty years of the free-lance writer's life had habituated me to solitude and the solitary organization of a day's hours and a desk's drawers. I continued, amid the distractions of guilt and needy phone calls and the need to do my own laundry and feed myself, to get the words out – to get them out in the specialized sense of words to be printed, as smooth in their arrangement and flow as repeated revision could make them, words lifted free of the fearful imperfection and impermanence of the words we all, haltingly, stumblingly, speak.

Eddie Pritchard seemed to be taunting me when my first books met the criticism that I wrote all too well but had nothing to say: I, who seemed to myself full of things to say, who had all of Shillington to say, Shillington and Pennsylvania and the whole mass of middling, hidden, troubled America to say, and who had seen and heard things in my two childhood homes, as my parents' giant faces revolved and spoke, achieving utterance under some terrible pressure of American disappointment, that would take a lifetime to sort out, particularize, and extol with the proper dark beauty. *In the beauty of the lilies Christ was born across the sea* – this odd and uplifting line from among the many odd lines of "The Battle Hymn of the Republic" seemed to me, as I set out, to summarize what I had to say about America, to offer itself as the title of a continental *magnum opus* of which all my books, no matter how many, would be mere instalments, mere starts at the hymning of this great roughly rectangular country severed from Christ by the breadth of the sea.

What I doubted was not the grandeur and plenitude of my topic but my ability to find the words to express it; every day, I groped for the exact terms I knew were there but could not find, pawed through the thesaurus in search of them and through the dictionary in search of their correct spelling. My English language had been early bent by the Germanic locutions of my environment, and, as my prose came to be edited by experts, I had to arbitrate between how I in my head heard a sentence go and how, evidently, it should correctly go. My own style seemed to me a groping and elemental attempt to approximate the complexity of envisioned phenomena and it surprised me to have it called luxuriant and self-indulgent; self-indulgent, surely, is exactly what it wasn't – *other*-indulgent, rather. My models were the styles of Proust and Henry Green as I read them (one in translation): styles of tender exploration that tried to wrap themselves around the things, the tints and voices and perfumes, of the apprehended real. In this entwining and gently relentless effort there is no hiding that the effort is being made in language: all professorial or critical talk of inconspicuous or invisible language struck me as vapid and quite mistaken, for surely language, printed language, is what we all know we are reading and writing, just as a person looking at a painting knows he is not looking out of a window.

Alphabetical symbols stamped on blocks marked the dawn of my consciousness, along with the smell of oilcloth, the extra-fuzzy texture of the rug underneath the dining-room table, the eerie flexibility of my own hands, and the shine on other people's shoes. My early toys, kept in an old-fashioned country bushel basket, included three kinds of blocks: big, elemental ABC's, enamelled the colors of the rainbow and holding their letters in sans-serif intaglio that a finger and a wobbly crayon could trace; small blocks of a more intricate texture, with a serifed alphabet and primal objects like apples and bananas and railroad cabooses lifted in bas-relief from a flatness hollowed between rims that were in turn lightly incised; and a medium-sized set featuring, along with the numbers and letters, Walt Disney characters from Mickey Mouse to Horace Horsecollar. The second set, put in the mouth, tasted of wood, and was painted only on the raised parts, much as type is inked. What early intimations of the printing process tumbled in on me with my manipulations, my assembly and disassembly, of that bushel basket full of blocks, I can only retrospectively guess at; but I still carry intact within me my happiness when, elevated by the thickness of some books to the level of my mother's typewriter, I began to tap the keyboard, and saw the perfect letter-forms leap up on the paper rolled around the platen. It was a little portable Remington, with elite type. Its sound, as my mother typed away, in the front bedroom with its view of the Lutzes' and the Van Derherschens' and the Shillings', at the stories and novels that were mailed to New York in their brown envelopes and were then mailed back, rattled through the long narrow house, whose downstairs stretched from the front-door letter slot to the icebox on the back kitchen wall. The sound of her typing gave the house a secret, questing life unlike that of any of the other houses up and down Philadelphia Avenue. One of my few memories of being rebuked by my mother concerns a day when I was sick and home from school; the front room was somehow the sickroom as well as my mother's workroom, and, feeling revived enough to share my thoughts with her as she typed away, I was shocked when she asked me to be quiet. In my mother's head existed, evidently, an entire rival world that could not co-exist with the real world of which I was, I had felt, such a loved component. Perhaps I had not hitherto realized that I had, within my mother's sphere of attention, any competitors whatsoever.

The writing enterprise that so engaged her presented itself to me first as a matter of graphic symbols; the tangible precise indented forms of those alphabet blocks and the typewriter's smart little leap of imprintation were part of the general marvel of reproduced imagery, of comic strips and comic books and books and magazines and motion pictures. This last looks like the anomalous term in a sequence, the one that must be circled on the aptitude exam, but in fact, in that pre-television Thirties world, the world of the movies and the world of the popular press were so entwined, and the specific world of Walt Disney so promiscuously generated animated cartoons and cartoon strips and children's books and children's toys, that it all seemed one art. The projector in effect printed with its beam of light the film upon the screen, and the stylized activities one saw there were being simultaneously read in a thousand theatres. A potentially infinite duplication was the essence, an essence wed for me to the smell of inked paper, dead pulped paper quickened into life by the stamped image of Dick Tracy or Captain Easy or Alley Oop; the very crudities and flecked imperfections of the process and the technical vocabulary of pen line and crosshatching and benday fascinated me, drew me deeply in, as perhaps a bacteriologist is drawn into the microscope and a linguist into the teeming niceties of a foreign grammar.

I loved comic strips. I copied their characters onto sheet after sheet of blank paper; I traced my copies onto plywood and cut them out with a coping saw and set them in rows on the shelf in my bedroom; I cut my favorite strips out of the newspaper and bound them in little long books with covers of white cardboard, lettered by me in India ink and crayon, fastened together with those brass-colored nails like pairs of legs. The materials for all this derivative artistry – plywood, paper fasteners in various lengths, stiff cardboard in sheets wider than my arm was long – were readily available in the Reading area, which had a strong artsy-craftsy side and lacked the sophistication to cast a single chilling breath, that I can recall, upon my infatuation with popular graphic culture. On Saturdays, as I grew older, I was permitted to take the trolley and roam downtown Reading for an hour or two, and the hand-lettered signs and window displays also seemed part of a wonderful artificial empyrean susceptible to new install-ments but exempt from decay and weediness in the way of the organic world. In the five-and-ten-cent stores along Penn Square – Kresge's, Woolworth's, McCrory's – a counter toward the back would hold Big Little Books: chunky vol-umes, costing a dime, assembled from comic strips, with a panel on the recto page facing a verso page of simple text. I collected these, and traded them with bookish friends like Fred Muth and Tony Van Liew, and on Saturday mornings in Reading shelled out dimes not only for the fresh new issues but for the rare old volume, the vintage "Mickey Mouse" or "Felix the Cat" or "Terry and the Pirates," that would show up among the fat bright spines crammed on the counter in those years, before Big Little Books were swept into history along with dolls of real rubber and soldiers of real lead and tin toys stamped "Made in Japan."

As adolescence approached, my fervor for consecutive square panels and words inside "talk balloons" moved on to magazine cartoons, as printed in *Collier's* and *The Saturday Evening Post* and *Liberty*. I cut them out, making a hard choice when two were back to back, and pasted them in scrapbooks that became unwieldably thick.* The varieties of cartoon style – the shaky pen lines of Gardner Rea and Chon Day, the dashing washes of Garrett Price and John Ruge – offered endless matter for the eyes to ponder, endless escape, into linecut or finely screened black and white, out of Shillington and life's drab polychrome. And when, during the war, *The New Yorker* began to arrive, courtesy of Mr Miller and my father's Greenwich sister, the world of magazines expanded into a new dimension, of better cartoons better displayed, of a lovely and flexible make-up that ran columns of type around little "spot drawings" by Birnbaum and Thurber and Edna Eicke. Thinking the cartoons too high and complex a goal, and the prose and poetry quite beyond me, I used to send in my little ink-and-wash "spots," in brown envelopes appropriated from my mother's desk. Like her short stories, they would faithfully come back. The bounce of their return at least demonstrated that there was something solid out there, that this intoxicating vapor of printed material had a source, which a person might some day, by following some yellow brick road, reach.

The fierce reality that I had allowed this rumored Oz of cartoon syndicates and animation studios and magazine offices to assume within myself bespeaks, it might be said, some inner defect, some vacuum that nothing intimate and actual could fill, and my subsequent career carries coarse traces of its un-ideal origins in popular, mechanically propagated culture. The papery self-magnification and immortality of printed reproduction – a mode of self-assertion that leaves the cowardly perpetrator hidden and out of harm's way – was central to my artistic impulse; I had no interest in painting or

* All this saving a child does! At one point I even saved the box scores of an entire baseball season, both leagues, since Philadelphia played, haplessly, in both. How precious each scrap of the world appears, in our first years' experience of it! Slowly we realize that it is all disposable, including ourselves.

sculpting, in creating the unique beautiful object, and have never been able to sustain interest in the rarefied exercise of keeping a journal. I drew, in black and white, exploring the minor technical mysteries of lettering nibs and scratchboard, of washes and benday, and then I drifted, by way of Ogden Nash and Phyllis McGinley and Morris Bishop and Arthur Guiterman, into light verse, and very slowly – not until college age, really – into the attempt to fabricate short stories. The idea of writing a novel came even later and presented itself to me, and still does, as *making a book*; I have trouble distinguishing between the functions of a publisher and those of a printer. The printer, in my naïve sense of the literary enterprise, is the solid fellow, my only real partner, and everyone else a potentially troublesome intermediary between him and myself. My early yearnings merged the notions of print, Heaven, and Manhattan (a map of which looks like a type tray). To be in print was to be saved. And to this moment a day when I have produced nothing printable, when I have not gotten any words out, is a day lost and damned as I feel it.

Perhaps I need not be too apologetic about these lowly beginnings. The great temple of fiction has no well-marked front portal; most devotees arrive through a side door, and not dressed for worship. Fiction, which can be anything, is written by those whose interest has not crystallized short of ontology. Coming so relatively late to the novel, as the end-term of a series of reproducible artifacts any of which I would have been happy to make for a living if I could, I find I feel, after completing thirteen of them, still virginal, still excited and slightly frightened by the form's capacity. My assets as a novelist I take to be the taste for American life acquired in Shillington, a certain indignation and independence also acquired there, a Christian willingness to withhold judgement, and a cartoonist's ability to compose within a prescribed space. Carlton Boyer, my high-school art teacher, once gave me an underlined "excellent" in composition; it struck me as an authentic artistic compliment, one of the few I have received. My debits include many varieties of ignorance, including an only child's tentativeness in the human grapple and an invincible innocence about literature. After Big Little Books, I read books of humor by Thurber and Benchley and Wodehouse and Frank Sullivan and E. B. White and mystery novels by Ellery Queen and Erle Stanley Gardner and John Dickson Carr and Agatha Christie and Ngaio Marsh, with a garnish of science fiction. This diet pretty well took me up to Harvard, where I read what they told me, and was much the better for it. But certain kinds of novel, especially nineteenth-century novels, should be read in adolescence, on those dreamily endless solitary afternoons that in later life become so uselessly short and full of appointments, or they will never be read at all.

But the books I did read – bought, in the case of the humorists and cartoon collections, with pennies I saved, and borrowed, in the case of the mysteries, from the Reading Public Library or the lending library in Whitner's Department Store – communicated magic enough. The library, one of Carnegie's stately granite benefactions, sat next to Schofer's Bakery, where one could buy warm and wickedly sweet "bear claws," and Whitner's basement held the finest cafeteria-restaurant in downtown Reading; so a heartening association of books with things delicious was established. The sturdy transparent wrappers that Whitner's added to the publishers' gaudy jackets also implied something precious, like the orchid corsages in their plastic boxes. My middlebrow and resolutely contemporary diet of boyhood reading had the advantage of being thoroughly escapist, so my sense of a book was of a space one gratefully escaped into, rather than of a burden of wisdom that bent one lower to the ground. The firm implicit contracts that the humorist and the mystery-writer draw up with their readers (*I will make you laugh; I will concoct a murderous puzzle and then explain it*) remained with me as models of the literary transaction even when, belatedly, I encountered the exhilarating, bourgeois-baiting lawlessness of modernism. I had dimly known there was something of the sort, out there beyond Berks County, for in my teens I would make an abrupt foray like reading "The Waste Land" at a table in the public libary, or plowing through my mother's copy of *Requiem for a Nun*, or doing a high-school paper on James Joyce, of whom my English teacher seemed never to have heard. But basically I was a cultural bumpkin in love not with writing but with print, the straight lines and serifs of it, the industrial polish and transcendence of it.

What did I wish to transcend? My beloved Shillington – can it be? The assumption was in the air, like the high humidity and the eye-irritating pollen, that I should get out.* I was, it seemed, along with my parents and grandparents and the cherry trees in the back yard and the horse-chestnut trees out front and the robins and squirrels and fireflies, *in* something, somewhat like the trapped victims of the mine and cave disasters that frequently figured in the news of those dingy, coal-burning decades. In the something I was in, these inky strata that fascinated me, these comic strips and captioned cartoons were veins of a lighter sort, that led to a bigger, glossier part of the cave, this cave called America. Looking back upon my transitions from Shillington to Plowville, from Plowville to Harvard, from Harvard to New York, from New York to New England, I seem to witness a wriggling feat of spelunking scarcely less dreadful than the prison escape in that bygone radio play. Yet of course at each stage, even in the narrowest passage, I had air to breathe, daily comforts and amusements, companions, and the blessed margin of unforeseeing that pads our adventure "here below"

---

* "The entire town seemed ensnarled in my mother's myth, that escape was my proper fate. It was as if I were a sport that the ghostly elders of Olinger had segregated from the rest of the livestock and agreed to donate in time to the air; this fitted with the ambiguous sensation I had always had in the town, of being simultaneously flattered and rejected."

– "Flight" (1959)

– a frequent phrase of my grandfather's, locating this world in relation to a better. Here below, the obstacle in my vocal apparatus when I tried to scream a detailed apologia at Eddie Pritchard was one more thing to get around, and though it still crops up, this anxious guilty blockage in the throat, I have managed to maneuver several millions of words around it.

IV

On Not Being a Dove

One of those first summer months spent on Martha's Vineyard, where the mail was rendered sticky and soft by the damp salt air, as if permeated by a melting island unreality, I received a questionnaire from some British editors asking – in the manner of a book compiled, thirty years before, of opinions on the Spanish Civil War – "Are you for, or against, the intervention of the United States in Vietnam?" and "How, in your opinion, should the conflict in Vietnam be resolved?" Had the questions arrived on the mainland, where I had so much else to do, I would probably have left them unanswered: but in the mood of islanded leisure and seclusion that I had attained I sat down at my makeshift desk and typed out, with some irritation, this response:

> Like most Americans I am uncomfortable about our military adventure in South Vietnam; but in honesty I wonder how much of the discomfort has to do with its high cost, in lives and money, and how much with its moral legitimacy. I do not believe that the Viet Cong and Ho Chi Minh have a moral edge over us, nor do I believe that great powers can always avoid using their power. I am for our intervention if it does some good – specifically, if it enables the people of South Vietnam to seek their own political future. It is absurd to suggest that a village in the grip of guerrillas has freely chosen, or that we owe it to history to bow before a wave of the future engineered by terrorists. The crying need is for genuine elections whereby the South Vietnamese can express their will. If their will is for Communism, we should pick up our chips and leave. Until such a will is expressed, and as long as no willingness to negotiate is shown by the other side, I do not see that we can abdicate our burdensome position in South Vietnam.

My discomfort increased when the New York *Times*, in a story covering the publication of *Authors Take Sides on Vietnam* in England, gave my impromptu response a prominence it never hoped to have. I wrote this letter to the editor:

I discover myself named, in the *Times* of September 18, as the lone American writer "unequivocally for" the United States intervention in Vietnam. How could anyone not be at least equivocal about an action so costly, so cruel in its details, so indecisive in its results? My statement, given in answer to an English questionnaire in August of 1966, says, "I am for our intervention if it does some good – specifically, if it enables the people of South Vietnam to seek their own political future." In the year that has passed, reasons accumulate to doubt that it is doing enough good. The bombing of the North seems futile as well as brutal and should be stopped. Our massive military presence may be crushing the South Vietnamese initiative it is supposed to encourage. The abundance of terror and coercion on all sides, as far as an American newspaper reader can tell, severely diminishes the significance of that trusted instrument, popular election. No doubt the history of our involvement in this land includes unscrupulousness and stupidity; no doubt the Viet Cong feeds upon actual discontent and injustice. I suspect the point is approaching, as for Spain in 1939, when peace at any price, even under a tyranny, is preferable to a continuing struggle. These – presented with consciousness of ignorance, by one too old for military service, and whose sons are too young – are my present feelings: these, plus the, I think, general dismay at the huge waste of material resources, the growing cost in lives, and the unaccountable influence of our party politics upon decisions vindicated in human blood.

I differ, perhaps, from my unanimously dovish confrères in crediting the Johnson administration with good faith and some good sense. Anyone not a rigorous pacifist must at least consider the argument that this war, evil as it is, is the lesser of available evils, intended to forestall worse wars. I am not sure that this is true, but I assume that this is the reasoning of those who prosecute it, rather than the maintenance of business prosperity or the President's crazed stubbornness. I feel in the dove arguments as presented to me too much aesthetic distaste for the President, even when not lifted to the paranoid heights of *Mac-Bird*; even the best of the negative accounts of our operations in South Vietnam, such as Mary McCarthy's vivid reports or Jonathan Schell's account of the destruction of Ben Suc, too much rely upon satirical descriptions of American officers and the grotesqueries of cultural superimposition. The protest seems too reflexive, too Pop; I find the statements, printed with mine, of Jules Feiffer and Norman Mailer, frivolous. Like W. H. Auden, I would hope, the sooner the better, for a "negotiated peace, to which the Viet Cong will have to be a party," and, like him, feel that it is foolish to canvass writers upon political issues. Not only do our views, as he says, "have no more authority than those of any reasonably well-educated citizen," but in my own case at least I feel my professional need for freedom of speech and expression prejudices me toward a government whose constitution guarantees it. I recognize that what to me is essential may well be, to a peasant on the verge of starvation, an abstract luxury.

My letter, long as it seems, actually went on for another page, which the *Times* cut, and in which I said, my wheels beginning to spin, that "I would enjoy being released from the responsibility of having an opinion on the Vietnam involvement" and "indeed, I would be glad to be freed of all the duties of living in a powerful modern state – while continuing to accept, of course, the benefits," but that "I cannot pretend to believe, though it would be convenient to do so, that our unilateral withdrawal from South Vietnam would serve the national interest or the cause of peace." I even had a concrete proposal:

My one concrete proposal would be that President Johnson decline to run in 1968. That as a last service he terminate his life of valued service to the country, including five years in its highest office. Then, under a new President, of either party, insofar as our role in South Vietnam is the inevitable product of our world position, it will continue; insofar as it is the special result of self-perpetuating mistakes of the present leadership, it should cease.

To dip into *Authors Take Sides on Vietnam* is to inhale the poisonous vapors of a polluted and fractious time. The responses by Mailer and Feiffer that I found frivolous run, in part, "The truth is, maybe we need a war. It may be the last of the tonics. From Lydia Pinkham to Vietnam in sixty years, or bust" (Mailer), and "The solution to the problem is so simple I'm amazed it hasn't occurred to anyone else. Lyndon Johnson should go on nationwide TV and say to the American people, 'Ah have goofed'" (Feiffer). I did not notice, twenty years ago, this gem of a cheering thought by James Purdy: "Vietnam is atrocious for the dead and maimed innocent, but it's probably sadder to be a live American with only the Madison Avenue glibbers for a homeland and a God."

The *Times* to the contrary, I was not the only non-dove: James Michener, an old Asia hand, gave a lengthy geopolitical explanation, ranging from Thailand to Australia, as to why "I am driven by experience of the past and concern for the future to support my government's stand in Vietnam," and Marianne Moore in typical cadence responded, "It is short-sightedly irresponsible, I think, to permit communist domination and acquiesce in the crushing of the weak by the strong. Can negotiation be imposed by force? Winston Churchill thought appeasement solved nothing." W. H. Auden wrote, sensibly as always, "It goes without saying that war is an atrocious corrupting business, but it is dishonest of those who demand the immediate withdrawal of all American troops to pretend that their motives are purely humanitarian. They believe, rightly or wrongly, that it would be better if the communists won. My answer to your question is, I suppose, that I believe a negotiated peace, to which the Viet Cong will have to be a party, to be possible, but not yet, and that, therefore, American troops, alas, must stay in Vietnam until it is." There was a great deal of discussion, in those pages from 1966, of the global threat posed by China, and of the Viet Cong; who could have foreseen that the Viet Cong, what was left of it after the Tet offensive, would be ignored by the North Vietnamese in their successful conquest of the South, or that China would become an uneasy friend of the United States and an enemy of the consolidated, militant Vietnamese nation?

My apologetic letter to the *Times* – blaming myself, as contritely as a victim of the Red Guards, for caring about freedom of speech – ended my public pronouncements on Vietnam. My usefulness as a sometime editorialist in the *The New Yorker*'s "Talk of the Town" came to an end some months later, with a brief "Notes and Comment" on President Johnson's surprise announcement in late March of 1968 that – just as I had proposed – he would not run again. My little piece praised his decision as "a victory of imagination, for in one stroke he has added credibility to his search for peace, heightened the dignity of his office for the remainder of his term, and compelled the United States to take its electoral process seriously. The political stage, without him, seems rather thinly populated; and, in the matter of Vietnam, the real alternatives may be more confining than we had imagined. Yet fresh opportunity and option have been created, and we can only be grateful for this unexpected gift." In a last-minute discussion over the telephone with the magazine's editor, the part of the penultimate sentence following the semicolon was cut. "We can't go saying he might have been right after all" was the argument. I acquiesced – after all, these anonymous pieces spoke for *The New Yorker* not me – and henceforth left "Notes and Comment" to other, more leftish, hands.

It pained and embarrassed me to be out of step with my editorial and literary colleagues, with the bronzed and almost universally "anti-war" summer denizens of Martha's Vineyard (including Feiffer and the fiery Lillian Hellman), and with many of my dearest Ipswich friends, including my wife. How had I come to such an awkward pass? In politics, ever since the hair-raising shouting matches that flew about my burning ears in Artie Hoyer's barber shop, my instinct had been merely to stay out of harm's way. By honorable double inheritance I was a Democrat: my father, raised as a Republican, had become a Roosevelt Democrat when thrown out of work at the outset of the Depression, and my grandfather Hoyer was a kind of Jacksonian Democrat, rooted in the dark soil of old Pennsylvania politics with its passion over tariffs and agrarianism. In his comfortable orotund manner Pop Hoyer would speak of the "business interests" and the "financiers" that occupied the sinister urban territory – steamy, malodorous Philadelphia and unspeakable New York – beyond Berks County's rural idyll.* Nearby Reading had a Socialist mayor when I was a boy, and its society was pretty much divided between those who owned the factories and those who worked in them. The mill owners, in their Wyomissing mansions and behind their iron fences in Heidelberg Township, were legendary figures, inaccessible ogres of wealth in my small-town boy's sense of things, scarcely less grand and remote than Pittsburgh multimillionaires like the Andrews Carnegie and Mellon, whose names were as romantic to my father as those of rock stars to a contemporary teenager. Elsewhere, in the miles of tight row houses throughout the bulk of Reading and its suburbs, lived the rest of us – "the people."

I was comfortable with being a Democrat. In my piping voice I defended Roosevelt and Eleanor and Henry Wallace against my Republican peers at the elementary school, much

---

* "'Had the northern manufacturers been half so concerned with the slaves in their own mills as they were with those in the fields of the South, they would have had no need to make the war for the sake of munitions profits. But they were jealous. Their hearts were consumed by envy. They had taken a beating in the Panic of '57. The civilization of the South menaced their pocketbooks. So as is the way with monied minority they hired a lawyer to do their dirty work, Lincoln.'"

– John Hook, in *The Poorhouse Fair* (1957)

as I competed in recess-time soccer tussles of the A's against the B's, or enlisted in the Philadelphia Avenue troops in mock-battles against the Second Streeters. A war was going on, and political differences, however shrill, were submerged in our common identity as young Americans doing our bit to defeat Hitler and Mussolini and Hirohito. The Republican party was understood to be that of the rich, or of those small businessmen who, like Artie Hoyer, for some reason identified with the rich; whereas the Democratic party was that of the common man, of the unrich. When I went to Harvard, my being a Democrat fit nicely into the liberal strain of establishment and undergraduate thinking: I sat in the Lowell House common room amidst a sardonic crowd loudly watching Nixon's televised Checkers speech (that strained piety! that lugubrious appeal to Pat's "good Republican cloth coat"!) and with my Unitarian, tennis-sneakered, pony-tailed girlfriend carried placards for Stevenson in front of a Cambridge polling place in 1952. There was a small, scarcely noticed difference, however, between the Harvard-Radcliffe Democrats and me that was to emerge in the Vietnam years: they, Unitarian or Episcopalian or Jewish, supported Roosevelt and Truman and Stevenson out of enlightenment, *de haut en bas*, whereas in my heart of hearts, I, however veneered with an education and button-down shirts, .was *de bas*. They, secure in the upper-middle class, were Democrats out of human sympathy and humanitarian largesse, because this was the party that helped the poor. Our family had simply *been* poor, and voted Democrat out of crude self-interest.

I first voted, pulling the Democrat lever, in New York City, after standing in line behind our Thirteenth Street landlord, who had had, fascinatingly, a piece of his ear bitten off by a young lover in a rage or amorous paroxysm – my wife and I naïvely speculated which. And she and I naïvely thought Stevenson might actually beat Ike this second time around. In 1960, transposed to Massachusetts, I was happy to vote with most of my fellow Bay Staters for our young native son, Jack Kennedy. And in 1964 I went to considerable trouble to vote inside the Soviet Union, casting at the American Embassy in Moscow my absentee ballot for Lyndon Johnson and against that warmonger Barry Goldwater; my peace-loving Russian hosts were as relieved as I at the Johnson landslide. One source of my sense of grievance against the peace movement when it came was that I hadn't voted for any of its figures – not for Abbie Hoffman or Father Daniel Berrigan or Reverend William Sloane Coffin or Jonathan Schell or Lillian Hellman or Joan Baez or Jane Fonda or Jerry Rubin or Dr Spock or Eugene McCarthy. I had voted for Lyndon Johnson, and thus had earned my American right not to make a political decision for another four years. If he and his advisers (transferred intact, most of them, from Kennedy's Camelot) had somehow got us into this mess, they would somehow get us out, and it was a citizen's plain duty to hold his breath and hope for the best, not parade around spouting pious unction and crocodile tears. Vietnam seemed to me a tight place we had got into and must close our eyes to squeeze through; Johnson, like me a few years earlier, had "tried to do too much," but, like Copper caught in the drainage pipe, perhaps he could wriggle free.

The protest, from my perspective, was in large part a snobbish dismissal of Johnson by the Eastern establishment; Cambridge professors and Manhattan lawyers and their guitar-strumming children thought they could run the country and the world better than this lugubrious bohunk from Texas. These privileged members of a privileged nation believed that their enviable position could be maintained without anything visibly ugly happening in the world. They were full of aesthetic disdain for their own defenders, the business-suited hirelings drearily pondering geopolitics and its bloody necessities down in Washington. The protesters were spitting on the cops who were trying to keep their property – the USA and its many amenities – intact. A common report in this riotous era was of slum-dwellers throwing rocks and bottles at the firemen come to put out fires; the peace marchers, the upper-middle-class housewives pushing baby carriages along in candlelit processions, seemed to me to be behaving identically, without the excuse of being slum-dwellers. At a White House dinner in June of 1965, I saw what seemed to me a touching sight: Johnson and Dean Rusk, as they moved among the tables, crossing paths and giving each other a brief hug in passing – two broad-backed Southern boys, trying to hold the fort.

It was hard to explain, even to myself, my feelings. The peace movement's predecessor and progenitor, the civil-rights movement, had posed no emotional problem. I had been proud, really, of my wife's going off to march in Selma, coming back with sore feet and a slight tan and stories of transracial sexual overtures (rebuffed, I was assured). Feverish with a cold, I marched with her in a large, singing, well-meaning crowd from Roxbury to the Boston Common one raw damp day, braving pneumonia in the process,* and we were charter

---

* "For a few blocks they marched between cheering tenements from whose topmost windows hung banners that proclaimed END DE FACTO SEGREGATION and RETIRE MRS HICKS. Then the march turned left, and Richard was passing Symphony Hall, within whose rectangular vault he had often dreamed his way along the deep-grassed meadows of Brahms and up the agate cliffs of Strauss . . . The new Prudential Tower, taller and somehow fainter than any other building, haunted each twist of their march, before their faces like a mirage, at their backs like a memory. A leggy nervous black girl wearing the orange fireman's jacket of the Security Unit shepherded their section of the line, clapping her hands, shouting freedom-song lyrics for a few bars. These songs struggled through the miles of the march, overlapping and eclipsing one another. 'Which side are you on, boy, which side are you on . . . like a tree-ee planted by the wah-ha-ter, we shall not be moved . . . this little light of mine, gonna shine on Boston, Mass., this little light of mine . . .' The day continued cool and without shadows. Newspapers that he had folded inside his coat for warmth slipped and slid. . . . Incredibly, they were traversing a cloverleaf, an elevated concrete arabesque devoid of cars. Their massed footsteps whispered; the city yawned beneath them. The march had no beginning

---

members of the local Fair Housing Committee, founded on the rumor that a black family had been finagled out of an Ipswich house they were on the verge of buying. I went to meetings and contributed to the NAACP and even lent a black man we slightly knew some money that he never repaid – I was all for people getting a break, if the expense to me wasn't inordinate.

By my mid-thirties, through diligence and daring, I had arrived at a lifestyle we might call genteel bohemian: nice old house (broad floorboards, big fireplaces) rather diffidently furnished (Danish modern always coming unglued, DR sofa in need of cleaning, five-and-dime kitchenware, a smattering of auction antiques), walls occupied by semi-abstract canvases painted by the Mrs and pine bookshelves hammered together by the Mr, scruffy back yard (uninhibited forsythia hedge, a rope swing hung from a dying elm, bare spots in the rough shape of a baseball diamond), four dusty but healthy children with Sunday bests at the backs of their closets, two cars, one of them a convertible, and, for dinner, lots of rice casseroles and California wine. To me, this was prosperity. Out of those shadows of debt and financial reversal that had darkened the Shillington house I had emerged into a kind of sunlight; I made more money than we spent, and we, with our modest reach of consumption, lacked for nothing. Casting my mind back to that Sixties domestic bliss, I recollect an evening when we headed off to the house of another couple who, with a rather more sumptuous outlay of broadly striped rugs, embroidered velvet pillows, and mohair antimacassars than had occurred to us to acquire, epitomized genteel-bohemian comfort. They cooked on a big black wood stove in giant pots

---

and no end that Richard could see. Within him, the fever had become a small glassy scratching on the walls of the pit hollowed by the detonating pills. A piece of newspaper spilled down his legs and blew into the air. Impalpably medicated, ideally motivated, he felt, strolling along the curve of the cloverleaf, gathered within an irresistible ascent."

– "Marching Through Boston" (1965)

and had encrusted their decor with those Hinduish trinkets and hangings that could be bought in "head shops," suggestive of inner freedom and mystical self-enhancement. We were, all four, to go off to a party on a rented steam boat on the Piscataqua River, and I realized, arriving in their house with its layered look and cozy potpourri of various fumes, that I was not dressed sportily enough. Inspired by a quick drink, I ran downtown to the clothing store, which was a mere block away and stayed open Friday nights; I bought myself yellow slacks, a boat-neck jersey, and blue topsiders, paid cash, and returned in a matter of minutes, to noisy admiration of my new outfit – such were the convenient economies of Ipswich life, for us dashing genteel bohemians.

Another image of mixed communal and financial happiness in those years that comes to me is of winter Wednesday mornings when, in the slanting light of our large living room, two or three housewives and one male doctor, who took Wednesdays off – the same who diagnosed that if I fainted I could breathe – would assemble for our weekly trip north, to ski in New Hampshire. He and I and our little bundled-up harem would crowd our bodies and our equipment into a station wagon and head for Gunstock Mountain or Sunapee or Cranmore or, at the farthest feasible reach of a day trip, Wildcat or Cannon, three hours away. Sleep still blurred our aging faces, the children had just been sent off to school, the housewives looked cuddly in their parkas and tight ski pants, and cups of coffee and bits of gossip were quickly passed around as we waited for the last of our group to appear on the snowy street outside. One woman, I remember, used to wear après-ski boots of a synthetic fur dyed in stripes, and these jaunty boots, with their pointed toes and vaguely psychedelic sheen, greatly charmed me, as symbols of what we could now afford. Our trips to the tonic north country squeezed us all into one smoky automobile and felt like a holiday back into adolescence. We would become a pack, welded together by the day's fatigue and bruises and beer. I seem to remember, on one endless drive back home in the dark down Route 93, while my wife sat in the front seat and her hair was rhythmically irradiated with light from opposing headlights, patiently masturbating my back-seat neighbor through her ski pants, beneath our blanketing parkas, and taking a brotherly pride in her shudder of orgasm just as we hit the Ipswich turn-off.

At other moments of suburban relaxation, in our circle of semi-bohemian homes, we smoked pot, wore dashikis and love beads, and frugged ourselves into a lather while the Beatles and Janis Joplin sang away on the hi-fi set. I was happy enough to lick the sugar of the counterculture; it was the pill of anti-war, anti-administration, "anti-imperialist" protest that I found oddly bitter. I was, perhaps, the most Vietnam-minded person I knew. Those who deplored the war fit what protesting they could into their suburban schedules and otherwise dismissed it with a gesture of automatic distaste; the technocrats of our acquaintance, the electronic engineers and stockbrokers and economics professors, tended to see the involvement as an administrative blunder, to which they could attach no passion. But I – I whose stock in trade as an American author included an intuition into the mass consciousness and an identification with our national fortunes – thought it sad that our patriotic myth of invincible virtue was crashing, and shocking that so many Americans were gleeful at the crash. I felt obliged to defend Johnson and Rusk and Rostow, and then Nixon and Kissinger, as they maneuvered, with many a solemn bluff and thunderous air raid, our quagmirish involvement and long extrication. My face would become hot, my voice high and tense and wildly stuttery; I could feel my heart race in a kind of panic whenever the subject came up, and my excitement threaten to suffocate me. It was the argument with Eddie Pritchard all over again, only now I was claiming that not only I but the President (whoever he was) was not an ostrich.

Of all the contending parties with which it might have been possible to sympathize – the Viet Cong in their tunnels,

118

fighting off bombers with punji stakes; the North Vietnamese and the old Viet Minh, condemned to fight war after war; Ho Chi Minh, with his innocently lifted eyebrows and saintly white goatee; the napalmed children; the defoliated trees and poisoned rice paddies; the self-immolating Buddhist monks; the American soldiers, derided and mocked at home and surrounded by inscrutable, implacably hostile villagers in Vietnam – I felt compelled to identify with the American administrations and to a lesser extent with those South Vietnamese, from Diem and Ky and Thieu down to the village chiefs buried alive and otherwise gruesomely assassinated, who were trying to run a non-Communist country. Gorge-deep principles of fairness and order were at issue; it greatly distressed me, for example – it wasn't *fair* – that American liberals could so blithely disown what was clearly a typically and historically liberal cause, intervention against a Communist bully. Carl Oglesby, addressing the SDS at a Washington rally in 1965, said it clearly:

> The original commitment in Vietnam was made by President Truman, a mainstream liberal. It was seconded by President Eisenhower, a moderate liberal. It was intensified by the late President Kennedy, a flaming liberal. Think of the men who now engineer the war – those who study the maps, give the commands, push the buttons and tally the dead: Bundy, McNamara, Lodge, Goldberg, the President himself. They are not moral monsters. They are all honorable men. They are all liberals.

I was a liberal. The political position I had wormed into on Artie Hoyer's barber's chair – holding my tongue, but inwardly scorning this frantic Republican hatred of governmental activism – had unfairly gone unfashionable on me. If we approved of Roosevelt's nudging us toward World War II, and of Truman's bouncing us into Korea one impetuous Sunday, why were we turning up our noses at Vietnam? What was Vietnam but Korea again, Korea without an overt invasion, without a UN resolution, and without a Syngman Rhee, but all the more honorable a cause for its added difficulties? Were the people in the State Department utterly stupid to think we shouldn't let Southeast Asia go down the drain? Were we really secure enough – high and mighty and smug enough – to become a pacifist nation? You don't get something for nothing. If there was one lesson my upbringing had instilled it was our earthly insecurity: a Depression, a disease, a swindler smarter than we can come along and take everything from us. My father was a patriot: he had been ready in 1918 to board the troop ship in World War I; he had been Uncle Sam in the victory parade after World War II; when McCarthyism had imposed a loyalty oath on public-school teachers in Pennsylvania, he had taken it without demur. I must have questioned him about it, for I remember his saying mildly that he had no trouble swearing that he was loyal to the United States. He was loyal, and so was I. I would rather live under Diem (or Ky, or Thieu) than under Ho Chi Minh and his enforcers, and assumed that most South Vietnamese would. Those who would not, let them move north. But the foot traffic, one could not help noticing in these Communist/non-Communist partitions, was south, or west, away from Communism. Why was that? And so on.

I wanted to keep quiet, but could not. Something about it all made me very sore. I spoke up, blushing and hating my disruption of a post-liberal socio-economic-cultural harmony I was pleased to be a part of. I recall, on Martha's Vineyard, the puzzled expressions on the faces of Bernard Taper and Philip Roth* as I argued on, defending poor Johnson and his

---

* On the dizzying verge of publishing *Portnoy's Complaint*. We were sitting, with wives, sweethearts, and children, in the amazing shack Taper rented, at the end of a grassy lane in West Tisbury, so small he had to type outside under a tree; the interior, one big room, was furnished entirely, it seemed, with driftwood, pots and pans, and a large Japanese kite in the shape of a fish. It was the ultimate of genteel bohemianism – it made our Ipswich attempts look pokey and padded – and I always felt agitated with happiness here, like a child invited to a party. A party, as it happened, I was spoiling.

pitiful ineffective war machine. In my mind I was beset, defending an underdog, my back to the wall in a world of rabid anti-establishment militants. At one point Roth, in the calm and courteous tone of one who had been through many psychiatric sessions, pointed out to me that I was the most aggressive person in the room. It gave me pause. On reflection, it seemed possibly true. Why *was* I so vehement and agitated an undove? I did not just have a few cool reservations about the anti-war movement; I felt hot. I was emotionally involved. "Defending Vietnam" – the vernacular opposite of being "anti-war" – I was defending myself.

My wife of those years offered an interesting idea: that Johnson was a former schoolteacher and I identified him with my father, whose inability to maintain classroom order had been a central trauma of my growing up, a childish cause for fear and pity. For three years, from seventh grade to ninth, I had been one of my father's students and had been torn by the wish to be a loyal son and the itch to be a popularity-seeking cutup. In my anxious dreams about him – naked but for a barrel, pelted and hooted on the steps of the town hall – things had "gotten away" from him, much as the country had gotten away from Johnson. The protest movement, which had begun in the solemn Fiftyish pronouncements of the Port Huron Statement and the orderly civil-rights strategies, by the time of the '67 Washington march and the '68 convention had become a Yippieish carnival of mischievous voodoo and street theatre and, finally, a nightmare of anarchy, of window-smashing and cop-bopping and drug-tripping and shouting down. The shouting-down part of it, the totalitarian intolerance and savagery epitomized by the Weathermen* but to

* For years I carried in my wallet, like a fortune-cookie slip somehow more than amusing, a statement from the underground Weathermen: "We are against everything that's good and decent in honky America. We will loot, burn, and destroy. We are the incubation of your mother's nightmare."

some extent adopted by student radicals everywhere, amazed and alarmed me. Authority to these young people was Amerika, a blood-stained bugaboo to be crushed at any cost. To me, authority was the Shillington High School faculty, my father and his kindly and friendly, rather wan and punctilious colleagues, with whose problems and perspective I had had every opportunity to empathize. I had overheard their mild-mannered conversations in the hall when the thundering hordes of unruly students had left; I was allowed to visit the boiler room, and see the male teachers at ease in their shirtsleeves, smoking and joking while the janitors lounged at the workbench and the boilers roared and chugged down another giant gulp of pea coal. Authority to me was Woody Coldren, the superintendent of the Lutheran Sunday School and eventually town burgess, loudly leading us children in the singing of carols on Christmas morning in front of the blank screen of the movie theatre. It was my grandfather and the town crew, tarring the tidy streets. It was the three town cops, in their comically different sizes. Such were the village elders whom I visualized tortured and executed by the Viet Cong, to show us peasants that the only possible social order was theirs.

Yet there was another side to it. Hadn't "the system," in losing my grandfather his money and my father his job, let us down just as I was being born? My mother, who had walked out of a classroom where she had been stationed as a student teacher, had with this gesture rejected the place the system offered her, and in her eccentricity – her private revolution – showed me the gravitational pull of other systems, more far-fetched possibilities. The town authorities, and all the hard-working churchgoing burghers of Shillington, struck me really as stodgy and not to be emulated. At heart I scorned them. Who would want to be a Thirty-second-degree Mason, or the top Oddfellow? Who, by extension, would want to be President of the United States? And my Harvard education, acquired in the mauve afternoon of modernism, amid Eliotic shades of irony and fastidious ennui, strengthened my impression that political concern was vapid and played small part in the civilized life. That, perhaps, was what angered me most about Vietnam; it made it impossible to ignore politics, to cultivate serenely my garden of private life and printed artifact. These butterfingered Washington fat cats in their three-hundred-dollar suits had dropped us all into a mess of blood and shame and frustration and embarrassment, and here I was, stuck with defending them.

Was I conservative? I hadn't thought so, but I did come from what I could begin to see was a conservative part of the country. Conversative in dress, in mores, in attitudes. The Germans of Berks County didn't move on, like the typical Scots-Irish frontier-seeking American. They stayed put, farming the same valleys and being buried in the same graveyards, one generation after another. Before the Germans came to southeastern Pennsylvania, there had been the Quakers, and these, too, were conservative, thrifty, accumulative, suspicious of all but inner revolutions. The cautious spirit of Ben Franklin's maxims still lived in the air. A penny saved is a penny earned; wilful waste makes woeful want; a fool and his money are soon parted: my grandfather quoted these often, as inherited wisdom to be passed on. My father's bitter economic experience supplied some darker maxims. Another day, another dollar. Dog eat dog. You don't get something for nothing. I had been reared in the static, defensive world of the Depression, to which the World War added a coloring of embattlement and patriotic pride. At the height of the Vietnam troubles, in the late Sixties, my family in loving exasperation gave me for Christmas a large American flag. I was, as an American Protestant, the beneficiary of a number of revolts – Luther's, which dumped the Pope; Cromwell's which dumped the monarchy; and Sam Adam's, which dumped the British – and saw no need for any more. I was, furthermore, a Christian, and Christ said, "Render unto

Caesar those things which are Caesar's." I was, by upbringing, a Lutheran, and Luther had told the "murdering and thieving hordes" ["*die räuberischen und möderischen Rotten*"] of rebellious peasants to cease their radical turmoil and submit to their Christian princes.* Faith alone, faith without any false support of works, justified the Lutheran believer and distinguished him from the Catholic and Calvinist believer. In all varieties of Christian faith resides a certain contempt for the world and for attempts to locate salvation and perfection here. The world is fallen, and in a fallen world animals, men, and nations make space for themselves through a willingness to fight. Christ beat up the money-changers in the temple, and came not to bring peace, He distinctly said, but a sword.

My thoughts ran as follows. Peace depends upon the threat of violence. The threat cannot always be idle. Privately and in the aggregate, we walk through life with chips on our shoulder, and when the chip is knocked off, we must fight. "You *must* fight," none other than a Russian had told me, in late 1964, in the Soviet Union, concerning Vietnam. Ho Chi Minh had knocked off our shoulder the chip that Dulles and Eisenhower and the SEATO treaty had placed there. We had

---

* Paul Tillich, a Lutheran, paraphrases Luther's "positivistic authoritarianism" in his *History of Christian Thought*: "The power of the state, which makes it possible for us even to be here or for works of charity to be done at all, is a work of God's love. The state has to suppress the aggression of the evil man, of those who are against love; the strange work of love is to destroy what is against love. It is correct to call this a strange work, but it is nevertheless a work of love. Love would cease to be a power on earth altogether without destroying that which is against love. This is the deepest insight into the relationship between power and love that I know. The whole positivistic doctrine of the state makes it impossible for Lutheranism, from a theological point of view, to accept revolution. Revolution results in chaos; even if it tries to produce order, it first produces chaos and disorder increases. Thus, Luther was unambiguously against revolution. He accepted the postively given gift of destiny." Even the admitted fact that the Lutheran church readily submitted to Nazism does not alter Tillich's tone of fond wonder as he insists, "Luther broke the back of the revolutionary will in the German people. There is no such thing as a revolutionary will in the German people; that is all we can say and nothing more."

tried to subvert the North, we had tried to train and arm ARVN so it could defend the South, and neither had worked. We had to fight, though it meant pitting ourselves, with our white faces, against the other guy's nationalism, halfway around the world, and picking up all the bad checks the French had scattered about in a century of conspicuously ruthless colonialism. It was all very well for civilized little countries like Sweden and Canada to tut-tut in the shade of our nuclear umbrella and welcome our deserters and draft evaders, but the United States had nobody to hide behind. Credibility must be maintained. Power is a dirty business, but who ever said it wasn't? In the Bhagavad-Gita, Krishna told Arjuna, "Therefore you must fight. . . . Freedom from activity is never achieved by abstaining from action. . . . The world is imprisoned in its own activity, except when actions are performed as worship of God." The Vietnam war – or *any* war – is "wrong," but in the sense that existence itself is wrong. To be alive is to be a killer; and though the Jains try to hide this by wearing gauze masks to avoid inhaling insects, and the anti-abortionists by picketing hospitals, and peace activists by lying down in front of ammunition trains, there is really no hiding what every meal we eat juicily demonstrates. Peace is not something we are entitled to but an illusory respite we earn. On both the personal and national level, islands of truce created by balances of terror and potential violence are the best we can hope for. Pacifism is a luxury a generous country can allow a small minority of its members, but the pacifism invoked in the anti-Vietnam protest was hypocritical and spurious. Under the banner of a peace movement, rather, war was being waged by a privileged few upon the administration and the American majority that had elected it.

My father-in-law, a Unitarian minister, had been raised as a Quaker. I loved hearing him 'thee' and 'thou,' without self-consciousness, in his gentle Midwestern voice, his wife and two daughters. By marrying his elder daughter, I had become an honorary Unitarian, and the Unitarians that I came to know were, every one of them, charming – lively, gracious, intelligent, and twinkly. They lived in big wooden houses on the tree-lined side streets of Cambridge, or in lovingly reclaimed old farmhouses up Vermont roads, or in solid brick establishments in the academic enclave of Chicago's Hyde Park, within a wary walk of the Meadville Seminary – my wife thrilled me by describing how she used to walk the dog with a knife in her stocking, in case the nearby black ghetto produced an assailant. Unitarians were at first as exotic to me as Bantus. Though the denomination claimed the Spanish physician, theologian, and martyr Michael Servetus (1511–53) as a kind of founder, the American church dated from the second quarter of the last century, and its living members still breathed the spirit and quoted the words of Emerson, Channing, and Parker. I could not understand why anyone would build and attend churches without believing in the divinity of Christ or the actuality of God, in miracles or sacraments or immortality, but the churches were there, and handsome large structures they were, full of fine choir music, lofty prayers, and learned sermons. Though my gentle father-in-law and I had some tense early arguments in which I, blushing and stammering, insisted that an object of faith must have some concrete attributes, and he suggested that our human need for transcendence should be met with minimal embarrassments to reason, at bottom I loved him, and Unitarianism, too; it lacked that greasy heaviness of Lutheranism, the gloom of its linoleum-floored Sunday-school basements and the sickly milky tints of its stained-glass windows, the thick yellow sheen of its varnished pews and altar furniture. Unitarianism seemed, instead, all air and light and good humor. It was classy, and friendly. My in-laws crackled around me like straw in a dry nest. Whether God's number be three or one or zero, human kindness and decency are clear enough, the twinkle in their pale-blue eyes seemed to reassure me. And they seemed to like me; my busy brains, which in

Pennsylvania had inspired distrust if not animosity, were valued up here, in this frostier clime, this thinner, bluer New England air. The rest of me – the Pennsylvania mud, the something starved and voracious, scabby and choked – my Unitarian acquaintances politely ignored.

By "Unitarians" I mean partakers in an ethos as much as a creed; I include those Harvard people, from my wife's circle of friends, whose minds and spirits had been washed clean. They wore pale clothes and their hair and skin looked bleached; they spoke so quietly I had to strain to hear. I could hardly believe my ears, one day, when, in discussing global pollution, the husband of the lovely lanky blond couple who occupied our basement apartment in Cambridge before we did, a fledgling astronomer, told me that of course I had reconciled myself to personal extinction, and therefore the future life of the planet had to concern me. I didn't have the courage to admit that I had reconciled myself to no such thing, and that I didn't care about the future of the planet except as it involved my own. It was and is still my fate to like the settings and the personalities that enlightenment creates without wanting, myself, to be thoroughly enlightened. Unitarianism early laid hold of the costumes and concerns of what would become the counterculture: natural purity, pioneer dress, sentimental feelings for country life, political activism. Unitarians and desynagogued Jews led liberal causes; in his Chicago years my father-in-law, based in his incongruously Gothic church just off the Midway, worked mightily to build bridges between the black and white communities of the South Side – though he was not entirely pleased when his older daughter threatened to fall in love with a blind black man. Indeed, I now wonder if he accepted me so graciously into his family because, rough-hewn as I was, and shaky as my artistic ambitions must have looked, I was the least radical romantic venture she had lately undertaken. His social idealism seemed to me, like his Vermont country place and his handsome Chicago parsonage, an appurtenance of my upward mobility, and I had no quarrel with it, or with his daughter's. Indeed, I admired, in the dry Unitarian spirit, its latent spark of revolutionary will, so dampened in my German forebears.

Yet the possibility exists that, along with my authority-worshipping Germanness and my delusional filial attachment to Lyndon Baines Johnson, my wife's reflexive liberalism helped form my unfortunate undovish views – that I assumed these views out of a certain hostility to her, and was protesting against our marriage much as campus radicals were blowing up ROTC buildings, government research centers, and, on occasion, themselves to declare (it was theorized even at the time) that their parents had been insufficiently loving. All noisy protest, I suppose, has some affinity with a baby's crying – it seeks to attract attention and affection. My wife and I must have discussed the war (the "Vietnam conflict" it was called, never earning the Korean epithet of "police action"). I remember my children wincing and leaving the room when the subject came up at the dinner table. But what we said I almost totally forget. I do recall her saying, of the Vietnamese and Vietnam, "It's their place" – about as succinct and cogent an argument for non-intervention as there could be. But my most vivid politico-marital memory of those superheated Sixties was her coming into the bedroom one morning in 1968 and waking me with "Now do you know what they've done? They've shot Bobby Kennedy!" This strange "they" – the implementers of chaos and destruction – was a shadowy army that neither of us, surely, sided with.

We had met at Harvard-Radcliffe and were children of light; I liked this about us, but not entirely. My notions of heterosexual love had been derived from Hollywood movies and pornographic comic books and then such modernist benchmarks of sexual realism as *Lady Chatterley's Lover*, the last chapter of *Ulysses*, Henry Miller's *Tropic* books, *The Story of O*, and the memoirs of Frank Harris; perhaps I was disappointed when an overworked mother of four failed to follow these scripts. I may have further felt that a generalized love for mankind, like a too-intense love for dogs and birds, rather delocalizes Eros. But, politically, I expected dovishness and liberal sentiments in women, as part of their nurturing, pitying nature. In the long haul of nearly a quarter-century between my wedding vows, I was more than once attracted to women to the left even of my first wife, and once had to control a shudder of revulsion when an adored beauty confided to me, from her side of the bed, an intention to vote for Goldwater.

Nevertheless, there was a theological animus; down-dirty sex and the bloody mess of war and the desperate effort of faith all belonged to a dark necessary underside of reality that I felt should not be merely ignored, or risen above, or disdained. These shameful things were intrinsic to life, and though I myself was somewhat squeamish about sex and violence and religion, as my childhood self had been squeamish about fingerpaints and spiders and tomatoes, they must be faced, it seemed to me, and even embraced. It was the reality-embrace I wanted – the admission, from all doves however vehement and wives however sleepy, that we had been led into the Vietnam mire plausible step by step, that the mire was U.S., us. A dark Augustinian idea lurked within my tangled position: a plea that Vietnam – this wretched unfashionable war led by clumsy Presidents from the West and fought by the nineteen-year-old sons of the poor – could not be disowned by a favored enlightened few hiding behind college deferments, fleeing to chaste cool countries, snootily pouring pig blood into draft files, writing deeply offended Notes and Comments, and otherwise pretending that our great nation hadn't had bloody hands from the start, that every generation didn't have its war, that bloody hands didn't go with having hands at all. A plea, in short, for the doctrine of Original Sin and its obscure consolations. "In Adam's Fall/ We sinned all," began that seminal American text, the *New England Primer*. New England had moved beyond this, and took a quite silly pride, I thought, in its haughty old disavowal of the Mexican–American War.*

Two other factors, it occurred to me at the time, inhibited me from taking the handy dove position. I had been to Russia, and I had not served in Korea, which had been my generation's war to fight. I had hid out at Harvard, and then had not even gone into the peacetime Army. I felt guilty at being 4–F, all the more guilty for being glad at the time, and hustling ahead with my career in those two years that I should have spent in barracks and canteens and the kind of boring clerical work that Philip Roth in his fiction has inflicted on Zuckerman. I would never know what I had missed, and read Roth's fictional versions of his Army tour with envious interest.† If Roth said, as he did, that the generals and presidential advisers knew no more about Vietnam and its alleged strategic importance than we did sitting in Bernie Taper's little driftwood shack, he had earned the right, it seemed to me, in a way I hadn't. He had paid his dues. If Norman Mailer wanted to march in Washington and be briefly jailed and then write a funny, inflated, shrewd,

---

* "'New England, Mr Buchanan, is no place to look for national policy. Adams is dying; he is their last voice of consequence. They may rant their sermons on the misery of the nigger, and a few retired men of means may spend a night in jail for refusing to pay their taxes, but since Massachusetts played the traitor's role in Madison's little war, and disgraced the Federalist party so it died of shame thereafter, this region is a thorn in our side merely. Howl though the Bostonians may, their descendants will not disdain to prosper in a nation squared off from coast to coast. To be President of the United States, sir, is to act as advocate for a blind, venomous, and ungrateful client; still, one must make the best of the case, for the purposes of Providence.'"

– President James Polk, in *Buchanan Dying* (1974)

† Recently reading my esteemed contemporary's own venture into autobiography, *The Facts*, I discovered that he served only one year, having been given a medical discharge for a back injury sustained in basic training at Fort Dix. So I feel only half as envious/guilty/inferior as before.

skewed, pop-apocalyptic account of it, he, too, had earned the right, risking his life in the South Pacific against the fanatic Japanese while I, for my heroic part, was flattening tin cans in my grandfather's chicken house. If Kurt Vonnegut, having survived capture by the Germans and the Allies' firebombing of Dresden, wanted to fulminate in his woolly way against the powers that be, more power to him; he had paid a fair price for his skepticism and indignation. I had paid no such price; in fact, I had had a fine peaceful time being an American male in the middle of the twentieth century. Defending the war (or, rather, disputing the attackers of it) was perhaps my way of serving, of showing loyalty to a country that had kept its hackneyed promises – life, liberty, pursuit of happiness – to me. When asked, in 1964, to go to the Soviet Union for a month as part of a cultural-exchange program, I consented partly because this would constitute a small patriotic service, a wearing abroad, at last, of my country's colors.

The month was an eye-opener: to see the birches and the wooden villages, St Basil's and the Hermitage; to visit Yasnaya Polyana where shelves held the very books, including one by Upton Sinclair, that Tolstoy had handled and read; to venture into a rather slummy part of Moscow where Dostoevsky had once resided and where his nib pen and wire spectacles were preserved in a glass case; to see vistas and experience atmospherics right out of Chekhov and Nabokov; to drink vodka with Yevtushenko and Vosnesensky past midnight and then again with Writers' Union apparatchiks at ten the next morning; to visit ballet schools and music conservatories where solemn and stately young females twirled in a glaze of sweat and played great galloping fistfuls of Chopin; to travel by swaying train and bouncing airplane to Armenia and Georgia and the Ukraine; to be dragged before English classes in some murky educational building and presented as a "progressive" American writer; to be made much of, in this or that "people's artist"'s studio or dacha, where the comfortably broad women fetched trays of sweets and bowls of fruit to accompany the slivovitz shot through with sunshine; to bandy words through a translator whose labors gave every conversation the ghostly grace of slow motion; to mingle with babushkaed and fur-clad citizens in the streets and subway; to participate marginally in the exalted, perilous whirl of Soviet literary circles; to attend the vast readings their poets give and, when introduced, to stand and be bathed in the mighty applause that the Soviet young awarded Americans, on no merit of our own, but as a kind of protest of their own; to improvise flowery ceremonial speeches; to be hauled about in Zil limousines to lavish old-fashioned hotel rooms full of brass bears and hidden bugs; to feel the musty closeness of the czarist past; to inhale the nostalgia, intrigues, and cooking odors of another, semi-Asiatic sort of civilization; to be at the heart of another empire; to be, oneself, a center of intrigue, the object of advice and confidences from both sides of the Cold War – all this was novel, heady, and congenial.

I liked the warm-hearted, boisterous, mischievous, many-layered Russians; I liked not only my celebrated literary peers like Yevtushenko but the party officials with their gold teeth and steel smiles and iron stomachs and the shy students reaching out with Oxford-accented English and the insolent languid sloe-eyed shopgirls behind their piles of fur and amber and the utterly bald barber who tapped the top of my skull and grunted out the English words "This haircut" – meaning one I had had in Ipswich, six weeks before – "no good." I was thirty-two and showed a stamina and capacity for alcohol and blarney that surprised me, and a gift (my submissive Lutheran heritage, again) for "going along" with things. I had gone along at Shillington High School, I had gone along at Harvard, I could go along here. The Russian system, the few gears of it that engaged me, gave me no pain; the most oppressed people I saw were the tiny, grandmotherly attendants in the opera-house checkrooms, literally tottering as they hauled back and forth mountains of ponderous winter coats. Any system, in place, has a certain logic of inertia and quotidian practicality arguing for it; my Soviet escorts and hosts, being at home, were more appealing than the embassy Americans, who in their pinstripes and hornrims had the awkwardness of interlopers. I did what I was asked to do, and dutifully tried to be a good guest of the Soviet state.

And yet I came away from that month, and the two subsequent weeks in the Eastern Bloc countries Bulgaria, Rumania, and Czechoslovakia, with a hardened antipathy to Communism. The difference between our empires was not, as many were beginning to say, and were to say louder and louder during the impending Vietnam years, six of one and a half-dozen of the other. It was more like eleven of one and one of the other. It was Athens and Sparta, light and shadow. Ours was the distinctly better mousetrap.

What made me think so? Was it the glittering display of luxury goods and all the spandy-new runway equipment in the Zurich airport? After my weeks of quaint Communist drabness, Swiss efficiency and prosperity looked like a sci-ence-fiction movie. Or was it the little leaks of fear that would show while I was in Communist countries, the spurts of steam betraying the underlying pressure – suddenly impassive expressions, quick lapses into French to evade the eavesdrop-ping walls, a burst of real, scurrying terror from my escort when it appeared I had lost my passport? I had never before been in countries where people were afraid of their own government – where everything, in a sense, every motion of the mind and heart and pen, was politics. And there was something bullyingly egocentric about my admirable Soviet friends, a preoccupation with their own tortured situations that shut out all light from beyond. They were like residents of a planet so heavy that even their gazes were sucked back into its dark center. Arthur Miller, no reactionary, said it best when, a few years later, he and I and some other Americans riding the cultural-exchange bandwagon had entertained, in

New York or Connecticut, several visiting Soviet colleagues. The encounter was handsomely catered, the dialogue was loud and lively, the will toward friendship was earnest and in its way intoxicating, but upon our ebullient guests' departure Miller looked at me and said sighingly, "Jesus, don't they make you glad you're an American?"

I *was* glad, and resented having my native land, with its treasure of natural resources and enlightened institutions and hopeful immigrant peoples, being described as Amerika. The peace movement's branding our government with a swastika seemed to me insanely blasphemous and itself fascist and, like Eddie Pritchard's insults, inarguably obtuse. The United States of my pre-pubescent years had been many-sidedly, all-involvingly at war, and I saw no atrocity in its continuing to possess an army and a military-industrial complex. In any case, it wasn't for me, a dermatological 4–F, to condemn a war other men were – if not enthusiastically, then stoically and stubbornly – fighting, and that our elected officials and their advisers found, from one administration to the next, essential to the national honor. To say that war is madness is like saying that sex is madness: true enough, from the standpoint of a stateless eunuch, but merely a provocative epigram for those who must make their arrangements in the world as given. In Sunday school, I had been much impressed by the passage where Peter denies Christ three times before the cock crows. My undovishness, like my battered and vestigial but unsurrendered Christianity, constituted a refusal to give up, to deny and disown, my deepest and most fruitful self, my Shillington self – dimes for war stamps, nickels for the Sunday-school collection, and grown-ups maintaining order so that I might be free to play with my cartoons and Big Little Books. I was grateful to be exempted from the dirty, dreary business of maintaining the overarching order, and felt that a silent non-protest was the least I in gratitude owed those who were not exempted.

* * *

And yet . . . wasn't there simply something of the high-school show-off, the impish contrarian "getting attention," in my refusal to take the unexceptional position that neither God nor good reasons for our being in Vietnam existed? My religious and Vietnamese opinions were clearly allied; both made me feel vulnerable, excited, apologetic, and angry, and both were, in my adopted social milieu, rather original. Among the repulsions of atheism for me has been its drastic uninterestingness as an intellectual position. Where was the ingenuity, the ambiguity, the humanity (in the Harvard sense) of saying that the universe just happened to happen and that when we're dead we're dead? Where, indeed, was the intellectual interest of saying that Johnson and Nixon were simply dreadful Presidents? Truth had to have more nooks and crannies, more ins and outs than that.

I distrusted orthodoxies, especially orthodoxies of dissent, and preferred to elude classification. Just as I enjoyed my distance as an artist (and a profit-making arist with a sly little national reputation!) from my neighbors, I enjoyed the anti-bohemian gesture of my deadpan churchgoing – my immersion, those many Sunday mornings, in the naked and guileless light of the Congregational nave and the plain rites descended from the Pilgrims. Thus blended among my neighbors, I felt out of harm's way. The basic dread that all religion offers to assuage drove me there, but there was a side benefit in the distance churchgoing put between me and the stereotypical writer, my disenchanted Manhattan counterpart. This distance seemed to me a professional asset: I was still somewhat enchanted, and that was artistically useful, since Western culture from Boethius to Proust had transpired under the Christian enchantment, and the psychological tensions that this enchantment generated were, really, almost all there was to say.

(And yet how different from this blithe formulation was the sad ecclesiastical reality! I wanted my children, though they lived in a different world and time, to have the Sunday-school experience, to begin their life's journey from. Our church affiliation, what with my wife's indifference and my own Barthian dandyism, was less than half-hearted, and the church itself a rather feeble, impoverished, merely surviving thing, occupying a precious old example of Carpenter Gothic built in 1846 and ignited by lightning one June Sunday in 1965. Not long before it burned down, I had been in the dim and dingy narthex alone, and was startled to see posted there, on a string of cardboard lamps containing the names of parish children, my older daughter's name. We rarely pushed her to attend the struggling little Sunday school; this pencilled enrolment implied an ideal, omnisicient community of belief pathetically at odds with the attenuated reality – a matter of weak stabs, of token belonging, of a credo faded to the palest sentimentalities, of a church family in which my children instinctively felt uneasy, of an affiliation on my part that may have been intended to preserve a distance from not only Manhattan but my Unitarian wife.*

If the good sheep around me, those Sunday mornings, like my dutiful father before me, were too busy coaxing a living from this earth's stony soil to second-guess the President, then so was I. I found the peace movement interfering. The Sixties were a palmy time, professionally, for me. *The New Yorker* accepted most of what I sent down to it, and toward the end of the decade a book of mine made a million dollars. My success was based, I felt, on a certain calculated modesty, on my cultivated fondness for exploring corners – the space beneath the Shillington dining table, where the nap of the rug was still thick; the back stairs, where the vacuum cleaner and rubber galoshes lived; the cave the wicker armchairs made

---

* The situation is sexually reversed in *Roger's Version* (1986):
"'Where on earth are you going?' I asked her.
'Obviously,' she said, 'to church.'
'Why would you do a ridiculous thing like that?'
'Oh . . . To annoy you.'"

when turned upside down against the rain on the porch. I had left heavily trafficked literary turfs to others and stayed in my corner of New England to give its domestic news. Now along came this movement wanting to gouge us all out of our corners, to force us into the open and make us stare at our bloody hands and confront the rapacious motives underneath the tricolor slogans and question our favored-nation status under God. There are two ways to live happily with a government: to accept or to snub it, to identify with it and rejoice in its policies or to ignore it as an unworthy brawl that has nothing to do with one's self. I could manage neither.

It surprises me to find, in fiction written by women of roughly my generation, the period of protests and marches recalled as a wonderful time. From *Hot Flashes*, by Barbara Raskin, of the 1967 Washington march:

> Thousands of people are forging across Memorial Bridge on their March to the Pentagon. Their faces are resolute and defiant. They are committed to stopping the war in Vietnam and challenging Lyndon Johnson for control of the country. They are determined . . . Halfway across the bridge I found myself caught up in an ocean of political hysteria. Fervor and fury ignited everyone. I was carried along by a tidal wave of antiwar passion. After years of disarray, the Movement was on the move. I felt simultaneously subsumed and enlarged.

From *Superior Women*, by Alice Adams:

> But there on the corner of Fifth and 57th is a group of hippies, in their ruffles and rags, bare arms and feet. Several of them have bad skin and vacant stoned eyes, hollow smiles. But Megan notices that one of them, a boy who seems to be their leader, looks clean and alert, and happy, not just doped. He is tall and dark and nearsighted, in rimless glasses, but he looks, astonishingly, very much like Henry Stuyvesant. He is carrying a sign that says MAKE LOVE NOT WAR, of course. As Megan goes by, he gives her a friendly, sexy wink, to which she finds herself responding, and smiling, smiling.

The Adams novel's central romance, between Megan Greene and Henry Stuyvesant, takes it spark from the political dissent of the Johnson era, and sputters when Richard Nixon is elected: "Both Megan and Henry find it surprising that this event should be a factor in their personal lives, but the truth is that they are both so depressed by Nixon that they are stunned into a sort of immobility. . . . The Vietnam war will go on forever, they hopelessly say, or at least until everyone is dead – both countries beaten back into the Stone Age, in the immortal words of that general."

And from *Persian Nights*, by Diane Johnson: "The idea had been to walk along to the hotel where Lyndon Johnson was staying, chanting, 'Hey, hey, LBJ, how many kids did you kill today?' Thousands of people walking from the park near Pico to Century Boulevard chanting, and the day was sunny, so lots of people had begun with a picnic." The picnic mood is transferred to quite another insurrection; over a decade later, the novel's heroine, Chloe, finds herself in Tehran, and joins a march against the Shah:

> Chloe thought of the Los Angeles peace march and saw that this was different. These faces were sullen, as the faces of the police had been. . . . She grew afraid, but it was thrilling. . . . There were women, wearing white, in numbers, like beehives of nurses, arms linked like chums. . . . The throng, the shouting multitude would prevent them from crossing the square. But she wanted to see the whole sea, the whole black and white sea to the horizon of signs and shouting people, and the fists, for the fists went by them, pounding in the air, people chanted, and above them they saw cameras, television films being made. . . . She laughed aloud. . . . Here you were part of history.

Fists uplifted, women enter history. The clitoral at last rebels against the phallic. The long hair, the beads and bracelets, the floppy clothes of the peace movement made a deliberate contrast with the tight uniform and close haircut ("This haircut no good") of the military male. The fights for women's rights and gay rights emerged enmeshed with the Vietnam protest and have outlived it. Though not consciously resisting the androgyny, which swiftly became – as all trends in a consumer society become – a mere fashion, I must have felt challenged. My earliest sociological thought about myself had been that I was fortunate to be a boy and an American. Now the world was being told that American males – especially white, Protestant males who had done well under "the system" – were the root of evil. Law-abiding conformity had become the opposite of a refuge. The Vietnam era was no sunny picnic for me; I remember it as a sticky, strident, conflicting time, a time with a bloody televised background of shame. Hawk, dove, soldier, draft evader, and even middle-class householder were caught in a superheated mire as an empire tried to carry out an ugly border action under the full glare of television. The soap opera of the nightly news and the clamor of a college generation that had not been raised to be cannon fodder (raised, rather, on the demand feeding condoned by Dr Spock and the six-minute attention span instilled by television) permitted no one to look away.

My disposition to take contrary positions and to seek for nuances within the normal ill-suited me for the national debate; I found the country so distressing in its civil fury that I took my family to London for the school year of 1968–69. For the second presidential election in a row, I cast my ballot abroad, in an American Embassy. I voted, of course, for the Democrat, the shrill and embattled Hubert Humphrey. To my relief, he lost: Vietnam was no longer a Democrat's war, and belonged to the jowly, tricky Nixon I had hooted at in the Lowell House common room. I felt sorry for him, and knew just why he had to keep bluffing and bombing, but had no trouble voting in 1972, as the ghosts of my grandfather and recently dead father looked on, for the Democrat, the implausible rabbit-mouthed McGovern. I was in Africa, in January of 1973, when word came that Nixon and Kissinger had at last disentangled us, on shabby terms, from Vietnam;

I was sitting on a stage in Nairobi and a black professor sardonically asked me from the audience what I thought of the great American victory. I said, spontaneously and truthfully, that our getting out felt like a victory to me. The Americans in the audience applauded. We were all tired to death of it; even the protest had worn out its welcome, and was no longer fashionable. We could begin to enjoy being American again.

Now the involvement slowly settles into the historical past. War movies are made about Vietnam that sound more and more like other war movies, and there is even (so I read) going to be an attempt to do for it what *M*A*S*H* did for the initially rather unamusing Korean conflict. In an unforeseeable way, as the vets and evaders age together, and Maya Yang Lin's superb black-marble V-shaped memorial – decked out with personal memorials like a Shinto shrine, a calm and polished Hades of names that takes us below the ground and up again – consolidates its place on the Washington Mall and the national self-image, the years 1965–72 melt into a dream-like "crazy" time when grunts fragged officers and cops bopped hippies, when brutalized soldiers painted peace signs on their helmets and the daughters of Wall Street lawyers committed murders and robberies in the name of social justice, a baroque time of long-haired hardhats and alliterating Agnewisms, of Joplin and OM and home-made bombs, of national self-hatred and loudly promoted love, a time costumed in buckskin and sandals and camouflage khaki and dashikis and saffron robes and miniskirts right up to the crotch, a darkly happy in-between time after the Pill and IUD had freed sex from fear of pregnancy and before AIDS hobbled it with the fear of death,* a time when pot and rock

---

* "They [Jerry Rubin and Abbie Hoffman, in a manifesto of 1968] published a list of demands that included, in addition to ending the war, the legalization of marijuana, the disarming of the police, the abolition of money and, as an afterthought, a note that 'We believe that people should fuck all the time, anytime, whoever they want.'"

– Milton Viorst, *Fire in the Streets*

obtained in Danang as well as San Francisco, a time luxurious in the many directions of its craziness, since the war and the counterculture and the moon shots were all fuelled by an overflowing prosperity no longer with us, a historical time, after all, that in the long run will hold us united as the Civil War opponents are united in the silvery-gray precision of the daguerreotypes they posed for. What with Woodstock and *Barbarella* and *The Joy of Sex* and the choral nudity in *Hair*, there was a consciously retrieved Edenic innocence, a Blakeian triumph of the youthful human animal, along with napalm and defoliation. The Vietnam intervention almost shrinks to the big bad trip in an era of trips ("If you remember the Sixties," Robin Williams has quipped, "you weren't there"), but it discomfited me so much that I have avoided all of the movies about it, from *The Deer Hunter* to *Platoon*, lest they revive my sense of shame, of a lethal stickiness, of a hot face and stammering tongue and a strange underdog rage about the whole sorry thing.

Reading a little now, I realize how little I knew, for all my emotional involvement, about the war itself, a war after all like other wars, with strategies and weaponries and lessons for the war professionals. I read that the North Vietnamese found us almost as frustrating and tenacious as we found them; they wanted to trap us into another Dien Bien Phu, and tried at Plei Mei and Con Thien, but were always thwarted by our air power, our helicopter gunships pouring lead into the NVA troops from above, so that every set battle North Vietnam attempted proved to be slaughterous defeat. And I read that China and Russia, with each their own reasons for desiring detente, in effect encouraged Nixon to bomb, to punish Hanoi for continuing a struggle that had become a nuisance to every major power. As usual, the previous war had taught a lesson that was perhaps misapplied in the new instance; the great administration fear was of Chinese intervention, as had occurred in Korea, so the difficult intent was to win without seeming, in any triggering way, to be winning. At the time, it was hard to focus on the military and geopolitical nuances. One simply longed for the light at the end of the tunnel to dawn, for the body counts and B–52s and M–16s and Phantoms and Skyraiders and Hueys and Chinooks and Claymore mines and spider-holes and punji stakes and barking fragmentary-seeming names like Dak To and An Loc and Pleiku to be tucked into history, to slide over the waterfall, with that joy of riddance.

Was it possible, really, I had to ask myself, that, in being "for" or at least not unconflictedly "against" the war, I was less caring, less sensitive to suffering, than others? A man I had offended at the outset of the Sixties complained to my wife that my face showed no signs of having ever suffered. Alfred Chester, in reviewing *Pigeon Feathers* (1962), had complained of my being "profoundly untroubled," and Alfred Kazin, reviewing *Couples* toward the end of the Sixties, wrote of me as "someone who can brilliantly describe the adult world without conveying its depths and risks, someone wholly literary, dazzlingly bright, the quickest of quick children." Was I really so oddly isolated from adult depths? Had I in fact *too* successfully found a place for myself out of harm's way? Perhaps there *was* something too smooth in my rise and my style, something unthinkingly egocentric in my sopping up love and attention from my grandparents and parents and now my children, something that drained my immediate vicinity, and something distanced and cruel in my writing, with its vengeful element of "showing" people, of "rubbing their noses" in our sad human facts, just as I used to show Copper – dragging him, so the soft reddish fur fanned up around his stretched collar – the hole where he had nearly smothered. I had learned from Kierkegaard and Barth to say the worst about our earthly condition, which was hopeless without a scandalous supernatural redemption; but I harbored a hurt hostility, also, an anti-Christian or at least anti-ecclesiastical bias, toward the church itself – a rubbing of its nose in the antique absurdity of what it professed. All sides of an issue spoke to me, and the effect possibly was numbing.

Had my great dermatological defect produced by compensation a defective inner smoothness, an imperviousness such as Emerson spoke of when he said, "The dearest events are summer-rain, and we the Para coats that shed every drop"? The relentless domestic realism of my fiction implied a self-exemption from normal intra-familial courtesy, and my own handicaps left me, if anything, less than normally tolerant of others': confronted with another stutterer, for example, I wonder why he just doesn't stop trying to talk.

As a child, I had tortured my toys, talking aloud to them, fascinating and horrifying myself. In some spasm of indignation I had slit my rubber Donald Duck's neck, halfway only, losing my nerve, so that the cut was there, opening and closing like a little lipless mouth when I moved Donald's head. There was also a rubber Mickey Mouse, whose head came altogether off, and could be replaced, and a stocky four-legged Ferdinand – the benign bull, a proto-flower child. He had heft in the hand, like a potato or putty ball, and a brown back and beige belly, and a drugged smile. I would line them up, these smiling anthropoid animals, and bowl a softball at them as in tenpins, knocking them down again and again, and all the while taunting them in my mind, like some Nazi interrogating Resistance prisoners. On the other hand, I cringed when other children fished, or trapped a toad, or caught a grasshopper and proceeded to pull off its legs until just an immobile staring torso of living tissue remained. Whenever animals or insects were placed at the mercy of my fellow children, a sensation of dread led me to turn away, to shut my eyes and turn my back, much as I left the room, a few years later, in disgust and horror and perhaps inverted desire, when a peer of mine took down his underpants and began to masturbate for a small audience. I was, if selfish, also squeamish. Behind the freckled mask of "dear Chonny" I had become sore at the world – at its mud, its mess, its "dirty talk," its menace, its eventual victory over us in death. If a dirty war was being fought in Indochina, what was so unusual? What was worth protesting, decrying, getting self-righteous about? That was what the world was – a dirty war, somewhere or other, all the time. Wake up to reality, peace-niks. At heart, all I know about my political attitudes is that enough verbalized antiestablishmentism and right (that is, left) thinking, like some baby hogging attention with its blind pink confidence of being lovable, arouses in me a helpless itch to open the discourse to other possibilities.

Had I suffered enough? There was enough suffering in the Shillington house – my mother's fits of anger and my father's fear of poverty, my grandmother's choking and my grandfather's sitting and tapping his old-fashioned high-top shoes as he waited (he frequently proclaimed) to die, his feet in the meantime stirring up little fuzz-balls out of the carpet that were, with his cigar-smoking inside the house, among the things that somehow infuriated my sensitive, beset mother. But I felt exempted, sheltered, though my stomach ached at mealtimes from nervous tension and at one point my hair began to fall out, leaving a little bald patch my mother noticed when I set off to elementary school. My skin made me suffer, and the hay fever that later became asthma, but these were trivial complaints, really, compared with famine in Asia and the war in Europe, and somehow self-induced – somatic by-products of self-consciousness.

The critics who found me callow might be right: I had been lucky and, as the lucky will do, had become hard-hearted. I had been the apple of my parents' eyes. Our Shillington arrangements, precarious though they felt, had skirted disaster. I had avoided fighting in a war or incurring a fatal disease. I had not broken a bone until I was forty and could view it as a humorous exercise in machismo. I was spared appendicitis until I was fifty and could make an epiphanic short story out of it. I had held the whip hand in the romantic relationships of my life and brought all heartbreak upon myself. No plane had crashed with me in it, though several had appallingly bounced around, and the two auto accidents of my life had been skids in a jaunty Corvair that, according to Ralph Nader, nobody could have driven safely.

Actually, a large helicopter hoisting a party including my second wife and myself to the top of the Auyán Tepuí, in southeastern Venezuela, did crash; as it hoveringly descended, with its battering big rotor blades, toward the cross painted on a flat rock as a landing field, it swerved out of control and plopped down on a nearby set of rocks shaped like diagonally stacked loaves of bread. The amazed helicopter, its rotors still cumbersomely battering the air, came to rest at a sharp tilt, and the tipped interior of the plane was flooded with excited Spanish in which the word *puerta* distinctly sounded. I was next to the door, and deduced that the general wish was that I open it and jump out; this I did, running out from under the whirling blades. I assumed that my youthful wife would irresistibly follow, but evidently I should have stopped and let her jump onto me, for when another man, an officer of the American Embassy, saw her balk and attempted to help her down, both fell, and she sprained her ankle so severely I had to push her, a day or two later, in a wheelchair through the Caracas airport. It had been a hazardous trip; I had lost my suitcase at the beginning, and she her mobility at the end. Though we have subsequently arrived together at a dinner-party version of the incident in which my behaviour was cowardly, at the time I was impressed by my own inner coolness; almost alone of the party, I ate heartily of the lavish picnic that had been prepared for the *tepuí* top and walked around admiring the curious moonlike topography of this great mesa, from which descends Angel Falls, the highest waterfall in the world. Because of a band of clouds beneath us, we never saw the falls, either on the way up or the descent, via a little rescue helicopter, some hours later. Our moment of greatest hazard, it was explained, came after the crash landing: if the whirling rotors had struck the rocks an explosion might have resulted. My instinctive reaction, as when I broke my leg, was a certain exhilaration; my good luck had faltered but I had survived.

Some moments in my long history of car-driving cause me to shudder in retrospect. In Shillington, to win attention and approval from my classmates, I would get out on the running board of my family's heavy old black Buick and steer the car downhill through the open window, while my thrilled passengers squealed within. And on our last summer on the Vineyard, when my first wife and I had separated and divided the two months of rental, I went with my four large children and my son-in-law of the time to a party where pot was passed around, of which I partook, as well as, liberally, of wine. Perhaps only three of the children were present, my older son remaining in Ipswich with his mother and his job at the beach; but there may have been instead a large dog, a golden retriever who had recently been, in response to his own contributions to our domestic confusion, castrated. As these fragments of my shattered family piled into the last of my convertibles – a lime-green Mustang with white upholstery, once owned by the brief young wife of the Ipswich Ford dealer, who later remarried his first wife – I realized that I was stoned to the point of non-attachment. But in clinging to my sense of myself as the family patriarch, I did not think to let someone else drive. The other automobiles on the narrow curving road from Gay Head to Chilmark, the sweet expensive salt-grayed shingled houses, the wild roses in bloom all whizzed by in a dream, tinted clouds of maya, while my windswept passengers shrieked in what, from a great distance, through the mystical ringing in my ears, sounded like pleasure. Some of them had to stand, the convertible was so crowded; a head-on crash would have made a fearful mash and mush of flesh, and from a great abstractifying distance I fought to understand that life and death, a crash and non-crash, were *not* one within Brahman, as my religious mood claimed they were, and that I *must* steer straight, on the right side of the road, and return my cargo of living kin to our rented house. Wonderfully, I did. My visual memories of that five-mile drive are like little fluttering flags pinked on the edge of a void. As my unharmed, woman-sized daughters made dinner, my inner clouds slowly cleared and I realized how lucky I was. Suffering and I have had a basically glancing, flirtatious acquaintanceship.

Except for my teeth. There, a long history of pain endured opens up behind me like a tunnel triumphantly negotiated. At the far end is Ernie Rothermel, the tennis playing son of our family doctor, a tall balding man with a wisp of mint to his breath and an air of having not much wanted to be a dentist. In my memory, *The Breakfast Club*, with Don Mac-Neil, is always playing on the radio in his office on Lancaster Avenue, a block down from the high school, on the opposite side of the street, across from the tennis courts. "Good morning, Breakfast Clubbers/Good morning to ya," their song would begin, and then the march around the breakfast table, a clumping, hilarious purely auditory event that was inordinately vivid. These sound effects came from a world way out there, a painless world beyond the tennis courts, where both Ernie and I would rather have been. But his minty breath, his insistent hands, the whirring burr of the drill, the hilarity wafting from the Breakfast Club in the Allerton Hotel in far-off Chicago all pressed me into his chair, as leather straps held murderers into the electric chair whose executions were so cheerfully publicized in those primitive days. The drills, certainly, were primitive, and it was an hour's work to hollow out one or two cavities, with my eyes rolling higher and higher in my skull to keep away from the intensifying pain. Even when Novocain was used, pain teased the edges of consciousness, as the shadow of a piercing signal stymied within the nervous system. Ernie told me, once, that my nerves were exceptionally large, and this, along with Carlton Boyer's compliment to my sense of composition, struck me as unusually concrete information about that strange inchoate thing, my self. He would always tell me, considerately, when the absolutely final bit of drilling would take place, and children raised with the high-speed, water-spraying drills of today can have little idea how welcome this news was. As closest to the nerve, the last go was the most painful, but it could be endured, because it was the last. With a decisive, merciful gesture Ernie would push the drill arm away, into another compartment of the air. Then would come the soothing, squeaking insertion of the silver, and his soft-voiced, humorous, somehow regretful dismissal of me back into the Shillington sunlight – the traffic and trolleys of Lancaster Avenue, the walk home across the school grounds and softball field and the strip of corn and Shilling Alley to my back yard or, in later years, the block's walk east to the high school, if my appointment had been scheduled during a study hall.

I had begun as a patient of Ernie's when his office was on the other side of Lancaster Avenue on the Becker's Garage side, in a brick building next door to the one that Stephens' Luncheonette would some day share with the post office and that eventually would hold Admixtures, Inc. In that first office, the story was, a child had somehow died in the chair, under gas. This rumored tragedy perhaps contributed to Ernie's rueful, preoccupied air. He was one of those men who seemed to my childish sense of things a bit too intelligent and elegant to be happy in Shillington; I might grow into another – that was the subtle bond I felt between us – but in the meantime I was a child, and happy here.

The printed diagrammatic cards whereby he noted cavities seemed huge open screams, Felix the Cat mouths in a non-cartoon key – horrible, calmly surgical displays of what we really were. Decades later, in London with a toothache, I had my whole mouth X-rayed by a posh new machine that travelled around my face and took a continuous exposure; the ghastly grimacing negative, showing all my crooked roots and opaque crowns and thready root-canal fillings and stumpy gold posts and the single tilted tooth-implant shaped like a miniature vegetable-chopper – the entire panorama, in short, of a life of dental suffering – reminded me with a shudder of the silent screams on Ernie's cavity cards. But *The Breakfast Club* would keep playing on his little streamlined blond radio, or the Phillies game if it was an afternoon appointment, or one of the innumerable mid-day soap operas, and there would be a whiff of cloves as he doctored the hole he had just made, and I relaxed into the certainty that this was all one of the procedures of the world, whereby the self is painfully fitted in. During the war, Ernie became just about the only dentist in town, and one had to wait ruinous lengths of time for an appointment. Tastykakes and Hershey bars and fastnacht doughnuts soaked in powdered sugar ravaged, in those pre-fluorine days, my enamel; I don't recall ever coming away from a checkup without a cavity or two having been found, and sometimes as many as six or eight. The sweet pain of his curved pick working into a soft spot would make sweat spring up on my face and chest. Yet, returned home from my ordeal, I would soon seek out a nickel and penny in our Recipes box on top of the icebox and go buy a consoling treat at Hen Kieffer's store.

Dentistry pursued me into adolescence. While I was in high school, Ernie hired a hygienist, a friendly square-faced young woman saddled with enormous breasts. As she scraped and flossed her way across my mouth, one of her great spheres pressed warmly on my ear and with desperately flitting thoughts I tried to distract my penis from the erection it wanted to have as I lay, not limp enough, in the chair. I was fourteen or fifteen, I think – under driving age – when I had my first tooth pulled; we had moved from Shillington to Plowville and my father had to drive me back into town when the Novocain from an especially extensive drilling wore off and revealed an unbearable socket of pain. The relief of having the immediate pain cease cloaked the tragedy of dental loss. I was so young, the future still seemed infinite to me: aeons of time in which a new tooth might miraculously grow.

I was to have a number of teeth pulled in my young manhood, as I went from high school to college and marriage and a scattering of living sites. At the Harvard dental clinic, as I remember it, the young intern, having shot the anesthetic into what seemed to me the wrong nerve, could not stop grousing to a colleague, about some departmental grievance, for even a second as he yanked my screaming molar, and so brutally ignored the rest of me that, having spat the first gushes of blood into the swirling bowl, I ducked under his arm and walked out in silence – an ironical undergraduate performance, a parody of his own indifference, quite wasted on him. A few years later, married, returning to Boston from Lake Winnipesaukee with a sick tooth that had nagged me for much of this honeymoon summer, I went to a recommended extractionist in a tawdry office building on Tremont Street. There, a big black woman, with the inarguable wordless strength of a prison matron, clapped a sweet mask over my face and smothered my panicked moment of struggle.* When I awoke, it was in a gaseous haze, and even the cigarette butts on the metal stairs as I stumbled down looked beautiful. In Ipswich, a toothache nagged for attention through the bouncy communal bliss of our Sunday volleyball game, where the soft white ball darted this way and that in the sky as erratically as the erotic currents in our violent harem atmosphere: anxious, bare-limbed housewives got bumped and upended as we aging young bucks leaped and dived and spiked and saved. The bruised grass gave off a hayey scent as it was being trampled. After the game, my own dentist being

* ". . . at the moment of anesthesia she had panicked; she had tried to strike the Negress pressing the sweet, sweet mask to her face and through the first waves of ether had continued to cry that she should go home, that she was supposed to have this baby, that the child's father was coming to smash the door down with a hammer and would stop them."

– *Couples* (1968)

off on a boat on this high summer day, I phoned a competitor, who had just come off the golf course. He was a fellow Congregationalist, and agreed to meet me in his downtown office. I winced when he tapped the tooth; he pronounced it "gone" and matter-of-factly pulled it, and I was still not too late to make the post-volleyball-game drinks, where my little ordeal was worth a laugh from the men and some sympathy from the women. I was among people, now, whose parents had given them good dental care, even orthodontia, which was scarcely heard of in Depression Shillington. Our class beauty and May Queen, I noticed for the first time at our thirty-fifth reunion, has overlapping incisors; my own front teeth, both upper and lower, had come in crowded, and were fatalistically accepted. Yet Ernie liked my front teeth. "You'll have those as long as you live," he had once unexpectedly assured me, with a casual prophetical glance into my clouded dental future.

The tooth lost after volleyball had been a wisdom tooth that, in the absence of two adjacent molars, had leaned in to do their chewing; now, on the advice of my regular Ipswich dentist, when he got off his boat, I went to a specialist in Brookline, a man who had taught him at dental school and whom he revered as a "genius." The genius set about salvaging what was left of my dentition. The surviving back teeth with all their blackened fillings were ground into square stubs and fitted with gold-and-porcelain crowns. The process enchanted me, not least because it was expensive, in keeping with my rise in the world. Also it was nearly painless. The genius had an armory of equipment and a tank of exotic tropical fish undreamt of by Ernie Rothermel. To anesthetize the prick of the Novocain needle (which could be an agony, especially in the roof of the mouth) he sprayed a bit of mist from a bottle to numb the spot. He demonstrated a host of chemical and mechanical niceties – little copper cups of hot wax to take the impression of my dentine stumps, deft procedures in wax to make my temporaries, a veritable alchemy to cast and bond and temper the finished crowns, which were adjusted to within a hair by his sensitive drilling. I loved the golden painproof teeth he so meticulously manufactured and installed; he showed that redemption existed: there could be a new me.* He was a solemn short man, with glasses that made his eyes enormous, and once told me that he loved dentistry so much that he would do it for free if he had to. He seemed disappointed that writing, as I described it, was a relatively passionless and mercenary profession.

Through his successive renovations I was introduced, with trepidation, to the mysteries of root-canal work, administered by a variety of endodontists, usually in the wake of a toothache and an abscess. No more of my teeth, I realized, need be lost; the perishable soft nerves could be pulled and drilled and scoured from their anfractuous canals, and the canals filled with encaustic, long pink cones like little bits of lobster meat that sizzled when they were inserted, and made smoke float out of my mouth. Of my many endodontists I remember especially the cheerful brisk man who put a kind of awl against the side of my gums and pushed as hard as he could, to puncture a tough bubble of pus; and the little Chinese woman who dutifully, with her tiny wire files, pursued the nerve up to beyond where the anesthesia took hold and would sniff the file each time she removed it, for a clue from my depths; and the cool fellow who referred to each nerve as a "guy" – "This guy is tricky"; "We'll clean out that guy next time."

* "When Richard Maple, after thirty years of twinges, jagged edges, and occasional extractions, had all his remaining molars capped and bridges shaped across the gaps, the gold felt chilly to his cheeks and its regularity masked holes and roughnesses that had been a kind of mirror wherein his tongue had known itself. The Friday of his final cementing, he went to a small party. As he drank a variety of liquids that tasted much the same, he moved from feeling slightly less than himself (his native teeth had been ground to stumps of dentine) to feeling slightly more. The shift in tonality that permeated his skull whenever his jaws closed corresponded, perhaps, to the heightened clarity that fills the mind after a religious conversion."

– "The Taste of Metal" (1966)

Even when a tooth, in the course of its adventures, breaks off at the gumline, all is not lost, I discovered; the denerved root can be drilled and implanted with a small gold post, and the top of the post crowned. For fifteen years, more or less, I was happy in the care of the genius, as his tropical fish sickened, died, and were replaced by others even more garish and filmy, and each of his assistants succumbed to marriage and gave way to yet another white-clad virgin. One day, however, his X rays showed a dark shadow: I had bone loss, where his ingenious cantilevered bridge – devised to spare me the humiliation of a partial denture – had microscopically wobbled and admitted bacteria along the roots. I passed on to periodontal work, the highest and most frightening level of repair yet. My decadent oral cavity was invaded by glittering little knives, as I lay flat on my back and a gurgling vacuum sucked out my blood. Then, as the periodontist hummed show tunes, my gums were stitched back together with twirling lengths of black string. In one maneuver, a strip of the roof of my mouth was snipped out and sewn around an exposed root. In another, entire roots, which had worn through my eroding periodontal tissue, were snipped off, leaving clusters of half-teeth to crown. Though syringes of powerful anesthetic turned my opened mouth into a feeling-less void, a miracle of nothingness while the periodontist smilingly hummed a few inches from my eyes and his terrible tools flickered just below the rim of my vision, the *image* of what was being done to me was hard to bear. It took all my courage to keep my appointments, but keep them I did, at an office so elegant that this week's magazines were fresh in the rack and half of the dental chairs enjoyed an ocean view. In final solution to the problem of the tooth pulled after volley-ball on a merrier day, an implant, made in Germany, was driven into my lower jaw, much as a nail is driven into a board. Into a resistant board: blow after blow made my head bob as I shrank into the chair, and the periodontist, a thick gold chain about his neck and his face haloed by a Jewish

Afro, smiled down and said I was being a very good patient. He had grown huge above me, like a triumphant cat in an animated cartoon. *Hit me again*, I inwardly begged, as my vacuumed blood gurgled in my ears and a trio of visiting Danish specialists peered around his shoulder into the yawning, helpless theatre of prosthesis. Hit me again, for my sins, for my sweets, for my being born poor in a starch-loving locale.

As with my skin, I seem to be keeping just ahead of the curl of technology's latest wave. The periodontist has passed on my dire but not quite hopeless case to a dentist of his generation, armed with the newest tricks and with arcane polymers that leave unexpungeable pastel flecks on my lips and chin. Instead of an aquarium, this genius has a parrot in his office, and flocks of adoring women that swoop in and out. His hands seem larger than those of the older genius. One of my lesser disabilities, perhaps related to my troubles with breathing and speaking and swallowing, is stingy jaw motion: one playful day on Crane's Beach I discovered that I, unlike even my six-year-old daughter, could not pop a golf ball into my mouth. Now, as all the tools and tubes and gloppy compounds of postmodern dental science crowd down into my oral cavity, my face feels cruelly stretched, and a hellish wave of intrusive sensation and incidental pain floods my consciousness and blots out my will to live; I become purely a locus of saliva and claustrophobia and the desire to gag. It reminds me, as my father often used to say, of death. And of that fine firm line from the Book of Common Prayer, *There is no health in us*. Young women come as I suffer and peek into my mouth with all its stumps, its gaps of gum, its gleaming implant: what must they think? What shudder is frozen behind their smiles? I must remind them of death, too.

These many decades of dental endurance have persuaded me that I probably fall within the normal range of human cowardice. Called upon to invade the beach at Iwo Jima or Normandy, I flatter myself that I would tuck my head down with the others, jump waist-deep into the shocking, surging water, and wade numbly forward. If hit in the gut with a bullet, I would grunt and fall on the wet sand and wait for the next blow of a distant God. Who knows how one will act in an extremity? But we are all equipped with animal stoicism as well as with a tormenting imagination. Hemingway, introducing the collection of war writings he edited in 1942, wrote of recovering from his wounds in World War I:

> I was very ignorant at nineteen and had read little and I remember the sudden happiness and the feeling of having a permanent protecting talisman when a young British officer I met when in the hospital first wrote out for me, so that I could remember them, these lines:
> *"By my troth, I care not: a man can die but once; we owe God a death . . . and let it go which way it will, he that dies this year is quit for the next."*

We owe God a death. It helps to think of it thus. As for my patriotic debt to my country, I feel, as I age, less anxious about that also. In a number of fiscal years I have paid more income tax than the President, and must by now have covered the cost of a bit of a battleship or the tip of long-range missile. And one of the reasons that my teeth have been so troublesome is that during World War II months and months went by – over a year, at one point – when I, in a critical stage of my growth and decay, couldn't get a dental appointment with Ernie Rothermel. So I carry an earned wound: I gave my teeth to the war effort.

V

A Letter to My Grandsons

Dear Anoff and Kwame:

We are all of mixed blood. Your mother, my older daughter, is fair, descended from the people of Northern Europe with its mist and fog and snow – she is English, with a dash of Russian and French, on her mother's side,* and German and Dutch on mine. Your father is black, the pure black of West Africa, his color sealed off by the Sahara from the north and by the breadth of a continent from the infusions of Arab and Hamitic genes that have rendered East Africans comparatively pale. Genealogists tell us that we are all cousins, with common ancestors surprisingly few generations in the past; but when the strains that meet in you last met, it must have been early in the history of the human race, when men were outnumbered by lions and tigers. Your two parents are about as black and white as people can be, and that helps make them a beautiful couple. But they are beautiful, too, for sharing similar temperaments, both being good-natured and nurturing and artistic, and similar backgrounds, coming as both do from the international race of teachers and artists. Your black grandfather is an internationally known ceramicist, and your white grandmother paints pictures that hang on your walls. Your black grandmother, like your father and my father and my mother's father (John Franklin Hoyer, after whom I was named John just as John Anoff was named John

* Her mother's people, the Danielses, claim through the English Greenes, who came to Rhode Island from England in the seventeenth century, descent from royalty no less legendary than Hugh Capet, founder of the French royal line in the tenth century, and Rurik, the first king, in the ninth century, of medieval Russia.

after me), is a teacher; we are all, that is, people who are at home with pencils and paper, with the tools of education and art. There must be warriors and hunters in our background as there are in everyone's, but by the time I appeared the Updikes and the Hoyers had become peaceable, reasonable people, who valued civilization and trusted it to offer them a niche.

It seems curious to me that I am, half, a Pennsylvania Dutchman. My grandfather Hoyer had two sisters, who produced only one child between them. My grandmother, however, was the youngest of twelve Kramer siblings, and southern Berks County abounded with my second and third cousins, who seemed to me, a small-town boy with city aspirations, depressingly rural. We would sometimes visit these country relatives in their damp stone houses and claustrophobic country parlors with horsehair sofas and faded plush upright chairs and big framed ancestral photographs and black iron wood stoves. Hen Kramer was tremendously fat, and lay on his sofa eating from a box of chocolates that rested on his belly. Scott Eshelman was the gravedigger for the Plow Cemetery in Plowville, and the leading citizen of that tiny community. Uncle John Spotts was the most ancient – the most ancestral – of all the relatives. He had married my great-aunt Hannah, and was a small gnarled man with deep eye sockets and a wheezing voice,* who lived to be ninety-six. His and Aunt Hannah's house was rather grand, set at

* "Even older than my grandfather was Uncle John Spotts, his sister Hannah's husband. Uncle John, shorter than five feet, with a hook nose and large-lidded eyes in deep sockets, spoke with an antique voice, an old-fashioned super-palatal wheeze that merged with the dark, somehow tropical greenery outside his house and the smells of fresh-baked pie dough and unused plush parlor chairs inside. Though his hand bunched into blue knobs as it gripped the curve of his cane, he was dapper, in starched pinstripe shirt and broad suspenders, and his inner knit, I felt as a child, was as clean and tight as the wickerwork of his porch chairs. . . . His kindly, eerie wheeze of a voice, sighing 'Johnny' with a caressing tone of lament, arose from a green world where men would not breathe again, a Pennsylvania dying about us, though its buildings like bones remained."

– *Buchanan Dying* (1974)

the end of a walk that went past flower beds and great drooping hemlocks; one hemlock shaded a spring whose cold water, walked on by water striders and jumped into by frogs, was supposed to be somehow thrilling; you drank from a tin dipper that rested on one of the rocks that rimmed the precious spring. The Spottses' son, Cousin Elmer, kept chickens and tuned pianos, and had a scarred chin and a sly smile. He had studied piano tuning in Richmond, Virginia, so he wasn't as hopelessly mired in farmerishness as my other cousins. The chickens he kept in a row of little houses didn't strike me as too bad, since we kept chickens ourselves, at the bottom of the Shillington back yard. But people who kept pigs, and owned mules, and grew corn, seemed unbearably sad to me. The first funeral I went to was Aunt Hannah's in the Plow Church, in 1943. Her coffin was open and right up front before the altar, beneath a tall mural of the Ascension, of Jesus floating upwards while the colorfully cloaked Apostles gestured in amazement; her little profile, lifted on a pillow, was on view throughout the service, a yellowish color like that of old newspapers. My other great-aunt, Aunt Sally, lived a mile away in Plowville, and in one childhood memory we are leaving a bag of groceries on her back porch, but stealthily, frightened that she, an irritable recluse, will come out and scold us.

Who, though, were the Updikes? The name was unique in the county. To find others, you had to go east, and cross the Delaware. Here, too, people depressingly farmed. My father's first cousins George Sharp and Eugene Drake had farms near Trenton, New Jersey, and there we would go once a summer, at the height of the heat, and congregate on their porches and meadows, with a herd of sickly cats. The Sharps had a dairy farm and horses that my cousin Evelyn, with her wiry black hair down her back, loved to ride. She was a strange smooth olive color and her courage was strange, too. The few times I was ever up on a horse, I found it terrifyingly high, and the thing under me treacherously alive, with a skittish will of its own. Eugene and George and his brother Ed all had a mild nasal way of talking, the New Jersey rural accent, and my father when he was among them would begin to sound like them, and become boyish and happy, for he had played with these men when they were all boys. There was a hazy placidity to these get-togethers that reminded me of milk, which was pronounced "melk" in the accent and which Cousin George had many cans of in his barns and truck. The Updike men – George and Ed and Eugene were the sons of Aunt Annie and Aunt Lillian, sisters of my grandfather, Hartley Updike – together made an impression of great gentleness, tall quiet former boys talking and joking together, doing what their wives told them and moving in their soft obliging way through a haze and a milkiness unchanged from hot New Jersey summers when the century was young. Aunt Annie Sharp was still alive during my childhood visits to the vicinity of Trenton, a very small woman who yet was the liveliest and loudest person on the porch and at the long loaded dinner table. She and George's wife, Marian, did not always "get along." Eventually, Aunt Annie was put in a "home." The New Jersey Updikes went back for generations, were numerous, and held in their history a number of interesting little scandals like Aunt Annie and Marian not getting along.*

But the Updikes that really interested me, that did not depress me, were my father's siblings – Mary and Arch. Mary, though married, was still called Updike, for she had married her first cousin Don, the only child of Uncle Foster and Aunt Bessie. Mary and Don lived in Greenwich, Connecticut, where Don, an engineer who had once mined copper

---

* For example, the sad case of Rachel Updike, the daughter of Peter Updike and Louisa Terhune. Born in 1843, she was a dwarf, who never married. From a family history compiled by George Sharp: "The story goes that Great-Grandmother Updike was badly frightened by a turtle that was placed in a cupboard by a prankster. People thought it was the reason Rachel was short with turtlelike hands and feet. Great-Grandmother was pregnant at that time."

in Chile, was now a contractor. He built one home at a time, which his family lived in until it was sold, so that my mother felt sorry for Mary, always having to pack up and move; but after a while they settled in a big white house within a few blocks of the Post Road and downtown Greenwich. I would visit them there, with my parents and, as I got older, alone. They had one son, Peter, who had died when only two and a half, and one daughter, Jean, who was three years younger than I.* They had a sun porch, many rooms and books and magazines and board games, and people who came to "help out" with the housekeeping and the garden. They were in my eyes, rich. Uncle Don and Aunt Mary both smoked steadily and had a drink or two in the evening, and this seemed rich behavior. Sometimes Don would take us all out to dinner in Greenwich at the Pickwick Arms, and he acted happily at home there, in contrast to my father, who, when our little family went to one of the restaurants in Reading, would swear at the prices on the menu and on one occasion jumped up and left my mother and me stranded at the table. Though my father wore a suit all day teaching school, as soon as we went out in the evening he would take off his coat and roll up his sleeves, so that at a "nice" restaurant there was usually trouble about letting him in. Uncle Don, who was six foot six and had a big face with puffy eyes, a wide lipless mouth, and a little slicked-down haircut on top almost like a wig, knew

* And who early in life won commemoration in Edmund Wilson's journals, in this entry for late 1936:

"*Mary Updike's baby*. [Mary Updike had been my secretary at *The New Republic*, and she was living not far from me in Connecticut.] When I went over to Mary Updike's and used the bathroom to shave, it woke up the baby, who had been put to bed next door. She began to cry and went on almost all the time I was there – the most feminine and appealing crying I have ever heard a baby do: it was really more like warbling; she would repeat a phrase, as it were, as if she were singing, and it didn't sound distressed or distressing, but as if she were engaged in a kind of recreation which enabled her to express herself. – Later on, I saw her in their car – she was a homely but cunning little blond pale-eyed thing with a kind of flat button nose."   – *The Thirties*, edited by Leon Edel

how to act in restaurants. Also, he taught me gin rummy and had read *Ulysses*. He was worldly-wise. Aunt Mary had worked for *The New Republic*, gave us *The New Yorker* for Christmas, and once took me to the Museum of Modern Art. She had a flapper's boyish figure and a dry tough way of talking – she made "wisecracks" – and long flaxen hair wrapped in a big braid around her head. She and Don lived the way I thought people should live, in a big house just an hour, by commuter train or the Merritt Parkway, from New York City, its towers and wonders and lights and noise. I wanted to become rich in this way.

Uncle Arch was richer yet, but lived in Florida. He and Aunt Mildred, his wife, and my three Florida cousins came visiting us in Shillington one time. Cousin Virginia wore a floppy sun hat and had an exotic Southern accent; I always remembered her standing in Shilling Alley drawling and holding on to her hat like a visitor from another world. One of her brothers was Arch Junior and the other had my name, John. He was, as far as I knew, the only other John Updike in the world. For Updike, in Pennsylvania, was an odd name, that got a loud laugh in the movie theatre. When you told them your name, people thought you were being "fresh". Hotel clerks and telephone operators would ask you to repeat it, bringing on (in my case) a fit of blushing and stuttering. It was not until I moved to New York City, where the Dutch (the real Dutch, the Holland Dutch, not the Pennsylvania Deutsch) still had some presence, that a person, a salesman at Brooks Brothers, heard my name at first try and wrote it down, correctly, with a respectful nod. Even when people hear it they want to spell it with a "y." Among my father's burdens as a teacher in Berks County was the oddity of his name, which lent itself to all sorts of mocking twists – Downdike, Downditch. At Ursinus they had called him, affectionately, "Uppie," and the Houcks still did, the pet name out of these middle-aged mouths sounding strange in my ears. My father had many nicknames. His sister called him "Russ", after his middle name, Russell. In childhood he was called "Much," because he ate so much licorice. Arch called him "Wed," and to his fellow teachers he was "Wes." Among the high school students he was the middle member of the trinity "Bus, Russ, and Truss" – the last an unkind reference to another faculty member's hernia.

One gloomy afternoon, I was startled to hear "Uppie" ring out across a playing field in Andover, Massachusetts, where my older son, your uncle David, was playing soccer. Nobody has ever called me "Uppie" except one boy, a boy I called "Neil Hovey" in a short story. All my life, I have felt most at ease with other males of Neil's type – dark and stoical; and I suppose my father could be considered this type, too. The stoicism was there for me to admire every morning when he set out for school, even before we moved from Shillington to the farm and set out to school together. As to dark, he took a good tan and his hair kept most of its brown to the day of his death at seventy-two. Hartley and Virginia Blackwood Updike had five children, of whom the first- and last-born died in infancy; of the middle, surviving three, Wesley Russell, the youngest, was brunette, and his sister Mary was very blond, with eyes of palest blue and skin of an almost ghostly white, and Arch, the oldest, was a redhead.

This redness of hair was central to the mythical image we had of Arch: a ball of fire, a powerhouse. To my father his brother was a virtual superman, a tormenting force of nature. My father told, in one of his stories of Trenton life, how he had laboriously taught himself to juggle two balls in one hand; he demonstrated this trick to his brother, who took the two, added another, and juggled the three without having ever practiced. Arch had been a stellar athlete at Trenton High, it appeared, and a paragon of leadership and vitality.*

---

* However he had physical problems, as his daughter, Virginia, has written me: "He started out in life as a puny premature baby and in later years developed severe back trouble at which time the doctors discovered he was missing some cushioning and bone formation in his spine, but a

He was a "go-getter," an expression my father used with ostensible approbation and yet with a sly implication of ruthlessness, of ultimately futile hyperactivity, somewhat as Jesus spoke of rendering Caesar his due. I, too, was a "go-getter" in my father's litany, and this flattery made me wonder if I wasn't devouring him from below, as Arch had pressed him from above. My father, in the running portrait of himself he offered aloud, was not, to his sorrow and our loss, a "go-getter."

Arch managed, after years of ups and downs – of busts and freezes in Florida – to build a little empire of orange groves around Lake Wales, an empire big enough to employ his sons and son-in-law and, eventually, his grandchildren and afford them all a comfortable inland-Florida lifestyle, with Cadillacs, golf memberships, and business trips north. Though rumblings of "taking Wes in" sometimes issued from this Southern enterprise, they were very faint rumblings, and my mother was fierce about keeping her husband and son independent of the other Updikes. I had no wish to pick oranges, and I could not imagine my father as other than a schoolteacher, so her ferocity seemed to me excessive and rhetorical; I took comfort from the presence of rich, red-headed Arch and sophisticated, Greenwich-dwelling Mary in the background of our modest Berks County life as I inched upward from grade to grade, looked forward to Christmas and then to summer, slowly outgrew my clothes from Croll & Keck and my shoes from Wetherhold & Metzger, borrowing my mystery novels from Whitner's and my P. G. Wodehouses from the Reading Public Library, bought big salty soft pretzels on Penn Street and licorice pipes and coconut strips from Henry's Variety Store

---

fusion surgery in 1943 remedied that problem and took the back pain away." He was completely deaf in one ear as a result of mastoid surgery and was turned down by the Army when he left Princeton at the end of his junior year to enlist; determined to do his bit for *that* war effort, he helped build barracks at Fort Dix. His wife's parents had been afraid she would be left a young widow, but Arch lived to be sixty-seven.

on Lancaster Avenue, played roof ball and box hockey at the playground and strained for glimpses of girls' underpants as they swung on the swings and skinned the cat on the jungle gym – as I grew, that is, into my self in the comfortable confines of the local institutions, ethnic tilt, and accent.

The existence of Mary and Arch meant to me that there were other Updikes in the world besides our own little lost pocket in Shillington. It meant, too, that my father, for all his self-advertised deficiencies, had had something that neither I nor my mother would ever have: siblings. The very way he spoke of his brother and sister, with an unfaltering assumption of natural affection and bond, came from a kind of human experience I would never know, and that I vowed to give my own children, and that you two boys now know as well. Without wanting a brother or sister for myself – where would they sleep? what would they eat? who would prevent them from using my toys and pencils and crayons? – I enjoyed this aspect of my father, and felt that these branchings of our shared blood also extended me.

Children's attention tends to wander during tales of the past; the Trenton of my father's childhood was to me a sketchy place, haunted by some deep disarray, some wound, in the family fortunes. I pictured dark streets, and a blizzard. My father, to help out the family, used to deliver papers, and would come home so exhausted that, one Christmas morning, greeted upon his return by a set of gifts on the kitchen table, he swept them aside and rested his head in his arms on the table: he told this story himself. It was my impression that everything he did, as a boy, hurt. Prematurely tall, he wore braces on his legs. Yet he played baseball as a catcher, squatting down and getting hit in the face and fingers by the balls, much as, in college, he played football, in the line, and kept getting his nose broken. Arch and Mary seemed to move into adulthood with a certain confidence and drive, but my father, the youngest, was caught in some awful undercurrent of discouragement, and failed or refused to finish high school.

My father was sinking, and some good soul saw it, and advised that he be sent to where her son was enrolled, St Stephens' Episcopal Boarding School on the Hudson, which later became Bard College; and there he was brought to order, and earned his high school degree. He went on to Ursinus College, where he met my mother and marched, in my sense of him, toward my creation.

But after Ursinus, in the year of their graduation, 1923, the Trenton situation took a turn for the worse; the family suffered a dispersal that finally left its fragments in Florida, in Greenwich, and in Pennsylvania. What went wrong? At the center of the mythic disaster a sick man is being carried onto a boat in New York; I picture him sometimes as in a wheelchair and at others on a stretcher. This man is my grandfather, Hartley Titus Updike. There is a crowd in attendance – his children and wife, who are going on the boat with him, and onlooking relatives, from that big New Jersey brood of Sharps and Drakes. Someone remarks, "Hartley looks tired." His wife, my grandmother, née Virginia Blackwood, famously responds, "Hartley was *born* tired."

My mother, your great-grandmother Updike, is my main, oral source for this family history. Both you boys have been held by her, on occasions you will have forgotten: Anoff sat in her lap, she has told me, for a peaceful long time when the three Cobblahs visited Plowville in 1986, and in June of the following summer she held Kwame for a few minutes on a sunny afternoon in Concord, on the festive occasion of his outdooring, with all four of his grandparents in attendance, and most everybody decked out in Ghanaian robes, in Transcendentalism's home town, on a day that also happened to be my mother's eighty-third birthday. Your mother was never held by *her* great-grandmother, but in June of 1955, I remember, when she was three months old and we had freshly returned from England, we laid her on the bed where my

165

mother's mother, whose musical full name was Katie Ziemer Kramer Hoyer, lay all but paralyzed by Parkinson's disease and the rigors of her eight hard-working decades. With her hawkish quick look she stared down at the baby, but was unable to enunciate a word. These two females, then, just barely touched in the great minuet of the generations, in that curtained upstairs bedroom where my mother, as I write this, lies staring at the ceiling wondering whether to live or die, and where, over four decades ago, my grandfather would cough his deep, heart-tearing cough to the distress of my adolescent ears. He died in September of 1953, at the age of ninety, in order to avoid (my mother claims) meeting my father-in-law, the Unitarian minister, who was bringing my bride and me down from Vermont, where we had worked at a camp in Lake Winnipesaukee. We arrived a minute or two after my grandfather had risen from his bed, was tackled by my grandmother and gave up the ghost.* My father-in-law went upstairs and, a pastoral intimate of death, felt for my grandfather's pulse, and found none. Thus the two men touched, but never met. My grandmother died – "passed away," as they say, in her sleep – three months after sharing a bed with your infant mother.

A photograph exists of me as a baby being held by Virginia Emily Blackwood Updike, my witty paternal grandmother, but I have no memory of it. She is stout and dark and stately, in the photograph, and was to die painfully of diabetes, after a foot was amputated in the early Thirties. I was recently handed, to my surprise, evidence that my grandmother and I corresponded. A letter from her of June 25, 1938, addressed to me at 117 Philadelphia Avenue, begins, "My dear Johnnie

---

* "He thought the bed was on fire and sprang from it; she clung to him and in their fall to the floor he died. But not quite. My mother rushed up the stairs and cried, 'What are you doing?'

"'Why, we're on the floor,' her father told her with level sarcasm, and his heart stopped."   – "The Blessed Man of Boston,
My Grandmother's Thimble, and Fanning Island" (1961)

Boy – You will never know how much good it did me to receive that memorandum of your activities for the past ten months. You were so explicit that my eyes followed your descriptions. You are standing in front of your birthday dogwood. You look so benign in your daddy's hat, and so animated too. I like the idea of school – of tap dancing – of singing but – John – I hurt all over when I heard you had been so ill* – you had forgotten how to dance. Im glad of your promotions. You will get thru high school and the Shirley Temple girls you associate with," and it ends, sadly and in spots illegibly, "John – my right arm is so painful has hurt[?]! – muscular – I believe – it may be rheumatism – maybe not – Love my dear boy – to all there [?] Grand Ma Updike." And there are two penny postcards, sent from Sebring, Florida, in 1937 and 1938, calling me "Chunny Boy" and "Chun." The second runs, "My dear – My nice Big Chun – Tell your father – Arch has a hideous carbuncle at base of brain – It has been exrayed and has a seepage today. He has not stopped work. I hope you come & bring your father & mother Xmas It is very windy & cold here Lovingly Gran Mommy. 10 – 4 – 38".

She came from a Missouri family of many girls. Her letters are written in a headlong handwriting that brooks little punctuation. My cousin Jean has transcribed some written early in her marriage. "Mr Updike is not very well and I shall be more than rejoiced when we get home. He is homesick and tired out. So much work and worry is attached to the ministry. I'm surprised that anybody in that vocation lives to a ripe old age." That was written from a parish in Blair, Nebraska, in 1892; from Livonia, Indiana, she wrote four years later, "We will not be here longer than Nov. So many have died & moved away that it will be impossible for us to live on what the people can pay. They want us to stay & have

---

* The bad case of measles in February, I presume, which induced my psoriasis.

paid more than they ever did, but it falls short over two hundred dollars. There are no vacancies near us, so that a long move with all its attendant woes will be necessary." That same year, according to my grandfather's obituary in the Trenton *Evening Times* of December 29, 1923, he left the ministry: "In 1896 a throat affection [*sic*] compelled his retirement from the ministry and he came to Trenton and engaged in the real estate business with his father." The family legend, in my mother's version, has it that he quit out of hurt feelings when he overheard a parishioner saying that Mrs Updike would make a better minister than he.

My cousin Virginia writes of our grandmother: "She had a good quick mind and a terrific love of people and the talent for getting up in front of people to speak on programs. Mother showed me a newspaper clipping which had a write-up stating Mrs Hartley Updike filled the pulpit during her husband's illness . . . Dad said his mother always had guests for dinner on Division Street in Trenton when they were growing up. They were poor and couldn't entertain lavishly but Grandma was a terrific cook and knew how to stretch the food. She invited people from all walks of life and anybody in the vicinity knew to drop by for a meal. Jenny said she wanted her children to be good at conversation and learn from the scholars and every day people all they could." My father remembered those feasts with melancholy, as a straining of perilously limited resources, but his inveterate, infuriating, ever-hopeful gregariousness makes sense as undying obedience to his mother's injunction to perfect the conversational art and to learn from everyday people all he could. Arch, according to Virginia, remembered that when the food ran low, his mother would signal "F.H.B.," meaning "Family Hold Back," and simultaneously offer the guests another helping. Aunt Mary liked to tell how, once unable to cross a Trenton street exactly when she wanted to, her mother threw her pocketbook into the middle of it and thus halted traffic and successfully crossed over. Virginia Blackwood Updike, in the Bible of family memory, walked on water and miraculously fed the multitudes.

She was not pleased when my father married my mother, in August of 1925. One story has it that she fainted on hearing the news. Another gives her response as the remark that only colored people got married in August. The bridegroom received a letter from his mother containing the one sentence, "You are a God-damned coward!" He also received a most gracious and reassuring letter from his older brother:

Sept 13, 1925

Dear Wed,

I wrote you on notice of your marriage but just see I have neglected to mail the letter so will answer you rather tardily.

Mary and mother were apparently disturbed at first because you did not give notice but are all OK now as far as I see and both wish you and Linda much happiness and success.

For my part I think you did the right thing. You love each other, have known each other for years and it is hell to be perpetually separated. I was engaged for six years and know from experience. Don't feel you have any obligation directly to mother, Wed. I know how you feel and that [you] will do your part when you are called on but mother has done well in real estate in fact there is every reason to believe that she will be independent by Xmas and that will relieve your mind. Keep what you make for your wife and coming family. That is the best advice I can give you. You must accumulate by your own labor the capital for a home, furnishings, life insurance, and many other fixed expenses. May God help you and give you health, strength and wisdom.

Remember me to Linda. Tell her she is a welcome addition to the family and that we all take her in with open arms. I wish you both many years of happiness and prosperity and may your only troubles be "little ones." . . .

My mother had not been there on the dock in 1923 as the boat set out for Florida, but had met her future father-in-law some months before, in May, when my father took her to the

Updike house on Edgewood Avenue in Trenton. The young couple were about to graduate from Ursinus; not quite nineteen, she wore one of the flashy dresses her own father was still prosperous enough to buy for her – a rose-colored dress – and Hartley's blue eyes, on his bed of debility, took notice. She remembers how blue his eyes were, and how they twinkled though he didn't speak, and how curiously high his bed seemed. He smiled at her. Behind his pale mustache, he wanly smiled. Her welcome into the family was wan, but then the family's resources were stretched perilously thin. She was part of a larger crisis, an upheaval in the Updike fortunes.

Here is my picture of it, gathered from her description, with some research of my own. My grandfather Hartley, born in 1860, was a bookish shy boy who was always in the hay mow reading. He attended the Pennington Seminary and upon graduation in 1879 gave an oration called "Moral Courage." He then went to Princeton and graduated in 1883. He did well at school and was considered erudite; a family joke about him was that he kept quiet in twelve languages. He attended Princeton Seminary for two years and took the third year of his theological course at Union Seminary in New York. He was licensed by the presbytery of New Brunswick in April of 1886 and ordained early in 1887. The necrological report of *The Princeton Theological Seminary Bulletin* says, in its specialized language, that he was "stated supply" to the church at Poplar Bluff, Missouri, from June of 1886 to January of 1888. It was there that he met Virginia Blackwood, who had been abandoned, another story went, at the altar when about to be married to another man. Her wedding to Hartley did not take place until July 21, 1891, by which time he had been stated supply to two other Missouri parishes and pastor for two years of a church in Lebanon, Illinois. From there they went on to churches in Blair, Nebraska, Little Rock, Arkansas, and Livonia, Indiana. Their first child was stillborn in Livonia. Virginia wrote from Livonia to her sister-in-law Lillian Updike Drake a twelve-page letter describing her ordeal, adding this upside-down postscript: "I forgot to tell you that Hartley stood right by me thro it all and has hardly left me since. He waits on me most of the time, and suffered as much as I did. Perhaps more. For I believe it is easier to bear than to look on." The next year, however, Arch was born, and in 1896 she wrote Lillian that "Hartley can not bear to think of you all not seeing the Baby before he gets so large." This same letter discusses the possibility of taking a church in Illinois, but "it is so far to move and so expensive"; and presumably in Livonia he had overheard the opinion that his wife would be a better minister than he, and his affected throat gave out.

Back in Trenton, he joined his father's firm, which sold real estate and life insurance. The firm stationery begins to be headed "Archibald Updike & Son" in 1897. Hartley's much-younger brother Lincoln, born in 1874, later became active in the firm. "Uncle Linc" was a phrase that would fall from my father's lips like a single metallic word, and that often rang out in the summer air of those visits to the Sharps and Drakes, where Lincoln's widow, Aunt Marty, was featured in the cast of kin – a rather snappy-looking elderly lady with thin legs and plenty of rouge. By the time my mother came onto the scene in the early Twenties, my great-grandfather Archibald was dead, and his widow, née Titus, was dying of a broken hip, and the firm was doing poorly. Uncle Linc was having financial trouble, for which rumor blamed Aunt Marty's extravagance. Updike pride prevented my grandfather Hartley from declaring bankruptcy. In his quandary, he contracted pneumonia, and had a series of little strokes, and became bedridden.

The family assets were now reduced to the house in Edgewood Avenue, where they had moved, in 1915, from Division Street; this move to a more fashionable neighborhood, in my mother's version of the saga, had been urged by

Arch and Mary's burgeoning ambitions and aspirations. My father always spoke of Division Street with warmth and of Edgewood Avenue as a grand place that had not much to do with him; the move had left him with a lifelong dread (which I have inherited) of living beyond one's means – of finding oneself in a pretentious shelter that is draining one dry. The Shillington house must have seemed to him a bit that way, which helps explain his willingness to leave it in 1945; he was happiest, really, on the move, and mourned the nomadic comradely life of his job with the American Telephone and Telegraph Company, for whose pole-planting operation he was working and travelling when I was born.

In the summer of 1923, in flight from sickness and disgrace, the Updikes left Trenton for a territory where their story becomes, for me, even harder to grasp. Virginia Updike's sister, who had married a man called Burt, had a thirty-acre farm in Zolfo Springs, in south-central Florida; a creek flowed through the acres, complete with alligators and water moccasins. At this point in her telling of the story my mother begins to laugh, perhaps because she, so loyal a Pennsylvanian, finds something irrepressibly droll in the idea of this desolate bit of flat hot inland Florida being the answer to anybody's problems. Arch, it seems, was already there, having become discontented with the Trenton real-estate business. With the proceeds from the Edgewood Avenue house, the Zolfo Springs place, or part of it, was bought. This family on the lam took to teaching: Mary taught school at near-by Wauchula, and my father became a school principal, at the age of twenty-three, in Green Cove Springs, way to the north, south of Jacksonville. His father died the day after Christmas, of one last stroke, and my father brought the body north, to be buried in the family plot in Pennington.

Both my father and Mary, eventually, stayed north, leaving in Florida Arch, who eventually prospered, and their mother, who eventually died, in 1939. She had left Zolfo Springs when Hartley died and lived in Sebring, where Arch for a time headed the Chamber of Commerce. My cousin Virginia remembers her in Sebring: "She was called Aunt Jenny by the town folk and was called upon to help the sick and lonely and even to do nursing. The town always had her as first aid nurse at the city's annual picnics. I always felt so proud to see my Grandmother performing such an important task and my friends thought I was the luckiest of us all to have such a grandmother." Her gift for feeding multitudes endured: "For Arch, John, and me she'd put on a kids' party out of nothing and on the spur of the moment and kids loved to come. Her speciality was doughnuts and she could whip up dozens in a flash." Fifty years after her death, she remains considerably more vivid than the man she married.

Of Hartley the most vigorous impression seems to have been made upon his only daughter, my aunt Mary. In a "grandmother book," she jotted down for the information of her descendants, "Dad was about 6 ft., blonde perfectly beautiful skin and hands" and "We went to Bethany Presbyterian, about six blocks away. Dad walked fast, so he led the parade, Mother next and the three kids trailed." In the Edgewood Avenue house, Mary recalled to Jean, her father, when angry with his wife, would go down into the basement and swear, the curses perfectly audible to his children as they listened at a vent in the attic – a virtually diagrammatic enactment of unsuccessful repression. Her mother's nickname for him, Mary claimed, was – based upon his middle name of Titus – Tightass. The few letters of his that I have read often strike a plaintive note of timid health and are almost pathologically dull. To his sister Anna in Pennington he wrote from Princeton in 1880:

> I intended to have come home to-day, but the walking was so bad that I concluded to stay. . . . I was out to Grand-pa's two weeks ago to-day and they told me that you have been at the funeral. I intended to have gone, but I had such a cold and the walking was so bad that I concluded to stay at home.

He was born tired. His life smells of financial failure and of the guilt and shame that attaches to such failure in these United States. It was the inspiriting genius of Calvinism to link prosperity and virtue, to take material thriving as a sign of salvation; and Presbyterians would be especially sensitive to this link. A failure of economic fortune must be a moral failure: in my mythic sense of my family the stain of unsuccess ate away at my grandfather's life as if in some tale by Hawthorne. A lurid quality attached to my father's memory of his own boyhood – snowstorms, wet shoes, sleeplessness, the rejected Christmas gifts, a miserable helpless pity for his failing father. "I couldn't help him," he would say to me. "I didn't know how to help the poor devil." My grandfather, I shadowily felt, was doubly damned – for leaving the ministry, and for failing in the real-estate and insurance business.

There is little physical evidence that he ever existed, this man who kept quiet in twelve languages. My mother has in her possession a wooden sign that says FOR SALE and, beneath it in slightly smaller letters, H. T. UPDIKE, BROAD STREET BANK BUILDING, 5686. And she has passed on to me a silver napkin ring, engraved *H. T. Updike* in script, and, inside, with these barely legible words:

> *From the Presb' Church,*
> *Lebanon, Ill.,*
> *Xmas, 1890*

Six more years would go by, years of being "homesick and tired out," before he would leave the ministry and embark upon his equally disappointing career in the world of business. I imagined this career as a kind of abyss, howling with sadness; his three children each set themselves to climbing out of the abyss, to "making good" out of so total a ruin that, in my father's case, it was a two-step process that left it to me to establish, on the platform of his doggedly held place in Shillington, a redemptive prosperity equivalent to Arch's and Mary's. Within the kinship network, I am helping carry Hartley to the boat.

He had come from robust stock. A cheerful slant on the New Jersey Updikes is offered by *The Op Dyck Genealogy*, written by Charles Wilson Opdyke and privately printed in Albany, New York, in 1889. Hartley's grandfather, Peter, appears on page 333, in telegraphic but glowing terms:

> Born 1812 at Cherry Valley near Princeton; farmed three years near Dutch Neck, a few miles south of Princeton; later bought a fine farm near Pennington. He was a good, kind man, a prosperous farmer and a very patriotic citizen. Was tall, and weighed 236 pounds at his death in 1866. His widow died 1887. [*sic*] His sons are all nearly 6 feet in height; Archibald and George each weigh about 200 pounds, and Edward 185 pounds.

Archibald, my great-grandfather, fairly leaps off the page to greet the genealogist:

> *Archibald* was the first Updike whom the author had ever seen. In the Summer of 1886 he was mentioned as a representative man, well acquainted with those of his name in New Jersey and best fitted to assist in placing them in the family tree. A letter was sent him, and he kindly undertook to interview the oldest Updikes who could be discovered in Somerset and Mercer Counties, and also offered his carriage and company to visit the oldest graveyards and localities connected with the family. The author gladly accepted and, on meeting Archibald Updike, at once recognized him as a relative; was in fact astounded at the similarity of features and characteristics to those of his own *Opdycke* relatives, although they were removed six generations from a common ancestor with the New Jersey *Updikes*. Together they visited the old Updike Road where every farm for miles had once been owned by an Updike; they forced their way through the bushes and briars in the old burial-ground of William Updike, explored the graveyards of Princeton and Dutch Neck, and called upon several branches of the family.

They forced their way through the bushes and briars – the Updikes were a big, bumptious race, and no strangers to earthly success. The genealogist, Charles Wilson Opdyke, was the son of a dry-goods millionaire, George Opdyke, who became in 1861 the first Republican mayor of New York and faced down the Draft Riots of 1863. In the genealogy account, Archibald's brother Furman, acting upon "a conviction formed in his early youth that farming was too slow and the West was the place for a man of small means and large aspirations," made his way to Nebraska by the summer of 1875 and "commenced picking up cheap lands." The Indians, led by Sitting Bull, were on the warpath; to avoid them, Furman camped out in the Rocky Mountains. "He left the Mountains in October, after a delightful Summer of camp-life in a country abounding with game and trout. Then opened a real estate and loan office at Hastings, Neb., and this proving successful, has kept an interest in the business ever since. . . ." Thus was founded the Nebraska Updikes, a prosperous banking clan that Furman's brothers Edward and George and sister Mary went west to join. My delicate, scholarly grandfather hailed from a race of giants, with "large aspirations," and was furthermore the oldest son. After the "bushes and briars" sentence, the account continues:

> Archibald married a great-granddaughter of Mary Updike (Johnson) who was daughter of John Updike and Mary Bragaw. He is living in a large brick house on a fine farm two miles from Pennington; has been twenty years Trustee of the Pennington Presbyterian Church; is successfully engaged in placing western mortgages among the best citizens of Princeton and Trenton. He has children: Hartley T., 1860, a graduate of the Princeton Theological Seminary, and now a Presbyterian Clergyman at Poplar Bluff, Mo.; Lilian A., 1864, married to Eugene P. Drake, a farmer near Princeton; Anna L., 1866; D. Foster, 1872; Lincoln, 1874; George A., 1880; – all living.

Here the printed genealogy stops, and the imagination must leap to Poplar Bluff, Missouri, where the Updike line would entwine with a Southern, Baptist, Irish strain. My parents once visited Poplar Bluff on a western trip of their own, and found it a disheartening place.*

The Updikes came to this continent in two installments. The first and more distinguished, the Wesel Updikes, arrived in New Amsterdam, in the person of Gysbert op den Dyck, before 1638. Gysbert – like Peter Minuit, the first governor of New Netherland – came from Wesel, a small city located on the lower Rhine, where it meets the Lippe. Wesel (which was all but demolished by air raids in World War II) is now part of western West Germany; in 1605, when Gysbert was born there, it was part of the duchy of Cleves, and though officially neutral in the Dutch–Spanish war, suffered incursions and hardship. A continuous line of Op den Dycks there went back to Henric, a Burgomaster and City Treasurer born late in the thirteenth century. Though no certain connection can be proved, the Wesel Op den Dycks are thought to be related to the family of the same name in Essen, which was of knightly rank, used armorial bearings (involving a pineapple, a star, and what seems to be a serrated tongs), and became extinct in the sixteenth century, "leaving their name attached to an estate and to a castle." For six generations after Henric, Op den Dycks occupied civic office in Wesel; in the seventh, Lodowick (b. 1565) became a brewer and an innkeeper. The genealogy assures us, "An explanation of his undertaking these somewhat humble occupations is to be found in the great decadence suffered by Wesel in his life-time." The war and the confusion arising from the death of the Duke of Cleves without male issue had curtailed commerce and finally

* "Strangely, the town had not changed; it looked just as he had imagined, from his father's descriptions: tall wooden houses, rain-soaked, stacked on a bluff. The town was a sepia postcard mailed homesick home and preserved in an attic. My father cursed: his father's old sorrow bore him down into depression, into hatred of life. My mother claims his decline in health began at that moment."   – "Son" (1973)

resulted in the siege and occupation of the town by a Spanish army in 1614. The Spanish stayed in Wesel for fifteen years, until 1629. After 1615, Lodowick disappears from the Wesel town records, and it seems probable that he and his son Gysbert, then aged ten, joined the many refugees seeking asylum in Holland, which had already thrown off the Spanish yoke.

Gysbert makes his first appearance in the records of the New World as an officer of the Dutch West India Company, and specifically as the Commander of Fort Hope, on the present site of Hartford. It was his ungrateful task to hold this fort while the English colonists from Massachusetts were overrunning the fertile Connecticut Valley. Failing to receive the reinforcements he needed, he resigned in late 1640 and "returned to the Fatherland," only to reappear in New Amsterdam in 1642 and, the following year, to marry Catherine Smith, the daughter of Richard Smith, the possessor of vast tracts on the west side of Narragansett Bay. Land was easily laid hold of in the New World; Gysbert himself owned all of Coney Island – then three separate sandy masses, of which the easternmost was called "Gysbert's Island" – as well as two farms on Long Island and a residence on Stone Street, in lower Manhattan. One's holdings were not always secure, however; the more numerous English brushed aside the Dutch claims to Connecticut, and the Indians were still a threat. Gysbert frequently sat on the Governor's Council and helped fashion Indian treaties; he advised against the petition in 1643, of the Long Island settlers for permission to attack the Marreckawick Indians near Breucklen (Brooklyn); nevertheless, attacks and plunder occurred, and the Indian reprisals included the massacre of Anne Hutchinson and her family and the devastation of Richard Smith's extensive colony at Mespath. Both Hutchinson and Smith had sought refuge among the Dutch from religious persecution in the English colonies to the north; both New England and old England were jealous of the Dutch colonies. In 1664, Charles II awarded a patent for all New Netherland to his brother the Duke of York, and the Duke's ships plus Connecticut troops compelled the unpopular government of Peter Stuyvesant to surrender. Dutch rule on the North American continent ended. "After the English capture, nothing further is found on the records concerning Gysbert. . . . The tradition is doubtless correct that he went with his children to Narragansett, after the death of Richard Smith, Sr. in 1666, to take possession of the lands about Wickford bequeathed to the children of Gysbert's deceased wife Catharine."

Thus began the notable, even glamorous line of Rhode Island Updikes. Gysbert, whose name became Anglicized to Gilbert Updike was called "Doctor," though he was probably not a physician. "He was well educated; his associations, official positions, reports, even his signature, show this. He must have spoken German from his birth, Dutch from his emigration, and English from his marriage." The eldest son of that marriage, Lodowick (b. 1646), laid out the town of Wickford, once called "Updike's New Town"; his son Daniel (b. 1694) was tutored at home, visited Barbados and mingled in "the first circles of society on the Island," studied law, married the daughter of the governor, and was repeatedly elected Attorney General of the colony. *His* son Lodowick (b. 1725) was "regarded in his time as one of the most eminent citizens of Rhode Island. His qualifications were such as fitted him to shine either at the Bar, in political, or in military career. But he preferred the dignity and scholarly leisure of the private life of a large landed proprietor." The thirty thousand acres of wilderness John Smith had purchased from the Narragansett Sachems in 1639 had become, augmented by marriage and subdued to cultivation, the basis of a plantation society akin to that of the South and like nothing else in the North. Wilkins Updike, Lodowick's grandson, wrote:

> Their plantations were large, many containing thousands of acres, and noted for dairies and the production of cheese. The

grass in the meadows was very thick and as high as the tops of the walls and fences; two acres were sufficient for the annual food of each cow. . . . Large flocks of sheep were kept, and clothing was manufactured for the household, which sometimes exceeded seventy persons in parlor and kitchen. Grain was shipped to the West Indies. The labor was mostly performed by African slaves, or Narragansett Indians.

In this American Eden, roads and carriages scarcely existed, and the planter families rode horses back and forth through each other's fences in an incessant round of festivity and fox chase, entertainment and dance. The black slaves (among whom you, Anoff and Kwame, might have found distant relatives of your own – men and women speaking Twi like your African grandmother or Ga like your African grandfather, brought here in manacles from the Gold Coast) were allowed a reflection of such brilliancy:

In imitation of the whites, the negroes held a mock annual election of their Governor; when the slaves were numerous, their election was held in each town. . . . The slaves assumed the ranks of their masters, whose reputation was degraded if their negroes appeared in inferior apparel or with less money than those of masters of equal wealth. The horses of the wealthy landholders were on this day all surrendered to the use of the slaves, who with cues, real or false, head pomatumed and powdered, cocked hat, mounted on the best Narragansett pacers, sometimes with their master's sword, with their ladies on pillions, pranced to election at ten o'clock.

Lodowick – "tall and fine-looking; always wore wig and small-clothes, and was said to resemble George III" – had eleven children, who lived to the average age of eighty years. The eldest, Daniel (b. 1761), became Attorney General of Rhode Island the same year, 1790, that the state ratified the Constitution; thus he served an independent commonwealth in the same office his grandfather had held in the King's colony. Lodowick's youngest child, Wilkins (b. 1784), served for many years in the General Assembly, which upon his death in 1867 passed a resolution saying: "Resolved, that in the decease of Hon. Wilkins Updike, has passed away from earth almost the last of a generation of true Rhode Island men, worthy of our respect and imitation in the walks of private and of public life." And indeed, in the nineteenth century the noble line of Rhode Island Updikes did rather suddenly shrivel and diminish, as if their Narragansett paradise, with its lush grass and powdered wigs, its abundance of cheese and sheep and slaves, had been something of a dream. The genealogy for the Wesel family sputters out in a chord of unmarried bachelors and men moved to Pittsburgh. When, a few years ago, I visited Wickford, or North Kingston as it can be called, the only Updike in the telephone book was an "Updike Laundry" on Route One; the young woman behind the counter told me that "Updike" was an old name for Wickford, and that nobody of that name worked in the laundry. Even before the turn of the century, when Charles Wilson Opdyke visited the vicinity of Richard Smith's fabulous holdings, he found the family all but vanished: "A hundred years ago, Wickford contained so many of the name that it was often called 'Updike Town.' Very few of the blood and none of the name now reside there."

Yet Wilkins, the youngest of eleven, himself had fathered twelve children. One of his sons was grandiosely named Caesar Augustus, and he "was a fine public speaker, inheriting much of his distinguished father's wit and humor, and like him was a thorough Rhode Islander." Caesar practiced law in Providence, and became a member of the city Common Council, a member of the lower House of the General Assembly, and from 1860 to 1862 Speaker of the House. But at around the age of fifty he died suddenly, of heart disease, leaving his widow, who had been Elisabeth Bigelow Adams, and a teen-aged son. That son was Daniel Berkeley Updike, born in Providence in (like Hartley) 1860. Daniel's middle name commemorates the warm friendship between his great-grandfather – the colonial Daniel – and George Berkeley, the

Anglo-Irish cleric-philosopher, in those years, 1728–31, during which the future bishop resided in Newport.*

Young D. B. Updike was frail and shy, with protruding ears and a religious disposition – the Rhode Island Updikes were keen Episcopalians. His father's premature death necessitated that he abjure higher education and go to work; he began as an errand boy for Houghton Mifflin in Boston in 1880 and showed a fine aptitude for the niceties of typography and printing. He set up as a free-lance designer in 1893, and founded the Merrymount Press in 1896. He undertook all sorts of jobs but specialized in ecclesiastical work: the 1928 revision of the Book of Common Prayer was printed by him. A lifelong bachelor, he was meticulous, fastidious, and learned. He utilized and helped revive the historical roman and italic faces Caslon, Scotch, Janson, Bell, Poliphilus, Bodoni. From 1911 to 1916 he gave lectures on printing at the Harvard Business School, and these were the basis of his two-volume *Printing Types: Their History, Forms, and Use*, a work not only classic but still unsurpassed in its field. Daniel Berkeley Updike was, when I was a boy, the only famous Updike – the only one who could be found in the back of the dictionary.

Yet he, and all the Rhode Island Updikes, were not really my relations, or yours. No genealogical connection has been established between the Wesel Updikes and our own ancestors, the Holland Updikes, who came, it is all but certain, from Elburg, in Gelderland, on the eastern shore of the Zuider Zee. Op den Dycks left their traces on records there

---

* He was there waiting for his proposed American University to be funded, a university he wished to see located in Bermuda and devoted largely to the education and conversion of American Indians. The vision was never realized, but in 1866 Berkeley's name descended upon a relocated California college and its town, which it continues to adorn. It was Berkeley who wrote the famous line "Westward the course of empire takes its way" and in his *Principles of Human Knowledge* set forth the arresting idea that "All the choir of heaven and furniture of earth – in a word, all those bodies which compose the mighty frame of the world – have not any subsistence without a mind."

since the fourteenth century, and the baptismal names Louris, Johan, and Albert recur in both the Elburg records and the first American generations.*

Louris Jansen Opdyck came to New Netherland before 1653, at which time he resided in Albany and bought land at Gravesend, Long Island. His Holland antecedents are indicated by a written petition of 1653, in which he complains that the English inhabitants of Gravesend were determined "that no Dutchmen should get into the Magistry there," and by his widow's appealing, in 1660, to the "law of Holland" in claiming half of his estate. Our genealogist takes Louris's Dutchness as reason to launch a patriotic rhapsody, as of the seventeenth century:

> The cattle of Holland, grazing on the bottom of the sea, were the finest in Europe, its farm products the most valuable, its navigators the boldest, its mercantile marine the most powerful. Where of old were swamps and thickets, now dwelt three millions of people, the most industrious, the most prosperous, perhaps the most intelligent, under the sun; their love of liberty indomitable; their pugnacity proverbial; peaceful and phlegmatic, they were yet the most irascible and belligerent men of Europe.

Such is our proud, though oft-diluted, Dutch heritage.

Louris participated in the fur trade with the Iroquois at Fort Orange, a Dutch fort dating from 1614, on the site of Albany, and was granted by Governor Stuyvesant a small lot there. But his main activity seems to have been at Gravesend, a farming colony dominated by the English. Gravesend was the only Long Island settlement to defend itself successfully in the Indian uprisings that destroyed Mespath; in 1655,

* Almost no Updikes survive in Europe. The genealogist in 1888 found two families called Oppedyk living in Friesland, one of which adopted the name under Napoleon: the other family had been living in Ylst since 1654. When I visited the Netherlands in 1977, the only Updike my publisher could turn up was my first cousin Jean, who had married a Dutchman called Kramer and listed herself with the double name Kramer-Updike.

another Indian war made Gravesend unsafe, and Louris resided with his family in New Amsterdam, on Pearl Street. The population of Manhattan was then one thousand people, of whom a quarter lived on Pearl Street. Money was so rare that purchases were made with beaver skins; the first brick-yard and the first paved street had just come into existence; and cows were driven through the town gate at Wall Street to the public pasture at the present City Hall Park. The meadow for Gravesend was Coney Island, and one imagines that in this cozy wilderness community Louris and Gysbert must have sometimes met, and may have known each other well.

The lines diverged, however: one went northeast to Rhode Island, and the other southwest into New Jersey. Louris was dead by 1660, we know from a document whereby his widow, Christina (already engaged to marry again), divided his con-siderable estate of twenty-one hundred guilders among her three sons, Peter, Otto, and Johannes. The farm at Gravesend was sold and the family with its stepfather moved to Dutch Kills, in the jurisdiction of Newton, in what is now the Long Island City section of Queens. Peter disappears from the records after the English captured New York and may have returned to Holland; Otto apparently never left Newton. It was Johannes, the youngest, a boy of nine when his father died, who in the early summer of 1697, by this time the father of seven and the grandfather of three, led his family into the fertile territory of West Jersey, where, a contempor-ary report had it, "you shall meet with no inhabitants but a few friendly Indians, where there are stately oaks whose broad-branched tops have no other use but to keep off the sun's heat from the wild beasts of the wilderness, where is grass as high as a man's middle, that serves for no other end except to maintain the elks and deer." It was, an early settler sent back word, "as good a country as any man need to dwell in."

In wagons and carts, with horses and oxen and farming utensils, the Opdyke party – which included Johannes's sisters Tryntie, Engeltie, and Annetie, who were all married to brothers called Anderson – made their way across the hills to Flatbush to a ferry at the narrows, across Staten Island, up the Raritan to the old Indian trail called "the King's Highway," which they followed across the future state to the two hundred fifty acres Johannes had bought that April, "above the falls of the Delaware." The land lay near the present town of Lawrenceville, just above Trenton, in an area then called Maidenhead. Here Johannes lived and farmed and bought and sold land for thirty years, until his death at seventy-eight in 1729; and here, in the vicinity of Trenton, Princeton, and Pennington, Updikes stayed for two more centuries, their name passing from the land only in my father's generation. The New Jerseyites were more tenacious of the Dutch spelling of the name than the Rhode Islanders; Johannes signed his name Johannes Lourense, using the patronymic in the Old World style, and his children were entered into the church and civic records as op Dyck, or Opdyck, unless an English clerk did the recording.

Louris Jansen op Dyck had begot Johannes Opdyck, who begat Lawrence Updick (1675–1748), who begat John Updike (1708–90), who begat Peter (1756–1818), who begat Aaron (1784–1861), who begat Peter (1812–66), who begat Archibald (1838–1912), who begat Hartley (1860–1923), who begat Wesley (1900–72), who begat me (b. 1932), who begat Elizabeth (b. 1955), who begat you (b. 1985, 1987). On your mother's side, then, you are thirteenth generation Americans, offspring of a favored white minority. The Dutch colony had lasted a mere forty years; after it surrendered in 1664, without a shot being fired, the English Governor was instructed to treat the several thousand Dutch inhabitants generously, letting them keep their lands, language, and religion. Soon they were intermarrying with the English and forgetting their Dutch. It was an easy assimilation.

And you, my grandsons, how will you fare here? When Anoff was born – in the Hartford Hospital, on a brutally cold

Super Bowl Sunday – my instinctive thought was that he would do better if his parents settled in Ghana; that is, I trusted an African country to treat a half-white person better than my own country would treat a half-black. Now, I wonder. Ours is a changing, merging, exogamous world, and while racial prejudice operates in the United States against blacks in many ways overt and oblique, and the black ghettos, as drugs surge and industrial jobs vanish, are perhaps more dire places than they ever were, at least our laws now formally insist upon equal rights, and our best corporations and educational institutions recruit blacks in an effort to right old imbalances, and professional sports and television commercials constantly offer images of multiracial camaraderie. An ideal colorblind society flickers at the forward edge of the sluggishly evolving one. Slim black models pose in *Vogue*, and well-dressed, professional blacks work in the downtowns of the major cities: neither of these things was true of the America I grew up in. Further, the Latinization of North America – the influx of Hispanics – has softened the color line and the singularity of the original black population imported from Africa by pale planters from northern Europe. America is slowly becoming yours, I want to think, as much as it is anyone's; already, out of the deepest disadvantage, black Americans have contributed heavily to what makes the United States a real country, with a style and a soulfulness no purely white country has. If, some day, you come to read in its entirety this book dedicated to you, and not just this grand-paternal letter, you will notice in every chapter a touch or two of this pressing issue within the American psyche – the matter of the blacks brought here against their wills, and confined to the slave quarters of the society, and that yet fascinate us whites as a people strikingly other, with an otherness that perhaps we need. There is a floating sexual curiosity and potential love that in your parents has come to earth and borne fruit and that the blended shade of your dear brown skins will ever advertise. Self-consciousness includes consciousness of one's color, and an American is aware of his or her color as one color among many, as one site in a web of racial tension and mutual ethnic watchfulness.

While integration has overtaken the media image of ourselves, the reality lags behind. Until I went to college I had hardly met a black person. In my profession, though I have had polite exchanges with a number of black authors, I have never dealt with a black as an editor, printer, or publishing executive. Across the politest of exchanges between blacks and whites a shadow falls, an apprehensiveness and wary memory like the dapple under a trellised grapevine. In the Northern cities, the stereotypical black is a mugger, addict, dropout, and outlaw, inheriting the red Indian's role of native menace – the avenging angel, as it were, of the natural wilderness we assaulted by coming to America at all, with our Bibles and plows and guns. As blacks, you will shoulder here a load of history and mythology that may hide you from yourselves and cut into your freedom to pursue happiness. You will each be in subtle (at best) ways the focus of distaste and hatred and fear that have nothing to do with anything but your skins.

Still, we must all take our chances, and the world is not anywhere basically a friendly place, though our mothers and fathers and schoolteachers would make it seem so. If you boys do live your lives here, you will become something that neither of your parents are: black Americans. None of your kin can perfectly advise you in taking up this identity. Though exactly half white, you will be considered black, just as from the day of christening your African names have overpowered your English ones in the mouths of your kin, white and black both. Even as I write you this letter that you are not ready to read, I foresee how estranging my own whiteness may eventually become, and how certain unselfconscious moments now (the moment, for instance, when Anoff, visiting "Grandpa's house," wordlessly and confidently climbed into the fertilizer spreader to be given a ride, or the moment the other evening when fretful little Kwame let himself be walked to sleep on my shoulder) are the maximum we may ever achieve in mutual ease and trust. America is still to some degree waiting to be made, and will be for each of us what we make of it. May you both, if this old wilderness is to be your nation, find it "as good a country as any man need to dwell in."

What's in a name? My family history, which in its most distinguished and interesting chapters is really just the history of a name I happened to share, was much dimmer in my childish mind than the account just given, and yet did figure in my self-consciousness. I was an Updike, and this distinctive name conveyed that I was somebody, from a line of somebodies. Uncle Furman, Uncle Linc, Aunt Annie, Pennington, Edgewood Avenue – the legendary allusions flew from my father's lips, realer to him than last night's dream. Amidst all the unease and disabilities of his position in Shillington and then in Plowville – the somehow *wounded* air he had, and his odd quest for humiliation; his fondness for sidewalks and strangers, his fascination with the seediest sections of Reading; his strange way of taking off his coat and rolling up his sleeves as if the suit of a white-collar worker were a Nessus's shirt to him; his refusal to fit into either my mother's or the school system's or my own notion of correct behavior; his financial worries, his delicate stomach, his malfunctioning automobiles – for all this he carried himself boldly erect and had an energy of dignity and humor that impressed people. He was an Updike. So was I. Indeed, we were the only two around, since my mother was a Hoyer. And through my father's name I was connected to those Rhode Island planters and New Jersey farmers and lace-collared sea-daring heroes who had made their way to New Amsterdam when it was a little village menaced by Marreckawicks and wolves. It may have not been my *county*, quite – Berks belonged to my mother and her cousins – but the United States was my *country*. And I found it an easy country to love, easier than you boys will – perhaps easier than anyone your age will.

My sentimental treasures include a remarkable group portrait, the assembled Updikes on the occasion of the fiftieth wedding anniversary of my great-grandfather Archibald and his wife, née Mary Elizabeth Titus, in October 1909. My father, aged nine, is in it. He does not look happy. Actually, I possess two versions, having recently been sent a reproduction of this same group in a slightly different pose, with some of its peripheral members removed, and in this second version my father looks miserable, with a hunch and what seems a black eye, but trying nevertheless to smile. In the other, the one that hangs on my office wall, he merely looks pensive, staring into the camera with his deepset eyes and with no attempt to mask what I conjecture to have been an itchy state of boredom. His mouth is sadly beautiful. His ears stick out. His thick hair falls forward over his forehead just the way mine did as a boy; he used to tell me that I had inherited his "stubborn hair." He is wearing a high white collar with round tips. He is standing beside his brother Arch, who is inches taller and adult in expression – wised-up, a tug of amusement at his mouth. On my father's other side, slightly behind him, is a large smooth man, the stoutest in this lean tribe; this is Uncle George, after whom my father (who was born on Washington's Birthday) always said he should have been named. George went to Nebraska to be a banker and reportedly had a drinking problem. In front of my father are three little boys – Ed Sharp, George Sharp, Eugene Drake – whom I remember as big men, in suspenders, at those New Jersey reunions, with their dairy smells and runny-eyed porch cats, that I would be dragged to as a boy, through the shimmering, sticky traffic, across the Delaware, fighting carsickness and losing a precious day at the Shillington playground.

Down front, in 1909, the married couple sits, my great-grandmother as wizened as a monkey and my great-grandfather prim and squinting, with a close white beard and no mustache. He is the only one who does not seem to have moved an inch from one pose to the next. His bewhiskered face is a model of that unflinching Protestant hardness which pushed our nation straight out to the Pacific. When he died, on the last day of 1912, the Trenton *State Gazette* called him "one of the best known residents of Mercer county" but misspelled his name "Updyke." My grandmother Virginia stands on the extreme right of the second row in one photograph and in the next has moved to the first row, and is crouching down, her eyes closed, beside old Margaret Terhune, who wears a cap like a white dishcloth dropped onto her head. Archibald's father, Peter, who "weighed 236 pounds at his death in 1866," had, thirty years before, married a Louisa Terhune; she died in 1887, and Margaret was her sister.* The old lady has been placed with space around her and a rug beneath her feet. The Updikes were proud of their connection with the Terhunes, a family of French origins that numbered among its members the popular novelist Mary Virginia Terhune (1830–1922) and her son, Albert Payson Terhune (1872–1942), who was to write *Lad: A Dog* and other collie tales. My grandmother, who was to die of diabetes in Florida, bulks large here, with a large face wearing an expression of sly pugnacity, that of an Irishman sizing you up in a bar. The women born into the Updike family, as opposed to the plump women who married into it, have a relatively pinched and worried look. A little distance from Uncle Arch stands Aunt Mary, a girl of eleven in white, with long hair hanging down in ropey curls, and her thin features faintly

---

* She is mentioned in a note Hartley wrote his father from Princeton, in 1880:

"Dear Father

Aunt Maggie is about out of money and since she does not expect to receive any before the first of April she requested me to ask you for two or three dollars. If you have it to spare, I would also like to have about a dollar inasmuch as I will have to buy another book.

From Your Son
H.S.U."

pained by her intelligence. She was, I believe, the last person in this photograph to die, in 1985, in her house in Greenwich, blind but still smoking Kools and, she told my mother over the phone the last time they talked, "damn mad" about her decrepitude.

What a thing time is, to pull children up out of this photograph into the lives they led! October's fallen leaves dot the bit of lawn in front of them all, and the well-laid brick walk. Behind them, the house – Archibald's house in Pennington – is very vivid, its broad clapboards and jigsawed little porch brackets and tall paneled window shutters and fringed window shades and the wavy big panes, two over two; the smears of reflected light in the windowpanes look curiously modern, exempt from time. Isn't this the fascination and terror of old photographs, their irrefutable evidence that photons once bathed vanished and disassembled worlds just as brightly as they now bathe ours?

My grandfather Hartley stands in the back row, under a ghost of reflected light, his head slightly tipped, his brow large and pale, his mustache fair and drooping. He wears, uniquely among the men, a wing collar. His hair lies flat, and does not look stubborn, as Archibald's does, combed up in a cocky peak. Hartley would, in 1909, have been back from the West and out of the ministry for more than ten years. I may imagine it, but he already looks wry, haunted, and beaten. In the studio photographs of him as a boy which exist, he looks softer than an Updike should, with an oval face, pale eyes, and a full-lipped mouth nothing like his father's and much like his mother's and the mouths of those other petite, rather langorous Titus girls, Laura Adelaid and Abigail Emma, whose photos survive in the same old thick-leaved album. Around age twenty or so, Hartley has firmed up – his ears look a bit less huge, and he has already grown a mustache as if to hide his womanish upper lip. Folded into the album, fragile as a dried butterfly wing in its envelope (it cost two cents to mail, in 1922), is an awkwardly tender and formal letter he wrote to my father, who was at Ursinus College, playing football, working in the kitchen, and going out with my mother.

Sept 20th 1922

Dear Son Wesley,

   Your letter recd. Am sending you check for $10.00 which will help you out some no doubt. The condemnation proceedings of the Chambers Tract is being held at the City Hall and Arch is directing the cross questioning. He sits at Barkes' right and is right in it. The Commissioners are Judge MacPherson Harry Leavitt and Clifford Worthington. They got the City's witnesses pretty well tangled up yesterday. Mr Chambers witnesses will testify to-day. I hope they make out better than the City's did. I hope that you get along all right with your football and do not get hurt. I would be glad if you could get out of playing this year if you could do so honorably. You have done your share for the College it seems to me.

Yours affct. Father

The stationery bears the address 414 Broad Street Bank Building, Trenton, and identifies my grandfather as an agent of the American International Underwriters of New York. The handwriting is legible but not energetic and a bit uneven. The business decline of "Updike & Son" was presumably well advanced, and Hartley's physical woes were within fifteen months of killing him. My uncle Archibald was, however, "right in it," and the condemnation proceedings must have held some promise for the sagging Updike fortunes. My father, in the event, took his father's advice and did not play football his senior year. Nevertheless, he carried through his life a flattened, often-broken nose. Toward the end of his life, as his circulation weakened, his nose became bluish and grieved me to contemplate: in this, this helpless pity for put-upon, hard-working, battered Wesley Updike, Hartley and I are united.

* * *

Trenton has been preserved from drastic change by decades of relative stagnation. TRENTON MAKES, THE WORLD TAKES, big white block letters still proclaim on the metal bridge connecting the city with Morrisville, across the Delaware in Pennsylvania. A few tall glass-and-steel-skinned buildings rise along the river in the vicinity of the state capitol and the state offices, and a few blocks of State Street have been made into a pedestrian mall wherein an old-fashioned Woolworth's faces the pillared white First Presbyterian Church and its small cemetery; but away from the downtown the streets of brick houses, interspersed with factories, are intact. I visited Trenton, in an attempt to draw closer to my Updike grandfather, on a windy clear November day following an unseasonably early snowstorm. The Broad Street Bank Building still stands, not on Broad Street but at the southwest corner of East State and Montgomery – the biggest building in its vicinity, twelve stories high in its tallest section, with the New Jersey Division of Youth and Family Services now dominating its ground floor. Here Archibald and Hartley and Lincoln and then young Archibald came on their workdays, I imagined, making their way by trolley car, riding into a narrow city heart where no glass-skinned buildings reflected the lights, no shops were boarded up, and no stretches of rubble testified to the need for renewal. The solid little skyscraper held a bank of three elevators guarded by a young Hispanic man who, politely, asked me what I wanted in here. I couldn't exactly say, and left.

At the Free Public Library on Academy Street, I found the old Division Street address – number 128 – in a 1910 directory. The directory was interesting. Not just Updike & Son were listed in it, and Hartley T., but Updikes I had never heard of, or encountered in the genealogy – a Richard Updike, driver, for intance, and a William Updike, livery. Another William was listed as a tilesetter; a Lemuel L., as a carpenter; and a George, not my father's stout uncle, as another "driver." A driver of what, for whom? Could these

193

have been black Updikes, named after a slaveholder, perhaps of the Rhode Island planters or the Virginia clan (which was descended from "John Updike the tailor" [1718–1802], a son of Johannes Opdyck's nameless third son; this John had gone south from the vicinity of Philadelphia and fathered a bevy in Loudoun and Rappahannock Counties)? For that matter, the present-day Trenton-area telephone directory listed ten Updikes, about whom I knew nothing, and who startled me by being there. There were more Updikes in heaven and earth, evidently, than had been dreamt of in my philosophy.

A house-by-house map of Trenton as of 1905 showed "H. T. Updyke" inscribed across a double lot on Division Street, on the south side of town, opposite a large area labelled the Church of the Immaculate Conception. It came dimly back to me: my father as a child had lived across from "Catholic fathers," and had looked in at them over their wall. The wall is still there – an ugly six-foot gray-brown wall of textured cement block, with A-shaped holders for barbed wire in place, though without wire – and a large church, too, well behind the wall, along with parking lots and buildings that antedate 1905. Up the street, at the corner of Division and Hamilton, what was the New Jersey School for the Deaf is now a park, and a block in the other direction, the American Cigar Company building, prominent on the map, is FOR SALE OR LEASE, and most of its windows are walled shut. Division Street itself looked like parts of Shillington – a row of brick two-family homes built with square porches and a space between them just wide enough for an automobile. A man was working on his old tan Chevrolet in one such minimal driveway. The houses were taller than most Shillington homes, and a darker red, and lacked little front yards. At number 128, where the old map showed a single structure occupying a double lot with space all around, three narrow houses of a newer style had been squeezed in, set back a few paces from the sidewalk – bow fronts faced in thin orange brick.

Aunt Mary in her grandmother's book described the Division Street house with some pride: "We had an acre, 200 × 210. It was a frame six-room house with a barn in the rear of the property. There was a porte-cochere over the driveway with wisteria trained on it. The wisteria frequently sent its tendrils into the bathroom, but didn't bloom then. We had a wrap-around porch, roofed in tin across the front of the house and about ⅔ of one side. Two access doors opened on the porch; one to the living room; one to the kitchen, which extended the entire width of the house." No trace remained of this capacious house. A mean-minded renovation had forced three narrow residences into the space where once one had stood. A similar though less drastic change had overtaken my old Shillington home: the front sun parlor, where I used to read the newspaper to my grandfather Hoyer before his cataract operation,* had been expanded into a doctor's office that blocked out the generous side yard. This Philadelphia Avenue house, my mother thinks, had pleasantly reminded my father of the Division Street place – long houses with greenery around them, on busy streets – and its acquisition by the prosperous-feeling, retirement-minded Hoyers in 1922 may have significantly enhanced her marriageability in his

---

* "On the front-parlor rug was a continent-shaped stain where as a baby I had vomited. Myth upon myth: now I am three or four, a hungry soul, eating dirt from one of the large parlor pots that hold strange ferns – feathery, cloudy, tropical presences. One of my grandmother's superstitions is that a child must eat a pound of dirt a year to grow strong. And then later, at nine or ten, I am lying on my belly, in the same spot, reading the newspaper to my blind grandfather – first the obituaries, then the rural news, and lastly the front page headlines about Japs and Roosevelt. The paper has a deep smell, not dank like the smell of comic books but fresher, less sweet than doughnuts but spicy, an exciting smell that has the future in it, the smell of things stacked and crisp and faintly warm, the smell of the *new*. Each day, I realize, this smell arrives and fades. And then I am thirteen and saying goodbye to the front parlor. We are moving. Beside the continent-shaped stain on the carpet are the round stains of the fern flowerpots. The uncurtained sunlight on these stains is a revelation. They are stamped deep, like dinosaur footprints." – "Plumbing" (1970)

eyes. He was too urban a creature, it could well be, to have wed the resident of a little sandstone country farmhouse; and in that case I would never have been born. This shuffle of houses and family fortunes in the early Twenties caused my card, a decade later in the game, to come up.

At mid-day, Division Street seemed scarcely inhabited; the man fussing with his car, and two other men of the same age, wearing wool shirts and polyester windbreakers, plodded into the wind, past the shreds of yesterday's snowstorm, in the same stooped style, a rachitic, nicotinic style familiar to me from my years around Reading – the industrial workingman's style, simultaneously bleary, patient, bitter, stunted, and cocky. Such men must have patrolled the street eighty years ago, across from the same dingy ecclesiastical wall, in those years when the Roebling Company's works, fabricating wire and wire rope, occupied acres and acres not many blocks away. The block's social status, though, had probably sunk over the years, with consciousness of better neighborhoods rising on the edge of town. It was hard to imagine that a realtor and former clergyman lived now in any of these houses.

On the other, northern side of town, Edgewood Avenue is five blocks long, ending at Cadwalader Park. It has a low and a high side, and the houses on the high side, above wide terraces of ivy and lawn, are grand and stately single homes that perhaps once did back up to the edge of a wood; they looked to have been built later, after the low side. Number 913, given as Hartley Updike's address in the 1915 Trenton directory, was on the low side – the lefthand half of a large wooden duplex that had surrendered its initial symmetry to the years. Both sides were painted green, but 913 a paler green, and it had lost the full graciousness of the double-decker porch, with tapered pillars, possessed by its Siamese twin, number 915. But, unlike 915, 913 had kept its stained-glass upper window lights, and the ornate interlocking mullions of the third-story window, high in the shared gable.

Was it up there that the Updike children would crouch listening to their father curse in the basement? A Toyota station wagon was parked out front, and the street, unlike Division Street had trees – a double row of them, thinly golden at this time of year, receding toward the park. Again, I saw few residents, but all of those I did see – two men in overalls walking together and joking, a single woman with a serious face getting out of her car, another woman getting into hers with a slam and driving away – were, Anoff and Kwame, not Dutch or German or Scotch-Irish or English in ancestry, but African. Edgewood Avenue, to which the Updikes had aspired at their peril, is now a solidly black neighborhood.

Our family trips to the Trenton area had always taken us to the outskirts – to White Horse, where the Sharps had their farm, or Ewingville, where the Drakes lived, or Pennington, where the Updikes were buried. I had waited until now to visit these ancestral sites in Trenton. My father should have been with me. With what effortless details and reminiscences could he have animated the mute streets and enigmatic façades! He would have banished my uncertainties and rebuilt these neighborhoods before my eyes. But he was dead fifteen years and I was a lone pilgrim. Driving away, between the much-bridged Delaware and the grandiose state capitol, I realized that the Trenton he had planted in my head was a city not of bricks but of feelings – a city of expressionistic hills and chasms, of deep snowstorms and towering civic monuments, all impinging crushingly upon himself and his poor hapless father. It was a city of suffering, lit, like Thurber's remembered Columbus, by incongruous visitations: Woodrow Wilson, while Governor, had once been a guest in their house on Division Street, as well as the strange characters my grandmother's Southern hospitality irrepressibly conjured off the sidewalks. There were always strangers at the table, though there had been not enough food for the children. My father's growing legs, as my mother tells it, had been weakened by malnutrition. And then, supposedly, one of his shoulders had been left higher than the other because of carrying the papers on the famous paper route: his paper route, an epic ordeal of early rising and thankless perambulation in all weathers that had made him so sleepy at school he had finally dropped out entirely. The paper route had been undertaken to help out his poor failing father. Father and son, bound together by pity and struggle in a down-sliding world: that had been his re-enactment with me, those cold days when we rose to drive off to high school in our treacherous second-hand cars, those long evenings trying, on a wandering course, to get back to the farm and supper. Had my father been with me in Trenton, he could have pointed out to me the streets where he carried papers, and the house on Division Street where the German girl he had once loved had lived. Her family had been recent immigrants, and his family, good conventional Hun-haters during World War I, had discouraged the match. But he had gone off to college and found another German girl, my mother. We will do what we want in one guise or another.

I drove away feeling better about my grandfather Hartley's life. It had occurred, like everyone else's, half in daylight. He had daily dressed in gentlemanly attire and gone to work in a centrally located edifice veneered in granite and marble; he had made his way through the comfortable low close streets of a small city that yet had the pride and consolation of being its state's capital; he had lived near parks, and led his family to church with a rapid stride; his web of work and hope and pretense and respectability had held up until near the end; and he had left his name for not only his two sons but, remarkably, his married daughter to extend into future generations. He had carried his length of the genetic chain, though his constitution had probably never been strong. All lives are failures, regarded from the standpoints of their unfulfilled possibilities and their sorry ends. In the meantime, in places like Trenton, we manage. We move from day to day. We find food enough to eat and stay a step ahead of our creditors. We survive and breed.

Dear boys, the world I grew up in was raw and rough enough to threaten the survival of decent people, who paid their dues, revered their flag, honored God and their parents, tried to do the right thing. How often, in the household of my childhood, did I hear of people trying to do the right thing! That there *was* a right thing seems an old-fashioned notion now; the family I grew up in was so old-fashioned we quoted proverbs aloud, to give each other courage and direction. *Willful waste makes woeful want. A fool and his money are soon parted.* My maternal grandfather would pronounce these in a clear and elocutionary voice made melancholy by the suspicion that no one was listening. My father had evolved minimal consolations, which he often offered aloud: *No matter what happens to you, it will be a new experience. You don't get something for nothing. Dog eat dog.* Sitting in a chair, he would suddenly announce, *I hate everybody*, and a remarkably diverse number of things reminded him, he informed his immediate family, of death. I took these words to be pedagogically offered as a realistic counterbalance to my own innate optimism and capacity for self-serving fantasy. He was a teacher, by instinct as well as fate, and hardly a day goes by that I do not remember his telling me, with a satisfaction so keen as to have cosmic implications, *Water is the great solvent.* Artistically I have lived by his advice in regard to buttering bread: *Butter toward the edges; enough gets in the middle anyway.* My mother had fewer slogans, but in doing research for her often-revised but never-published novel about Ponce de León, she discovered a proverb she said was Spanish but perhaps exists in many languages: *Take what you want and pay the price for it.*

I envision my paternal grandfather as having been, like me, bookish and keen to stay out of harm's way; we aspired to the clerisy, and the price that we pay, we Americans who shyly wish to live by our eyes and wits, at our desks, away from the frightening tussle of human strength and appetite and intimidation and persuasiveness, is marginality: we live chancily, on society's crumbs in a sense, as an exchange for our exemption from the broad brawl of, to give it a name, salesmanship. My father, in his desperate economic straits in the years surrounding my birth,* once tried salesmanship, and walked the streets of Birdsboro offering insurance to other inhabitants of the Depression, and on returning to Philadelphia Avenue went to bed for several days, beaten. His father, too, does not seem to have been a good enough salesman, though he persisted at it longer. Trenton and its business matters were the price he paid for taking an exit from the ministry. But visiting the city left me with less sense of him as a "poor devil," and with much less sense of my father as an exile: I was struck by how much like Shillington and Reading the older streets of Trenton looked. Wesley Updike had in fact only slightly extended, another sixty miles, the westward trend that Johannes had set in 1697 when he trekked from crowded Dutch Kills to the fresh paradise of West Jersey.

* His employment record, in the difficult decade between his graduation from college and his becoming a math teacher at Shillington High in the fall of 1934, was always vague to me, and perhaps belongs with this attempt to account for my self. For the school year 1923–24 he was the principal of the high school at Green Cove Springs, Florida. The following school year, he taught in Harrington, Delaware. From July 1925 to January 1926 he was a field superintendent for a small oil and natural-gas field in New Waterford, Ohio; his bride's defection from this field hastened his own departure. In the year following, he lived in Shillington with his in-laws and served as desk clerk at a number of hostelries – the Wyomissing Club in Reading, the Reading Hotel on South Sixth Street, and the Colonial Hotel on North Sixth Street. His experiences, especially at the second place, gave him his intimacy with the low-life side of Prohibition-era Reading. An A.T. & T. crew planting poles west of Reading stayed at the Colonial and took a great liking to him and carried him off, for his five happy years (February 1927 to June 1932) on the road. His monthly salary in these years ran to no more than a hundred dollars, of which fifteen was faithfully sent to his mother in Florida. After being laid off, he babysat for me, worked for the WPA in the bitter winter of 1933, and accumulated education credits at Albright College, in Reading, qualifying him to teach in the Shillington public schools.

I am, it could be said, a New Jersey Updike who aspired to be a Rhode Island Updike; I heard of those other Updikes' far-off distinction and moved to New England and have become a typophile and an Episcopalian. But, in terms of life's continuum, my grandfather Hartley was more of a success than Daniel B. Updike, who left behind only a lot of beautifully printed pages, a name that lingered for a time in elite Boston circles, and a chaste little slate marker in a Wickford churchyard. Our ancestors lived that we may live. We reverence them because they participate in the mystery of our own being.

We are all of mixed blood, and produce mixed results. At a low time in my life, when I had taken an exit not from my profession but from my marriage, and left your mother and her siblings more in harm's way than felt right, my mother in the midst of her disapproval and sadness produced a saying so comforting I pass it on to you. She sighed and said, "Well, Grampy used to say, 'We carry our own hides to market.'" The saying is blunt but has the comfort of putting responsibility where it can be borne, on a frame made to fit. The comfort of my hearing it said lay of course in its partial release from tribal obligations – our debt of honor to our ancestors and our debt of shelter to our descendants. These debts are real, but realer still is a certain obligation to our own selves, the obligation to live. We are social creatures but, unlike ants and bees, not just that; there is something intrinsically and individually vital which must be defended against the claims even of virtue. *Quench not the spirit. Do not hide your light beneath a bushel basket. Do not bury your talent in the ground of this world.* In this grandfatherly letter about my paternal grandfather, whom I never knew, let me end by offering you, as part of your heritage, this saying ascribed to my other grandfather, John Hoyer, whom I knew well, who watched me grow from infancy and who lived in good health until he was over ninety. *You carry your own hide to market.*

Love,
Grandpa

VI

On Being a Self Forever

When I look up at a blank blue sky, or rest my gaze on a bright surface of snow, I become aware of a fixed pattern of optical imperfections – specks in my vitreous humor like frozen microbes – that float always, usually unnoticed, in the field of my seeing. These are part of my self. From the distant days when I wanted to be a graphic artist, I have an odd habit of tracing what I see with a mental finger or pen – outlining a shoe or foot, drawing diagonals across window-panes, tracing a curtain pattern while my real finger slightly twitches. This, too, this idiotic tic, is my self. Throughout each and every day of my life, scraps of old songs come into my head, most persistently and irresistibly, the opening lines of a faded tune from my high-school days called "The Old Lamp Lighter":

> He made the night a little brighter
> Wherever he would go,
> The old lamp lighter
> Of long, long ago.

And also, at other times, this catchy couplet –

> Your good-bye
> Left me with eyes that cry –

not to mention

> I'm bidin' my time;
> 'Cause that's the kind-a guy I'm.

These random bytes of recollection are part of my self, as is that ridiculous repetitive voice that, with its rehashed anxieties and blurred recollections, keeps me company during insomnia, and has an intelligence so feeble it sometimes forgets the Lord's Prayer.

When I sign my name, which I seem to do ever more often, to books and checks, I find it increasingly difficult to get past the "d" – something in the rhythm of the "Up" produces a forced rest, a freeze in the little motor muscles, at the top of the "d," so that the ink, if from a felt-tip pen, begins to bleed, and to make a blue star, and to leak through to the other side of the paper. This unprompted hesitation, in what should be a fluent practiced signature, I think of as my self – a flaw that reveals my true, deep self, like a rift in Antarctic ice showing a scary, skyey blue at the far bottom. And in the palm of my right hand, in the meaty part below the index finger, exists a small dark dot, visible below the translucent skin, a dot that is, I know, the graphite remains of a stab with a freshly sharpened pencil that I accidentally gave myself in junior high school one day, hurrying between classes in the hall, a moment among countless forgotten moments that has this ineradicable memorial. I still remember how it hurt, and slightly bled – a slow dark drop of blood, round as a drop of mercury. I think of it often. Our waking thoughts tend to be absurd. I think about whether or not my fingernails need cutting and why my shoelaces keep coming untied (obviously, because I didn't learn how to tie them properly in Miss Becker's kindergarten). Since adolescence, I have frequently noticed that, when I lift the first knuckle of the index finger of my left hand to my nose, I can detect a distant putridity, a faint bad smell that is always (somehow satisfyingly) there, no matter how often I wash my hands. Such embedded data compose my most intimate self – the bedrock, as it were, beneath my more or less acceptable social, sexual, professional performance. Do I really want it, this self, these scattered fingerprints on the air, to persist forever, to outlast the atomic universe?

Those who scoff at the Christian hope of an afterlife have on their side not only a mass of biological evidence knitting the self-conscious mind tight to the perishing body but a certain moral superiority as well: isn't it terribly, well, *selfish*, and grotesquely egocentric, to hope for more than our animal walk in the sun, from eager blind infancy through the productive and procreative years into a senescence that, by the laws of biological instinct as well as by the premeditated precepts of stoic virtue, will submit to eternal sleep gratefully? Where, indeed, in the vast spaces disclosed by modern astronomy, would our disembodied spirit go, and, once there, what would it do? The *New Yorker* cartoonist, to occasion a laugh, has merely to limn white-robed people on clouds, with harps – a popular image derived from a single Biblical verse, Revelation 14:2 – and haloes thrown in for added risibility. The Bible in fact says very little about Heaven, aside from the extensive measurements in Ezekiel and the glimpses of the crystalline city with streets of gold in Revelation 21. The founders of the Christian faith were not unaware, even in their relatively naïve cosmos, of potential posthumous absurdities; Jesus fended off the question of the Sadducees about the après-resurrection embarrassments of the often-married (Mark 12:18–27; Matthew 22:23–33; Luke 20:27–40), and Paul, as he expounds to his captors in Caesarea how Christ was the first of many to rise from the dead, is told by the Roman procurator that much learning has made him mad (Acts 26:23–24). Paul waveringly tends to construe resurrection metaphorically, as the spiritual renewal that righteousness in Christ brings, and to distinguish as if Platonically between the natural body and the spiritual body (1 Corinthians 15:44). He rejected, however, the Gnostic idea that the resurrection has already taken place (2 Timothy 2:18), and in 1 Corinthians 15:12–14 ringingly rebuffed doubters within the early Church: "How say some of you that there is no resurrection of the dead? But if there is no resurrection of the dead, then is Christ not risen; and if Christ be not risen, then is our preaching vain, and your faith is also vain." The church, in arriving at its orthodoxy, insisted no less firmly than modern materialism that the body *is* the person, and left us with a tenet, the resurrection of the dead, that has become unthinkable, though it remains part of the Apostles' Creed professed in chorus by millions every Sunday.

If we picture the afterlife at all, it is, heretically, as the escape of something impalpable – the essential "I" – from this corruptible flesh, occurring at the moment of death and not at "the last trump" as Paul stated and as hundreds of medieval sculptors tried to imagine on church tympani. The thought of this long wait within the tomb afflicts us with claustrophobia and the fear of becoming lost forever; where is our self during the long interval?* The winged heads on Puritan tombstones do not represent ascended angels but souls hovering in that abyss between death and resurrection. The idea that we sleep for centuries and centuries without a flicker of dream, while our bodies rot and turn to dust and the very stone marking our graves crumbles to nothing, is virtually as terrifying as annihilation. Every attempt to be specific about the afterlife, to conceive of it in even the most general detail, appals us. Our medically clever era has achieved many practical resurrections, and the testimony of these returnees from the beyond, their reports of a radiant tunnel and a suffusing love, have a kitschy triviality, a funhouse air, that allows an atheistic novelist like Kurt Vonnegut to incorporate them good-humoredly into his novel *Galápagos*. Our brains are no longer conditioned for reverence and awe. We cannot imagine a Second Coming that would not be cut down to size by the televised evening news, or a Last Judgment not subject to pages of holier-than-Thou second-guessing in *The New York Review of Books*. Not only do we feel morally superior to the Biblical notions of atonement and damnation, but our sharpened sense of fact and image resists vague reassurance. Another good-humored clear thinker, George Bernard Shaw,

---

* "Well, where is our soul, then, in this gap?"
           – "Pigeon Feathers" (1960)

at the age of ninety-two proposed that personal immortality would be an "unimaginable horror";* and we do find it hard to picture any endlessly sustained condition or activity that would not become as much a torture as live entombment.

In fact we do not try to picture the afterlife, nor is it our selves in our nervous tics and optical flecks that we wish to perpetuate; it is the self as window on the world that we can't bear to think of shutting. My mind when I was a boy of ten or eleven sent up its silent screams at the thought of future aeons – at the thought of the cosmic party going on without me. The yearning for an afterlife is the opposite of selfish: it is love and praise for the world that we are privileged, in this complex interval of light, to witness and experience. Though some believers may think of the afterlife as a place of retribution, where lives of poverty, distress, and illness will be compensated for, and where renunciations will be rewarded – where the last shall be first, in other words, and those that hunger and thirst shall be filled – the basic desire, as Unamuno says in his *Tragic Sense of Life*, is not for some *other* world but for *this* world, for life more or less as we know it to go on forever: "The immortality that we crave is a phenomenal immortality – it is the continuation of this present life."

Life as we know it is inextricable from change: our bodily growth and decay, the daily news and weather, the resolution

* In his preface to *Buoyant Billions*: of the Spiritualists, he says, "They believe in personal immortality as far as any mortal can believe in an unimaginable horror." Thirty-seven years earlier, prefacing *Misalliance* (1910), he struck much the same note: ". . . if some devil were to convince us that our dream of personal immortality is no dream but a hard fact, such a shriek of despair would go up from the human race as no other conceivable horror could provoke. With all our perverse nonsense as to John Smith living for a thousand million eons and for ever after, we die voluntarily, knowing that it is time for us to be scrapped, to be remanufactured [here Shaw offers some cold comfort, Life-Force variety], to come back, as Wordsworth divined, trailing ever brightening clouds of glory. . . . After all, what man is capable of the insane self-conceit of believing that an eternity of himself would be tolerable even to himself?"

of old adventures and the possibility of beginning new ones. The Book of Common Prayer concedes this by speaking of our "going from strength to strength" in some unspecified progress beyond the grave, and a puritan religion like Buddhism, founded by an atheist and austere even to the exclusion of deliberate austerity, acquires in popular application a heaven of bustling, bejewelled complexity – the Land of Bliss, the Buddha Realm of Amitabha. Ridiculous, excessive, unreasonable, you say? No more, the response must be, than existence as it is, than the worlds that are, with trees and flowers, ocean and sky, stars and stones, animals and insects and men. Our self is thrust into a manifold reality that is thoroughly gratuitous, and the faith in an afterlife, however much our reason ridicules it, very modestly extends our faith that each moment of our consciousness will be followed by another – that a coherent matrix has been prepared for this precious self of ours. The guarantee that our self enjoys an intended relation to the outer world is most, if not all, of what we ask from religion. God is the self projected onto reality by our natural and necessary optimism.* He is the not-me personified.

All mysteries are subject to the modernist dissolution. God having been, in the general intellectual mind, thoroughly dissolved into psychology and anthropology, the self itself, that core "I" which we imagine to be so crystalline and absolute within us, can also be attacked and analyzed as a construct that human society bestows, in widening rings out from the mother who first holds and feeds and talks to us and begins to fill our void with her substance. "*Je est un autre*," Rimbaud said a hundred years ago, and a best-selling contemporary novel's hero concludes that "Your *self* . . . is *other people*; all the people you're tied to, and it's only a thread,"

---

* "'We are natural believers,' Emerson says in his essay on Montaigne. 'Belief consists in accepting the affirmations of the soul; unbelief, in denying them.' It was Emerson's revelation that God and the self are of the same substance." — "Emersonianism" (1983)

and a less well-selling novel, *Friday*, by Michel Tournier, taking Defoe's islanded hero Robinson as its hero, observes of the self:

> A first point that must be noted, in attempting to depict the *self* unrelated to others, is that it exists only intermittently, and, when all is said, comparatively seldom. Its presence corresponds to a secondary and as it were reflexive mode of knowledge. What happens in the primary, direct mode? Well, the objects are all there, shining in the sun or buried in the shade, rough or smooth, light or heavy; they are known, tested, touched, even cooked, carved, folded, and so on; whereas I who do the knowing, the tasting, touching, and cooking, have no separate existence except when I perform the act of reflection which causes *me* to emerge – a thing which in fact rarely happens. In that primary state of knowledge my awareness of an object is the object itself, the thing known and perceived without any person knowing and perceiving it. We cannot use the image of the candle shedding its light upon objects. We must substitute another: that of objects shining unaided, with a light of their own. . . . Then suddenly there is a click. The subject breaks away from the object, divesting it of a part of its color and substance. There is a rift in the scheme of things, and a whole range of objects crumbles in becoming *me*. . . .

The frangibility and provisionality of the self is well within our modern competence to perceive. The modern science of psychology treats of the anomalies and discontinuities of self-awareness. The self of schizophrenics splits into voices they hear in their heads, friendly at first and then quarrelsome and strident. The child's ego-sense does not come at birth but slowly emerges from a confusion of its self with the mother's. We each chronically entrust our selves to the subconscious realm of sleep, of dreams where the self wanders among its own raw materials, in an unquestioning present tense, without those limits which give the waking world stability. To me, an astonishing thing about dreams is that we are not more astonished by them, and descend into them each night with so little fear and anticipation of their perils. In our dreams, without feeling a discontinuity, we become smaller or younger or even another person altogether, who leans up against our real self like a doleful contiguous bodyguard. And who can say in what sense self-consciousness resides within a cretin, a dog, an ant, a tree? Trees, it lately seems, communicate, and become anxious when the chain saw approaches. How much more distinctly individual are bees in a hive than the cells in our body, cells which apparently have appropriated organelles like mitochondria from some earlier stage of individuation? Is not the self, as understood in the United States of the "me decade," a precarious and luxurious invention quite different from the constantly shared and submerged self of a primitive tribesman, or the compacted identity of those Roman soldiers who would shout out, "Decimate us!"?

When does the self dawn? The impressions we acquire before the age of three remain subsconscious, though they flavor our lives forever. My own deepest sense of self has to do with Shillington, and (at a certain slant) the scent or breath of Christmas. I become exhilarated in Shillington, as if my self is being given a bath in its own essence. There – in the words of the Tournier quotation – objects shine unaided, with a light of their own. This light is less strong, now, around the white Shillington house in which I was raised than around those two bulky brick houses across from the new movie theatre, where the luncheonette and the post office once were, and where Ernie Rothermel performed his first dental operations upon my mouth, and at the back of one of which lived Carl Leh, our brave policeman, under some cloud of disgrace, and on the porch of another of which I used to wait for my father to get done counting athletic receipts in the living room of Fred Grimes. Fred was a cripple, like Shorty Wartluft – not a hunchback but with one leg in a brace, and an arduous, back-bending way of walking, of poling himself along. I believe he was also, like Shorty, a staunch churchman, or perhaps his patiently suffering smile made me imagine so. At any rate he was a solid Shillington citizen whose living room served as the locus of this fond vision, in the short story "In Football Season":

> I would stride through the hushed streets, where the rustling leaves seemed torn scraps scattered in the wake of the game, and go to Mr Lloyd Stephens' house [a transposition, since Walt and Boo Stephens' luncheonette had been two doors away]. There, looking in the little square window of his front storm door, I could see down a dark hall into the lit kitchen where Mr Stephens and my father and Mr Jesse Honneger [a fictional version of my cough-drop savior Al Richards] were counting money around a worn porcelain table. Stephens, a local contractor, was the school-board treasurer, and Honneger, who taught social science, the chairman of the high-school athletic department. They were still counting; the silver stacks slipped and glinted among their fingers and the gold of beer stood in cylinders beside their hairy wrists. Their sleeves were rolled up and smoke like a fourth presence, wings spread, hung over their heads.

This suggestion of a hovering angel should not distract us from the glinting center of the young voyeur's happy vision: the money, stacks of it, a glorious excess over the coins and worn bills in the Recipes box that sat on top of the icebox at 117 Philadelphia Avenue. It occurs to me now that these Lancaster Avenue houses, between the Borough Hall and the house and garage of our important relatives of the Beckers, represented to my innocent mind city life – the central, power-laden Shillington transactions from which my own family, for all their originality and pretensions to quality, was excluded.

Not only are selves conditional but they die. Each day, we wake slightly altered, and the person we were yesterday is dead. So why, one could say, be afraid of death, when death comes all the time? It is even possible to dislike our old selves, these disposable ancestors of ours. For instance, my high-school self – skinny, scabby, giggly, gabby, frantic to be noticed, tormented enough to be a tormentor, relentlessly pushing his cartoons and posters and noisy jokes and pseudo-sophisticated poems upon the helpless high school – strikes me now as considerably obnoxious, though I owe him a lot: without his frantic ambition and insecurity I would not now be sitting on (as my present home was named by others) Haven Hill. And my Ipswich self, a delayed second edition of that high-school self, in a town much like Shillington in its blend of sweet and tough, only more spacious and historic and blessedly free of family ghosts, and my own relative position in the "gang" improved, enhanced by a touch of wealth and celebrity, a mini-Mailer in our small salt-water pond, a stag of sorts in our herd of housewife-does, flirtatious, malicious, greedy for my quota of life's pleasures, a distracted, mediocre father and worse husband – he seems another obnoxious show-off, rapacious and sneaky and, in the service of his own ego, remorseless. But then, am I his superior in anything but caution and years, and how can I disown him without disowning also his useful works, on which I still receive royalties? And when I entertain in my mind these shaggy, red-faced, overexcited, abrasive fellows, I find myself tenderly taken with their diligence, their hopefulness, their ability in spite of all to map a broad strategy and stick with it. So perhaps one cannot, after all, not love them.

The New Yorker of the Shawn era (1951–87) was a club of sorts, from within which the large rest of literary America – the many other less distinguished and fastidious magazines, the coarsely striving book trade, the tawdry best-seller lists, the sharp-tongued quarterlies and partisan reviews – could be politely disdained. Our good self-opinion, which Shawn maintained with an intellectual confidence and Buddhistic serenity that transcended Ross's agitated perfectionism, made a useful shelter for me, a hard shell I didn't have to grow myself. While I can now almost glimpse something a bit too trusting in the serene sense of artist's well-being, of virtual invulnerability, that being published in *The New Yorker* gave me for over thirty years, the self who looked up into the empyrean of print from that muddy farm in Pennsylvania with its outhouse and coal-oil stove is not so remote from me that I can still think it anything less than wonderful to have become a writer. The very selves that make me most cringe to remember – the self of 1945–48, the little unwilling 4–H member with his strawberry project, picking them for hours in the buggy June heat and peddling them to old family friends in Shillington, and the pathetic undersized catechumen newly enrolled at the Robeson Lutheran Evangelical Church, sucking his bad postwar teeth and painful theological doubts in a class of beefy country cousins; and the self of 1950–51, beset by homesickness and hemorrhoids in his first New England winter and showing up at the *Lampoon* tryouts in slightly wrong clothes (they had a word for it: "wonky") in blissful ignorance of the social dimension of the bastion he is trying to storm – are yet the bravest boys, exiles clinging to a vision, to a belief in print, in ink, in a sacred realm of publication that will redeem them.

And then there are favorite, pet selves – the faithful little habitué of the Shillington playground, in his shorts and sneakers, getting in line for game after game of roof ball, playing checkers and braiding gimp in the shade of the playground pavilion; the lonely psoriatic explorer of Caribbean islands, again in shorts and sneakers, wandering with his poor baked skin through the jostle of tourists and natives, savoring the tattered, fragrant, sleepy traces of the old West Indies, before the jets made it too easy to get to; and the copyboy, in his penny loafers and tucked-back shirtsleeves, for the Reading *Eagle*. During my eighteenth, nineteenth, and twentieth summers (in my twenty-first, I was married), I fetched coffee and doughnuts for the editorial room and carried copy to the linotype room, responding to the shout of "Boy!," joking with the chummier reporters, and admiring the dashing look of the copy itself, the triple-spaced sheets rubber-cemented together in long festoons emended with loops and slashes by the darkest of dark pencils. The factory-like clamor of the linotypes, and the whiff of hot lead, and the operators each with his green eyeshade under his private lamp like so many monks in conical cells of yellow light: these phenomena gratified me, as did the air of early-morning Reading when I made the eight-o'clock coffee run to a diner on Penn Street – the sidewalks damp in spots and the young women tapping to work in their heels and taut skirts, the broad downtown blocks bestirring themselves for another busy weekday, every store from Whitner's up to Pomeroy's occupied in those last years before shopping malls gutted the inner city.

My morning hours were the busiest; by the time I came back from the lunch run with sandwiches for the diners-in, the paper had been put to bed, and there was little to do but perch on a desk and gab until the first run of papers came off the press around two. My remaining duties included taking a paper to Mr Hawley Quier, who owned both the *Eagle* and its morning counterpart, the Reading *Times*; he had a harelip, and I had trouble understanding, at first, his pleasantries from on high. Sometimes (I seem to remember) one took the paper to him at a little dive a half-block up Court Street, where he sat at a round table playing cards of an afternoon. Small-city rich have this engaging way of mingling, in shirtsleeves, with the common man. Reading was a friendly town; its mayors were friendly with racketeers and its mill owners with their tenant farmers and its sole newspaper magnate with a teen-aged copy boy. Like me, Mr Quier had his problems – not only the harelip but his unusual French name; the radio station he owned called itself the Hawley Broadcasting Company, rather than the Quier one. Once in a while, after I had distributed papers through the editorial room, someone would spot a typo bad enough to justify breaking the press run; then the city editor would give me a scrawled slip I would carry – *run*, boy! – down to the thunderous chamber where the presses themselves rotated their great curved plates and rivers of newsprint flooded forth. But generally these afternoon hours were idle enough for me to type, on a spare machine, poems on such topical subjects as the Rosenbergs' execution, or light verse that Jerry Kobrin might publish in his column, or a letter to my Radcliffe girlfriend. In my sense of myself I tap-danced through this palace of print disguised as the lowliest of employees, with my mother-ironed shirtsleeves nicely folded back and my shirt pocket cockily squared by a pack of cigarettes, of Kools in their minty, icy white and green or Philip Morrises in their old-fashioned pack of homely tobacco brown.

It seems marvellous to me that once I smoked. Old photographs in which I am holding a cigarette have in my eyes the black-and-white glamour of stills from Hollywood films noirs. I smoked a great deal, in fact, beginning at the age of fifteen (or could it have been fourteen?) when, as part of my campaign to become more "popular," I bought a pack in Reading, at the railroad station on Seventh Street, and lit my first cigarette as I walked along past the little banistered porches, beneath the buttonwood trees. At the initial puff, the sidewalk lifted as if to strike my forehead, but I fought the dizziness and persevered. The beckoning world of magazines (loaded with cigarette ads) demanded this, not to mention the world of girls. With some determined tutorial work in Stephens' Luncheonette, I learned how to inhale, to double-inhale, to French-inhale, and (just barely) to blow smoke rings. At Harvard, I was up to three packs a day, and my fingertips turned orange. In Oxford, the little stiff cardboard packages of five or ten Churchman's were a novelty, as was, at the back of the slideout part of the package, the lined blank space entitled "Notes" – conjuring up an empire full of Englishmen coolly taking notes, amid grapeshot and cavalry hoofbeats, on their cigarette boxes. In New York, getting worried, I began to experiment with holders, including that awkwardly long type which employs as a filter an entire other cigarette, replaced when it darkens through and through and drips with tar juice. By the time of the move to Ipswich, my self-glamorization in other respects had proceeded far enough that I almost felt able to do without cigarettes as a prop. Now I have long since, in deference to my emphysema, given up smoking, even the smoking of little cigars that, after I broke the cigarette habit, used to get me through the stress of composition. Also, I have given up salt and coffee in deference to high blood pressure and alcohol in deference to methotrex-ate. The big-bellied Lutheran God within me looks on scoffingly. "*Hunde, wollt ihr ewig leben?*" Frederick the Great thundered at his battle-shy soldiers – "Dogs, would you live forever?"

So writing is my sole remaining vice. It is an addiction, an illusory release, a presumptuous taming of reality, a way of expressing lightly the unbearable. That we age and leave behind this litter of dead, unrecoverable selves is both unbear-able and the commonest thing in the world – it happens to everybody. In the morning light one can write breezily, without the slightest acceleration of one's pulse, about what one cannot contemplate in the dark without turning in panic to God. In the dark one *truly* feels that immense sliding, that turning of the vast earth into darkness and eternal cold, taking with it all the furniture and scenery, and the bright distrac-tions and warm touches, of our lives. Even the barest earthly facts are unbearably heavy, weighted as they are with our personal death. Writing, in making the world light – in codifying, distorting, prettifying, verbalizing it – approaches blasphemy.

"Consciousness is a disease," Unamuno says. Religion would relieve the symptoms. Religion construed, of course, broadly, not only the form of the world's barbaric and even atrocious religious orthodoxies but in the form of any private system, be it adoration of Elvis Presley or hatred of nuclear weapons, be it a fetishism of politics or popular culture, that submerges in a transcendent concern the grimly finite facts of our individual human case. How remarkably fertile the religious imagination is, how fervid the appetite for significance; it sets gods to growing on every bush and rock. Astrology, UFOs, resurrections, mental metal-bending, visions in space, and voodoo flourish in the weekly tabloids we buy at the cash register along with our groceries. Falling in love – its mythologization of the beloved and everything that touches her or him – is an invented religion, and religious also is our persistence, against all the powerful post-Copernican, post-Darwinian evidence that we are insignificant accidents within a vast uncaused churning, in feeling that our life is a story, with a pattern and a moral and an inevitability – that, as Emerson said, "a thread runs through all things: all worlds are strung on it, as beads: and men, and events, and life, come to us, only because of that thread." That our subjectivity, in other words, dominates, through secret channels, outer reality, and the universe has a personal structure.

How gorgeously strange the religions of others seem! The world's outstanding believers these days are the Moslems: what forms has God taken in their heads – what does Allah mean to them as they surge forward in their Iranian human waves or Palestinian suicide missions? What common image animates all these close-packed male bodies bowing in unison on some dusty equatorial *masjid?* It is not the Christian God – or gods, for, out of Paraguayan Catholics, Vermont Congregationalists, Utah Mormons, and New Zealand Anglicans sprout as many gods as are carved on a Jain temple wall. The Jewish God, as best He can be glimpsed in the United States, wears yet a different face. He seems meatier, more unbuttoned than His Christian offspring; He does not excite the churchgoer's anxious either/or, that "Does He?" or "Doesn't He?" in regard to His existence, that angst-generating crux of faith. Christianity has somehow taken hold of religion at the wrong end of the stick – the inhuman, or wholly other, end. The Jewish attitude seems in comparison humorous and submissive: it's His choice, to exist or not. The Old Testament God seems brashly free, compared to the locked-in God of Aquinas or Anselm. What theologian was it who, asked for a proof of God's existence, answered, "The Jews"? As long as Jews exist, even as atheistic Marxists or Freudians, a chosen people exists, and in its existence indicates that of a Chooser. Meanwhile, the gods of the Australian aborigines are silenced as if by rotting telephone wires; the bedaubed and naked old men who know the rituals and the sacred places die away, leaving behind grandsons, in boots and bush hats, to whom all rocks are merely rocks. Picasso chastised Matisse for designing and decorating a chapel. Both men were professed atheists. Matisse retorted, "Yes, I do pray; and you pray too, and you know it all too well: when everything goes badly, we throw ourselves into prayer . . . And you do it; you too. It's no good saying no." All anger, a psychotherapist recently told me, is anger at God. "God" is a word, however problematical, we do not have to look up in the dictionary. We seem to have its acquaintance from birth.

For many men, work is the effective religion, a ritual occupation and inflexible orientation which permits them to imagine that the problem of their personal death has been solved. Unamuno: "Work is the only practical consolation for having been born." My own chosen career – its dispersal and multiplication of the self through publication, its daily excretion of yet more words, the eventual reifying of these words into books – certainly is a practical consolation, a kind of bicycle which, if I were ever to stop pedalling, would dump me flat on my side. Religion enables us to ignore nothingness and get on with the jobs of life. Perhaps there are two kinds of people: those for whom nothingness is no problem, and those for whom it is an insuperable problem, an outrageous cancellation rendering every other concern, from mismatching socks to nuclear holocaust, negligible. Tenacious of this terror, this adamant essence as crucial to us as our sexuality, we resist those kindly stoic consolers who assure us that we will outwear the fright, that we will grow numb and accepting and, as it were, religiously impotent. As Unamuno says, with the rhythms of a stubborn child. "I do not want to die – no; I neither want to die nor do I want to want to die; I want to live forever and ever and ever. I want this 'I' to live – this poor 'I' that I am and that I feel myself to be here and now."

The objections of material science and liberal ethics to this desperate wanting belong to the outer, sunlit world, of sense and the senses; our wanting and its soothing belong to the elusive dark world within. Emerson, in *Nature*, points out "the total disparity between the evidence of our own being, and the evidence of the world's being." Evidence of God's being lies with that of our own; it is on our side of the total disparity that God lives. In the light, we disown Him, embarrassedly; in the dark, He is our only guarantor, our only shield against death. The impalpable self cries out to Him and wonders if it detects an answer. Like the inner of the two bonded strips of metal in a thermostat, the self curls against Him and presses. The need for our "I" to have its "Thou", something other than ourselves yet sharing our subjectivity, something amplifying it indeed to the outer rim of creation, survives all embarrassments, all silence, all refusals on either side. The sensation of silence cannot be helped: a loud and evident God would be a bully, an insecure tyrant, an all-crushing datum instead of, as He is, a bottomless encouragement to our faltering and frightened being. His answers come in the long run, as the large facts of our lives, strung on that thread running through all things. Religion includes, as its enemies say, fatalism, an acceptance and consecration of what is.

The thermostat image needs adjusting: God is a dark sphere enclosing the pinpoint of our selves, an adamant bubble enclosing us, protecting us, enabling us to let go, to ride the waves of what is.

Early in my adolescence, trapped within the airtight case for atheism, I made this logical formulation:

1. If God does not exist, the world is a horror show.
2. The world is not a horror-show.
3. Therefore, God exists.

The second premise, of course, is the weaker; newspapers and biology lessons daily suggest that it *is* a horror show, of landslides and plagues and massacres and falling airplanes and incessant carnivorousness. And of – we cannot but be especially conscious these days – venereal disease: what more fiendish proof of cosmic irresponsibility than a Nature which, having invented sex as a way to mix genes, then permits to arise, amid all its perfumed and hypnotic inducements to mate, a tireless tribe of spirochetes and viruses that torture and kill us for following orders? Yet this and all bad news merits reporting because our general expectation is for good: an instinctive vision of health and peace underlies our horror stories. Existence itself does not feel horrible; it feels like an ecstasy, rather, which we only have to be still to experience. Habit and accustomedness have painted over pure gold with a dull paint that can, however, be scratched away, to reveal the shining underbase. The world is good, our intuition is, confirming its Creator's appraisal as reported in the first chapter of Genesis.

During that same adolescence, I reluctantly perceived of the Christian religion I had been born into that almost no one believed it, believed it really – not its ministers, nor its pillars like my father and his father before him. Though signs of belief (churches, public prayers, mottos on coins) existed everywhere, when you moved towards Christianity it disappeared, as fog solidly opaque in the distance thins to transparency as you walk into it. I decided I nevertheless *would* believe it. I found a few authors, a very few – Chesterton, Eliot, Unamuno, Kierkegaard, Karl Barth – who helped me believe. Under the shelter (like the wicker chairs on the side porch) that I improvised from their pages I have lived my life. I rarely read them now; my life is mostly lived. God is the God of the living, though His priests and executors, to keep order and to force the world into a convenient mould, will always want to make Him the God of the dead, the God who chastises life and forbids and says No. What I felt, in that basement Sunday school of Grace Lutheran Church in Shillington, was a clumsy attempt to extend a Yes, a blessing, and I accepted that blessing, offering in return only a nickel a week and my art, my poor little art.

Imitation is praise. Description expresses love. I early arrived at these self-justifying inklings. Having accepted that old Shillington blessing, I have felt free to describe life as accurately as I could, with especial attention to human erosions and betrayals. What small faith I have has given me what artistic courage I have. My theory was that God already knows everything and cannot be shocked. And only truth is useful. Only truth can be built upon. From a higher, inhuman point of view, only truth, however harsh, is holy. The fabricated truth of poetry and fiction makes a shelter in which I feel safe, sheltered within interlaced plausibilities in the image of a real world for which I am not to blame. Such writing is in essence pure. Out of soiled and restless life, I have refined my books. They are trim, crisp, clean, especially in the moment when they arrive from the printer in a cardboard box, before the reviewers leave their smudges all over them, and I discover, like a tiny flower that insists on blooming in the expanse of a shining level salt flat, the first typographical error.

Yet fiction, like life, is a dirty business; discretion and good taste play small part in it. Hardly a story appears in print without offending or wounding some living model who sees himself or herself reflected all too accurately and yet not accurately enough – without that deepening, mollifying element of endless pardon we bring to our own self. Parents, wives, children – the nearer and dearer they are, the more mercilessly they are served up. So my art, like my religion, has a shabby side. These memoirs feel shabby. Truth should not be forced; it should simply manifest itself, like a woman who has in her privacy reflected and coolly decided to bestow herself upon a certain man. She will *dawn* upon that man. My writing here about my religion feels forced – done at the behest of others, of hypothetical "autobiography" readers. Done, I believe, in an attempt to comfort some younger reader as once I was comforted by Chesterton and Unamuno. A *worthy* attempt, which is not, in a larger sense, good: the attempt to work an altruistic good through print is generally a mistake, a miscarriage. I am in these paragraphs struggling to expose what should be – in decency, to conserve potency – *behind*: behind the façade, the human courtesies, my perform- ance, my "act." But there seems, my having gone this unfortunately far, still this to say: one believes not merely to dismiss from one's life a degrading and immobilizing fear of death but to possess that Archimedean point outside the world from which to move the world. The world cannot provide its own measure and standards; these must come, strangely, from outside, or a sorry hedonism and brute opportunism result – a greedy panicked heart and substance abuse. The world punishes us for taking it too seriously as well as for not taking it seriously enough.

Wherever there is a self, it may be, whether on Earth or in the Andromeda Galaxy, the idea of God will arise. Religion, once the self has taken its hook, preaches selflessness. The self is the focus of anxiety; attention to others, self-forgetful- ness, and living like the lilies are urged, to relieve the anxiety. Insomnia offers a paradigm: the mind cannot fall asleep as long as it watches itself. At the first observed lurch into nonsensical thought we snap awake in eager anticipation, greedy to be asleep. Only when the mind moves unwatched and becomes absorbed in images that tug it as it were to one side does self-consciousness dissolve and sleep with its heal- ing, brilliantly detailed fictions pour in upon the jittery spirit. Falling asleep is a study in trust. Likewise, religion tries to put us at ease in this world. Being human cannot be borne alone. We need other presences. We need soft night noises – a mother speaking downstairs. A grandfather rumbling in response, cars swishing past on Philadelphia Avenue and their headlights wheeling about the room. We need the little clicks and sighs of a sustaining otherness. We need the gods.

The pragmatic undercurrent in this exposition troubles me. I am selling short something or Someone precious. It is not enough, surely, to strive for faith because it makes us more effective and holds off terror until the – as Gibbon said – "bad fifteen minutes at the end." Pragmatic belief becomes cynical belief, a papering-over of the secret conviction that eventual annihilation will harmlessly resolve this strenuous unease of living.* Religion and nothingness, that is, are successive doses of anesthetic, the first temporary and imperfect, in throwaway wrappings of dogma and Christmas tinsel, the second permanent and perfect. An age of anxiety all too suitably takes God as a tranquillizer, just as feudal times took Him as Lord or King, leaving us a language of piety loaded with obsolete obeisances, and other eras took him as a magical incantation, or an insatiable repository of blood sacrifice and self-mutilation, or an imperturbable Watchmaker, or a surge of the Life Force. The self's echo and companion must be not only that. One believes not only to comfort one's self but for empirical and compositional reasons – the ornate proposed supernatural completes the picture and, like the ingredient that tops up and rounds out the recipe, gives reality its true flavor. Similarly, in art one has to add a little extra color,

---

* Can the sweetness of riddance extend to *everything*? Emerson wrote in his journals: "Old age brings along with its ugliness the comfort that you will soon be out of it – which ought to be a substantial relief to such discontented pendulums as we are. To be out of the war, out of debt, out of the drouth, out of the blues, out of the dentist's hands, out of the second thoughts, mortifications, and remorses that inflict such twinges and shooting pains – out of the next winter, and the high prices, and company below your ambition – surely these are soothing hints. And, harbinger of this, what an alleviator is sleep, which muzzles all these dogs for me every day?"

some overanimation, to bring the imitation up to the pitch, the bright roundedness, the repletion, of the actual model.

Of my own case, looked at coldly, it might be said that, having been given a Protestant, Lutheran, rather antinomian Christianity as part of my sociological make-up, I was too timid to discard it. My era was too ideologically feeble to wrest it from me, and Christianity gave me something to write about, and a semblance of a backbone, and a place to go Sunday mornings, when the post offices were closed.

What I have written strains to be true but nevertheless is not true *enough*. Truth is anecdotes, narrative, the snug opaque quotidian.

Pennsylvania. There. Here. Staying in my mother's farmhouse. Yet again. I cannot count the times I have gone back over these years since 1950 – by train from Harvard, by car from New York and New England, and now most commonly by airplane, often on the way back from somewhere else.

My mother is old, she has not been well. This summer she fell in the kitchen, and the fall hurt her back and abdomen and has taken something out of her. She has taken to her bed, and says it is too painful to get up and walk around.

I don't know quite what to do about her. "She lives *alone?*" people ask me, with round eyes and an implication of filial neglect. In this conservative region family members tend to stick close to one another. Four generations of Mennonites live all together on the neighboring farm. I am waiting for her to tell me what to do about her. I find that the older she becomes, the more my image of her is of someone young: the young mother in the Shillington back yard with the fireflies and flowering cherry trees, the tall laughing college girl posing with my father in his football sweater, and even the little girl raised on this farm with a batch of complaining and ailing old people. She taught herself from books to name the birds and flowers, setting out a little wildflower garden under a black birch tree that, grown thick and lopsided, is still there, though now only weeds grow beneath it – weeds and wild raspberries and a few scraggly Japanese lanterns brought from the Shillington yard forty years ago. When she was very small, my mother once settled herself in a basket of clean wash in imitation of a nesting robin, and was scolded by her mother for it. An only child like me, she made her paradise, her escape hatch, out of the nature around her, leaving no living thing on her father's farm unnamed, much as I, once, could identify all the cartoonists in *Collier*'s upside down. Her diary, kept sporadically over the years, takes note of the weather and the songs of the birds, returning year after year, as they sound in the woods to the west, through whose branches the red sun sets. During these more than a dozen years since my father died, her voice over the telephone has always sounded young – quick and playful and interested in life, in the reality modulated by our "vocabulary," by our "gay-making" slant on the world. I am alarmed and depressed by what seems her withdrawal from the world – she stopped, after her fall, cooking, driving, watching television, writing, reading, and eating. All she manages to do is feed the dog and the cats and talk on the telephone to her well-wishers and to the numerous charity fund-raisers who call up relentlessly from Reading, asking an annual renewal of her little widow's mite of ten or fifteen dollars. There is no end of giving.

Her will to live, anciently involved with mine, has been slowly reviving this autumn. Tonight she let herself be driven out to dinner with some friends from Lancaster. Now we have returned, adjusted the dog and the thermostat, and gone to bed. Our bedrooms have between them a wall and door so thin we can hear each other breathe. My wife wonders how five of us once managed in this little house, all sleeping in this same upstairs, and all I can say is that at the time, to the child I was, it seemed big enough. My parents and grandparents each had a room and I slept in a bed in a space that served also as a kind of hall at the head of the stairs. There were voices, true – coughs and sighs and snoring, bedsprings creaking and the sound of my father patting my mother and making a humorous woo-woo noise that signified affection; but when one is young space curls up tight inside the blankets and it is not so hard to fall asleep through the hole that opens at the bottom of one's brain.

Now, it is harder. I am old, though not as old as my mother. It was not easy for me to drive her back from the restaurant, through an unseasonable sleet storm, early in this November. The wipers struggled against the freezing rain, the headlights coming at us were smeared and magnified, and she had been fearful that I was going to hit a deer, because deer did now and then cross this dark highway. Without saying so, I found her repeated concern rather sentimental and hysterical, especially since the deer would be slaughtered in hunting season less than a month away. Now the sleet patters on the windows and makes a crinkling sound in the fireplace, as the individual pellets tumble through, into the room. It would be cozy if the bed were not so cold, unwarmed by a woman. My wife stays away, as a gift, she says, to my mother. The room has two windows, a low ceiling, this never-used fireplace, and wallpaper, patterned with rosettes and little pink roses, that hasn't changed since I can remember. Even the decorative changes are slow: an uncompleted oil painting I did of my first wife was retired to a drawer around the time of our divorce, and more recently a felt piece of local kitsch I always disliked has been taken down. It showed an Amishman standing erect with a hammer and a carpenter's square, above the slogan WHAT A MAN DOES, THAT HE IS. I believe it but didn't like reading it. My suitcase is spread open across two straight chairs, and a Harvard yearbook and an early Peter Arno cartoon anthology sit on a bedside table; these books never change, and in the table's drawer are pencils so old their erasers don't erase and even the graphite has gone waxy and refuses to write. Time moves slowly here but does move, and is overtaking my mother.

Which visit will be my last? We do not know, or speculate. I can hear her breathe, with the loudness that signifies sleep.

The drive home from the restaurant, the unseasonable sleet, and my entire life all rankle in me. I have come here from some Midwestern university where I read and talked into a microphone and was gracious to the local rich, the English faculty and college president, and the students with their clear skins and shining eyes and inviting innocence, like a blank surface one wishes to scribble obscenities on. I need these excursions, evidently: they reassure me that I don't stutter, or stutter too much. They leave me feeling dirty and disturbed, as though I have wasted this time away from my desk, posing as an author instead of being one, and it is hard to get back from the academic unreality and ponderous flattery into my own skin. These leftover feelings are complicated by the sensations of enchantment and claustrophobia that occupy me now in this little overfamiliar room, surrounded by musty memories and the whisper of sleet and the sounds of my mother and the dog sleeping. My light is on and I feel this as a discordant note in the countryside; Plowville, once so empty that not another houselight could be seen from our house, is being invaded by developments. The farms are being broken up into two-acre lots. The thousands of acres between here and Morgantown once owned by Bethlehem Steel, and kept as forest against the potential exploitation of their low-grade iron ore, have been sold to a Chester County developer who has visions of golf courses and amusement parks and incinerators that will turn all of Philadelphia's trash into smoke. A raw new development begins on the other side of my mother's meadow, which she has not been able to mow this fall, since her injuries prevent her from getting up on the tractor. I can see its lights through my window, whose sash rattles. By my bedside light I am reading a book for review: book-reviewing is another superfluous chore that I do, like the public readings, for the money and for the easy exposure of it, the showing-off, the quick certification from a world that I fear is not hearing me, is not *understanding* me, like Eddie Pritchard long ago. And tomorrow (or is it the next day?) I must drive to Trenton, to research the fifth chapter of this exposition of my self-consciousness.

I rub my face. My forehead, full of actinic damage from all those years of seeking the healing sun, hurts. My public, marketable self – the self put on display in interviews and slightly "off" caricatures in provincial book-review sections, the book-autographing, anxious-to-please me – feels like another skin and hurts also. I look over at my younger self on the wall: a photograph taken in Earl Snyder's studio on Penn Street when I was five wearing a kind of sailor collar, the edges blurred away – "vignetted" – in old-fashioned studio style, an image cherished by my mother, nicely framed the workmanlike way they do things in Reading, and always hanging there, in this spot, for me to admire and remember: little Johnny, his tentatively smiling mouth, his dark and ardent and hopeful eyes. For a second he looks evil. He has got me into this.

In this room, with its cold clammy bed and cobwebbed corners and sandstone fireplace hearth, I have often on these visits had asthma, so that I slept only a few hours and woke with a pulse racing from repeated use of isoproterenol. But my asthma, like my stuttering, seems to be less a factor, as the actualities of aging overtake me, and the shadows lengthen around my walk in the sun. Earlier today, we had driven into Shillington, so my mother could visit her doctor. The doctor's office, as it happens, is next to the movie theatre where, seven years before, *Being There* had been playing while I waited for my lost luggage. Now the daughter whose failure adequately to tip the porter at Logan perhaps delayed the luggage is the mother of my two grandsons. Now the theatre, the last trace of fantasy to this small town, is closed; to see a movie in Berks County now, one must go to a shopping mall. The marquee bears the unchanging advertisement GRACE FELLOWSHIP; the building has become a church. Across Lancaster Avenue, the big orange brick duplex, with its aura of downtown power, that had held Stephens' Luncheonette and the post office and Carl Leh at the back and now Admixtures, Inc., and, next door to it, the taller, older, graver building where Fred Grimes had counted money and where Ernie Rothermel had first sat me in his chair, have been joined by a new, unharmonious structure in what had always been a vacant lot or generous side yard. My mother's doctor's office is in another new building on a site where, when I was a child, travelling fairs would set up their rides and stalls. One of the few times I ever sat in a saddle was on this land, at such a fair; I was small and seemed appallingly high up, on a huge, warm, smelly, rough-haired, nervous thing, though the animal was a mere pony, led by a boy not much older than I.

After the visit to the doctor, my mother and I had driven down Lancaster Avenue to the area of the Poorhouse Lane, now a shopping mall one of whose attractions was a medical center where she could have her blood drawn for some tests. Her young doctor seemed determined to keep her alive. As her arm, its dry skin extra loose from her weight loss since her fall, was pierced, she engaged in one of her flirtatious, slightly baffling exchanges with the nurse; how like, it now seemed, my father she was, spontaneously grappling with strangers, agggressively seeking contact in inappropriate places. In my embarrassment I wandered off and pondered the marvellous devices offered in this medical center for the use and easement of old age – canes and braces and pans and wheelchairs, and toilet seats thickened like a clubfoot's shoe, and long canelike pincers to retrieve what can no longer be bent over for: a veritable armory as complex as a medieval knight's, our Grail now simply the indefinite prolongation of life.

And then in this medical center, astoundingly, a miracle of sorts had occurred. In came a living relic of my Shillington boyhood – Reverend Rhoads, who had been, with Reverend Kroninger, one of the two pillars of the local Protestant clergy, the pastor of the Reformed Church up New Holland Avenue, a frequent and orotund speaker at high-school assemblies and civic observances. He had been a short owlish man with wobbly jowls and a strong voice. Under the impact of old age his face had as it were exploded into separate elements – plump cheeks, button nose, mottled forehead, thick throat wattles – but his voice was still vibrant and his eyes alert behind their bifocals; and his wife in all these years that had flowed by since I had left Shillington had turned white-haired but remained handsome and even frisky, with good trim ankles and a dazzling broad smile. She told me she remembered watching my mother carry me up New Holland Avenue. Did she mean carrying me in her arms, or carrying me in her womb? I tried to picture my mother, a young woman walking about Shillington at the outset of the Depression, her husband still off with the phone company, the automobiles in the street dark and boxy, the porches and brick housefronts of Shillington much then as they are now, and New Holland Avenue then as now slanting up to the cemetery and the tree-lined lane that led to Cedar Top past the Dives Estate. In this remoteness of time I had been somehow present, and the Rhoadses, and my mother, and here we all still were, standing in a geriatric emporium where once there had been a cornfield you could see from the trolley car, part of the poor farm. Our bodies since that earlier conjunction had been considerably worked upon by time – mine enlarged and strengthened, theirs somewhat shrunk and enfeebled, but *here* was what we were, quite animated in our ten minutes of pleasantries.

The Rhoadses' son, Bobby, had been two grades ahead of me in school and often stood with me in the Shillington playground roof-ball line. Indeed, a photograph of such a line exists. Bobby had inherited his father's position as the town's Reformed minister, in a new church built on a street that hadn't existed until the 1950s. My having moved away, first eleven miles and then hundreds, made the Shillington of my boyhood seem more remote than it really was – a mere fraction of a lifetime away, a ship sinking so slowly that many survivors still had their heads above water. Karl Barth, another Reformed clergyman, responding in an interview late in his life to a question about the afterlife, said he imagined it as somehow *this life* in review, viewed in a new light. I had not been as comforted as I wanted to be. For is it not the *singularity* of life that terrifies us? Is not the decisive difference between comedy and tragedy that tragedy denies us another chance? Shakespeare over and over demonstrates life's singularity – the irrevocability of our decisions, hasty and even mad though they be. How solemn and huge and deeply pathetic our life does loom in its once-and-doneness, how inexorably linear, even though our rotating, revolving planet offers us the cycles of the day and of the year to suggest that existence is intrinsically cyclical, a playful spin, and that there will always be, tomorrow morning or the next, another chance.

I hear my mother turn and breathe in her bed. The sleet sprinkles in the fireplace and a mouse scrabbles behind the baseboard beneath the table and the picture of me as a pretty child. My mother knows this mouse; she has told me that in the darkest of her post-fall, bedridden days, he, the mouse, used to come into her bedroom and, standing right there on the floor beside the baseboard, would vigorously make noises, trying to tell her something. His attempt to offer advice amuses her in the telling and she does not yet have the heart, nor perhaps the muscular strength, to set a trap for him.

So here I lie in this damp old Pennsylvania farmhouse listening to an animated mouse. My first artistic love and inspiration was Mickey Mouse – his piping voice, his yellow shoes, his nimble skill on any sort of musical instrument, his patience with Goofy and his courage against Peg-leg Pete, and the way his face would come bursting into Mr Shverha's movie theatre, radiating golden beams to the edges of the screen – and I have taken that jubilant commercial inspiration further than most of my fellow Shillingtonians would have predicted. But perhaps with an undue effort, with an attenuated result. My life behind me feels rickety. My sleeping mother and I seem to be out on a precarious, swaying limb. The house rustles and sighs, I feel up in the air, scared. In our chance encounter, the Rhoadses told me how much I resembled my mother, and I felt slightly offended, as though a dirty secret were being advertised. Standing there in the bright medical center I was aware of the little flecks of psoriasis at the edge of my mother's white hair, and in the wings of her nostrils, and of all the spots of actinic damage mottling her skin, which had once been as smooth and fair as the boy's in the picture. My mother was my future, as well as my past.

Now the dog heaves in its sleep, woofing at some dream-prey, its claws scratching on the soft old pine floorboards. Sleep will not come for me. The house is too noisy, the bed clammy as though I am already dead. I cannot escape myself. The sleet, the fear that we will hit a deer keep revolving in me. My brain buzzes with selfish, scared thoughts. We fall asleep in selflessness, when our thoughts turn self-forgetful. Masturbation and prayer both attempt this; I feel too old for either. I feel forsaken, lost. But when I am not looking, perhaps when I am thinking of the dog's dreams or of the old roof-ball line at the playground, sleep does come. I awake in light, feeling as if my soul has a slight sore throat, my membranes still chafed by the fear of earthly existence. I hear my mother and the dog talking downstairs. She is recovered enough now from her fall to get out of bed in the morning and go downstairs and make breakfast. She has turned on television, which rumbles with the barely suppressible urgency of a new day begun, in Philadelphia and nationally. The morning light gives the pale wallpaper a deep exciting sheen, a subtle luminosity from beneath the surface.

It has snowed during the night; through the window, as I rise to dress and shave, I see an inch or two of snow on the still-green lawn, and on the boughs of the pine tree holding the bird feeder. In this low-ceilinged room the light is antique, preserved from the Philadelphia Avenue house, my first tender winters in it, with their evergreen secret of Christmas. The light holds my first inklings of celebration, of reindeer tracks on the roof, of an embowering wide world arranged for my mystification and entertainment. It has the eggshell tint, the chilly thrilling taste, of my self.

The dread of death comes upon me in futuristic space movies,* and when, in early adolescence, I would read science-fiction, I dreaded those future aeons when I would not be present – an endless succession of days I would miss, with their own news and songs and styles of machine. The future will forget us, or get us slightly wrong, as our history books get the past wrong, and leave out the very texture of life lived now, what James called "the palpable present *intimate* that throbs responsive." Will the future understand, for instance, how much sex, with Freud's stern blessing, meant to us, or how much of our mental energy was spent fending off importunities – on billboards and television, by mail and telephone – to buy something? Or how much of our lives was spent in automobiles, and how largely their little curved caves of painted metal, speeding through a landscape

* " . . . while on the screen some mechanical dragon unfolded its wings or starships did special-effects battle with supposed laser beams, Fulham would be visited by terror: the walls of the theatre would fall away, the sticky floor become a chasm beneath his feet. His true situation in time and space would be revealed to him: a speck of consciousness now into its seventh decade, a mortal body poised to rejoin the minerals, a member of a lost civilization that once existed on a sliding continent. The curvature of the immense Earth beneath his chair and the solidity of the piece of earth that would cover Fulham's grave would become suffocatingly real to him, all in an instant; he would begin to sweat."   – "The Wallet" (1984)

of imploring advertisements and commercial desolation, and the powerful instant responses of their knobs and pedals, and the fine points of their amenities and costliness, and their aura of controlled explosion were part of our coming of age, our mating, our fulfillment of obligations, our thrusts of dreaming? An average American male became a man at the age of sixteen, with his possession of a driver's license, and every seventeen years thereafter he drove the distance to the moon.* Not just the robust but the timid and the crippled and the myopic and the senile and the certifiably insane daily hurtled about on the highways only inches and a flick of the wrist removed from murderous collision. Every pair of hands resting on the steering wheel held the power of death; the wonder is not that accidents occurred but that most of us daily lived through that siege of rushing miles. We even felt, while speeding along, a curious peace. But for a handful of sportsmen and Amish farmers, we had forgotten, in a few generations, the horse, and how ubiquitously horse power, horse manure, horseflesh and horse suffering and the smell and whinny and clip-clop of them had covered the city streets, the same streets we then choked and blanketed with millions of big self-propelled scarabs. The ages of chivalry and romanticism must be imagined from the floating, rocking height of a horse; our age was instead one of crouching behind a wheel, merging in a blur of mirrored others as the gaseous miles melted beneath the pressed accelerator.

Will the future understand our music, how it lulled us in dental chairs and electrified us in dance halls and was so universally applied a varnish to the backdrop of our lives that only the very rich and the unspeakably poor could escape its cloying urgency, its persistent rhythm urging that we move a litte faster, love a little harder? Out of millions of little plastic boxes, young men and women half-intelligibly proclaimed

* 238,855 miles. A recent *National Enquirer* reports, "Men drive an average of 13,962 miles a year, more than double the 6,381 miles driven by women."

some shift in their erotic output or input. Devices were invented whereby music could be carried like a pack of cigarettes and plugged into the ears, so that not a second of life need be spent without its comfort and community.

Music excites us to visions, and vanishes like a generation's bodily secretions. When I watch, say, televised film clips of Bing Crosby, or catch a honeyed bit of Doris Day on a Golden Oldies band, I realize how these singers are taking my life with them, into silence and then grave. And how remarkably young they were, at the time when they appeared ageless giants and set my nerves to tingling from thousands of miles away, from that Los Angeles or New York that exists only in the airwaves and in the mind of the receiver. Stars are young, it turns out; otherwise they would not be smooth enough and quick enough for the intolerant, impatient camera. Most of us, indeed, except for politicians, are young when we make our mark. And then we live and live, with our canes and blood tests and toilet seats fattened like orthopedic shoes.

In myself I observe the very traits that used to irritate me in men of late middle age whom I have known: a forgetfulness, a repetitiveness, a fussiness with parcels and strings, a doddery deliberation of movement mixed with patches of inattention and uncertainty that make my car-driving increasingly hazardous and – other, younger drivers indicate with gestures and honking – irritating to others. I feel also an innocent self-absorption, a ruminativeness that makes me blind and deaf and indifferent to the contemporary trends and fads that are so crucial to the young, invested as these passing twitches are with their own emerging identity and sexuality. My brain cells have accepted their program and are full. I used to find it difficult to talk to my first wife's father, an intelligent and sensitive man, because he didn't seem to be *up* on anything. Now, as I look over *The New Yorker*, its cartoons and "The Talk of the Town" bristle with allusions I don't quite catch, and a psychic music that isn't mine, any more than Thurber's and White's was mine. Part of my value, in the days when I so blithely and rapidly wrote for "The Talk of the Town," was the very youth that I feared might be a disadvantage; I was freshly arrived at the gates of print, helplessly full of the new music. William Maxwell once startled me by asking my advice on the purchase of a jazz record, as if there was something I knew that he didn't. I had assumed that, since he was older, his knowledge would include all of mine. Though we were young in our time, my generation was never exultantly young as the young of the Twenties were, or the Sixties; we never felt youth as an empowerment or as a license to do anything but respectfully escape our elders and then emulate them at a safe distance.

Also like my late Unitarian father-in-law am I now in my amazed, insistent appreciation of the physical world, of this planet with its scenery and weather – that pathetic discovery which the old make that every day and season has its beauty and its uses, that even a walk to the mailbox is a precious experience, that all species of tree and weed have their signature and style and the sky is a pageant of clouds. Aging calls us outdoors, after the adult indoors of work and love-life and keeping stylish, into the lowly simplicities that we thought we had outgrown as children. We come again to love the plain world, its stone and wood, its air and water. "What a glorious view!" my father-in-law would announce as we smirked in the back seat of the car he was inattentively driving. But in truth all views have something glorious about them. The act of seeing is itself glorious, and of hearing, and feeling, and tasting. One of my dead golf partners, Ted Lucas, said once within my hearing to another dear departed fellow golfer, John Conley, "Life is bliss." The remark had come about by I forget what circuitry, but I assume John must have somehow raised the contrary possibility; this was unlike him, for he was a good Catholic as well as a good golfer in his prime, with a smooth takeaway and sound hip motion. Ted also, on another occasion, while we were floundering around in the sunshine on a little friendly nine-hole course called Cape Ann, suddenly exclaimed, "Ah, to be alive, on a June day, in Ipswich, Massachusetts!" The course was actually in Essex, but I knew what he meant – a happiness above and beyond any particular cause for it. I was relatively young, and Ted and John were relatively old, and I was alert, during our Wednesday afternoons together, for what wisdom might fall to me. Ted came originally from New York City and, after what I gathered to have been a rakish early life, converted to Bahaism, and died in an instant, of a heart attack, while making a telephone call from the hospital to say he was being released.

I own many books full of my annotations, proving that once I read them, though I have no memory of it. In writing a sentence some twenty lines above, I had to get up and go ask my wife what the five senses were; I could think of only four. "Smell," she said, when I had named my four. She was in the bathtub, up to her neck in bubbles, and though the bathroom smelled nicely of vitamin-enhanced soap I was not sorry I had suppressed "smell," since of the five senses it delivers most unpleasantness to us, and least well illustrated the point I was trying to make. When I stopped smoking, a whole unwelcome new world of odors came upon me, of dead rats in the wall and what people had eaten for lunch hours before. When I get out of bed in the morning, my own smell surprises me: stale flesh, warmed over. My body's ugly obstinacy in keeping on living strikes me as admirable, like an ungenial but impressive moral position; it makes me, still half-asleep, stop and think.

As I age, I feel my head to be full of holes where once there was electricity and matter, and I wonder if, when my head is all hole, I will feel any more pain of loss than I do now. What we don't know, we don't know: the stoics are right at least about this. Ignorance is a kind of bliss, and senility, like drunkenness, bothers beholders more than the bearer.

My father used to pain and embarrass me greatly by wearing a little wool Navy watch cap;* it kept his head warm, yet also made him look like a cretin, or one of those rummies who tottered around in Reading, up around Seventh Street, the street given over to the railroad tracks. The Reading Railroad hauled anthracite from the coal regions of Schuylkill County to Philadelphia; I can remember standing, as a child, on the Penn Street sidewalk while what seemed miles of coal cars went by. At the turn of the century, at the time of the great anthracite strike, the coal lands were entirely controlled by the railroads and the Reading Company was headed by George F. Baer, one of American business's great self-righteous reactionaries, who wrote to a pro-labor Wilkes-Barre clergyman, in a letter which became public, "The rights and interests of the laboring man will be protected and cared for – not by the labor agitators, but by the Christian men of property to whom God has given control of the property rights of the country, and upon the successful management of which so much depends." Reading had a Socialist mayor while I was growing up, and the old class war between owners and workers, of which distant rumors reached me in my grandfather's stately voice – that, too, is part of my self. As is coal. It would be delivered to our Shillington house via a chute telescoped through the basement window from the truck out by the curb; from the front of the living room, where the Christmas tree stood in its season, I would watch the roaring cascade with a delicious sense of spying and illicit

---

* "On his head he wore a hideous blue knitted cap that he had plucked out of a trash barrel at school. Pulled down over his ears, it made him look like an overgrown dimwit in a comic strip. . . . The streetlight touched with a row of steady flecks the curve of his knit cap: the way Vermeer outlined a loaf of bread. . . . His father's head is a considering shadow pinced into the pinheaded cap that is for Peter the essence of everything obsequious and absurd, careless and stubborn about his father."

– *The Centaur* (1963)

delight; it was like watching Mr Miller approach with his leather pouch and then quickly lying in the front hall underneath the letter slot, where the mail would spill over me. The shiny black lumps, each marked with a red dot that signified good-grade anthracite, poured past under my eyes, like logs over a waterfall, to their riddance in our coal bin, where my grandfather could be heard, early on frosty mornings, shovelling them to their final doom. The coal in its rackety downward slide entranced me but frightened me as well, for we little Pennsylvanians were taught how coal was the compacted vegetation of incredibly ancient times – layer upon layer of giant ferns once as alive and as happy in the sunshine as I. An entire stretch of Paleozoic time, millions and millions of years before even the dinosaurs arose, was named after our state. The thought of it made me feel buried, and forever forgotten.

Now, I wear a watch cap just like my father, all winter, inside the house and out, and though my wife complains that I look foolish I discover, what my father in his turn had discovered, that there is no pain and a certain pleasure in looking foolish. Looking foolish does the spirit good. The need not to look foolish is one of youth's many burdens; as we get older we are exempted from more and more, and float upward in our heedlessness, singing *Gratia Dei sum quod sum*.

My mind is becoming full of holes but enough matrix remains to tap out sentences cheerfully confessing my deterioration. We live by a double standard. Evidence gathered in the light, away from that thermostat in the dark, only carries so far, like newspaper news. We secretly doubt it. As we get older, we go to more and more funerals, and sit there in a stony daze, somehow convinced that it will never happen to us, or if it does, we will be essentially elsewhere.

In church this morning, as I half-listened to the Christmas hymns and the reading of the very unlikely, much-illustrated passage from Luke telling how Gabriel came to Mary and told her that the Holy Ghost would come upon her and the power of the Highest would "overshadow" her and make her pregnant with the Son of God, it appeared to me that when we try in good faith to believe in materialism, in the exclusive reality of the physical, we are asking our selves to step aside; we are disavowing the very realm where we exist and where all things precious are kept – the realm of emotion and conscience, of memory and intention and sensation.

I have the persistent sensation, in my life and art, that I am just beginning.

But no, I am near the end. What is left to say, along these lines of self-consciousness? Of churchgoing, it might be added that it is among other things a social exercise, what small towns have where they lack concert halls and opera houses – a pooling of bodily warmth, in all our clothes, placing our bodies in synchronized positions of abjection, expectation, and celebration, confessing our selves, with an ancient creaky decorum, to one another in the corners of our eyes, as wood and bones and cloth crack and rub and rustle. Church in a small town is one of the places "where the people are," and the only cultural institution dealing in two-thousand-year-old rites and six thousand years of history. We all avert our eyes in going up to take Communion and returning, as if there was something immodest in the act. Both of my wives have had me go to church alone, making me commit a kind of infidelity.

Watching the Olympic Games ice-dancing the other night on television, I was struck by the primordial poetry of a man and woman together – each sex with its different fleshly center of emphasis and style of contour, each with its special biological assignment and evolved social expectations, but partnered, mutually compensatory, supportive and amusing and excitingly, maddeningly strange to each other, together making a single species. As the couples flashed and glided over the ice, intertwining, some sweet brute truth hulked dimly out of our animal past, from near where sex was invented by the algae and ferns, and I wanted to cry in joy, feeling humanity, mine and the ice-dancers', as a spot of warmth within vast dark coldness. The cosmic view materialism opens to our vision has a tragic grandeur, an inexorable unintended gathering of form out of dust. Darwin and Freud have the unsmiling augustness and numen of early church fathers, though they condemn us to trait and trauma, reflex and struggle and final nothingness. They and the great minds of physics have immensely extended the dark side of perceived reality. The universe itself we now know to be, like our individual lives, singular in its career, beginning in the Big Bang and ending in entropy. Our species, too, arose but once, through a set of unreproducible contingencies. And the planet Earth, once endowed, pole to pole, with all sorts of imagined abysses and wonderlands, now is seen as the extensive but finite thing it is, the projected outlines of its seven seas and seven continents confirmed by photographs from high in space. The Amazonian jungle, the very symbol of impenetrability, is displayed in the high perspective as fragile, diminishing, and unique, as vulnerable to the human animal as the buffalo, the whale, and the rhinoceros have been, and the ozone over Antarctica. Things in general take on a tragic once-and-doneness, displacing the ancient comedy, bred of ignorance, of infinite possibility and endless cycle.

Though the phrase "death wish" has passed from favor, there is that in us which seeks rest from the irritation and agitation of life. To be done with the dentist, with twinges and remorses and second thoughts . . . The self is not *only* self-protective and self-extending. It can condone its own end – witness suicides, soldiers, saints. Love and drugs and a good political cause can loom as greater goods than one's own life. Like a heap of loose iron filings, we want to be magnetically lined up. Only a transcendent magnet can do this. "Decimate us!"

* * *

Celebrity, even the modest sort that comes to writers, is an unhelpful exercise in self-consciousness. Celebrity is a mask that eats into the face. As soon as one is aware of being "somebody," to be watched and listened to with extra interest, input ceases, and the performer goes blind and deaf in his overanimation. One can either see or be seen. Most of the best fiction is written out of early impressions, taken in before the writer became conscious of himself as a writer. The best seeing is done by the hunted and the hunter, the vulnerable and the hungry; the "successful" writer acquires a film over his eyes. His eyes get fat. Self-importance is a thickened, occluding form of self-consciousness. The binge, the fling, the trip – all attempt to shake the film and get back under the dining-room table, with a child's beautiful clear eyes.

In my seventeen Ipswich years (during which I drove the distance to the moon), I felt well located artistically, in a place out of harm's – e.g., New York agents' and literary groupies' – way, yet one from which I believed reports would be news. It was a community vivid but transparent to me, exotic but valid as a metaphor, and only I was there to tell its tale. A useful sensation for a writer: to be a spy behind the lines, yet in touch, by passenger pigeon or telegraph wire, with the central switchboard and the paymaster's shack. Other places I have lived (Cambridge, New York, Beverly Farms) have been too trafficked, too well cherished by others, or else, like the environment my mother created in Pennsylvania, need too much special explaining, and don't read simply as America. I had been turned down by the Army but in Ipswich felt enlisted in actual life. Even returning now, to attend a funeral or a wedding, I feel actualized all over again, and "full of myself."

New England. I have been happy here.* For thirty years I have begrudged admitting it, out of loyalty to Pennsylvania. But I found, coming north to college, something flinty and

* "I have been happy at the Divinity School."   – *Roger's Version* (1986)

dry, witty and reticent, complex and venerable, breathable and lucid that suited me. I go south, and in the middle of Connecticut a mugginess takes over, and the sky turns from blue to gray, and there is a human abundance that flattens and masks the earth, and money begins to matter too much. I had not known the sea or the mountains until I came to New England. Lots of writers had been here of old, and had left their signatures on the air like those initials people with diamond rings used to carve on old windowpanes. There are distances in New England, hard to see on the map, that come from the variousness of regions set within a few miles of one another, and from a tact in the people which wordlessly acknowledges another's right to an inner life and private strangeness.

Happiness. Is it a subject? It is best seen out of the corner of the eye. Trying to picture an especially happy self, I come up with a Harvard student – a junior, I think, cockily at home by now in the English department – attending the first day of Professor Hyder Rollins's course in the later Romantic poets. Rollins was a Southerner, tall and thin and white-haired, of a primly pedantic turn of mind; his academic speciality was the "variorum" edition, a word he lovingly pronounced with a distinct prolongation of the third syllable. The idea of reading the tumultuous and short-lived Byron, Keats, and Shelley under the dry guidance of this gentleman of the old school struck me as a wonderfully Harvardian thing to be doing – rarefied and chaste. As I settled into the first lecture, in my one-armed chair, my heart was beating like that of a boy with a pocket heavy with nickels as he walks through the door (which has a bell, to alert the kindly old lady dozing behind the counter) of a candy shop. It would be bliss, I think I thought, to go on forever like this, filling in one's ignorance of English literature slot by slot, poet by poet, under the guidance of tenured wizards, in classrooms dating from the colonial era, while the down-drooping golden-leaved elm branches shivered in the sunlight outside in the Yard.

And the other morning, a Sunday morning, around nine, walking back up my driveway in my churchgoing clothes, having retrieved the Sunday *Globe* from my mailbox, I experienced happiness so sharply I tried to factor it into its components. (1) The Christmas season was over – the presents, the parties, the "overshadowing" – and that was a relief. (2) My wife and I had just made love, successfully all around, which at my age occasions some self-congratulation. (3) It was a perfect winter day, windless, with fresh snow heaped along the driveway by the plow and a cobalt-blue sky precisely fitted against the dormered roof-line of my house. I admired this blank blue sky and was not conscious of my vitreous-humor flecks. (4) Earlier that weekend I had mailed to New York a rather tedious critical piece I had reluctantly undertaken, with much procrastination; after getting out of bed this morning, I had glanced at a page of the photocopy and it seemed more interesting than when I was writing it. It would do. Good riddance. (5) I had the easy beginnings of preparing the final draft of this long-savored and -contemplated book ahead of me. (6) A visit from my daughter and son-in-law and two grandsons was scheduled for that afternoon. I take an idle aesthetic delight in my grandsons I was too busy to spare my children, except when they were asleep. (7) Or was it simply that I was walking back to enjoy the *Globe*'s sports headlines, Arts Section, and *Spider Man* (the only one of the "funnies" I still follow, as he juggles his tingling "spider sense," his improbable double career as a student and professional photographer, and now his marriage to the voluptuous Mary Jane), while I consumed my variable breakfast of Erewhon New England Style Honey Almond Granola and orange juice? Can happiness be simply a matter of orange juice?

* * *

For all the physical handicaps, neurotic symptoms, aberrant thought patterns, and characterological limitations touched upon in these pages, I think of myself, and believe that I "present" (as psychoanalysts say) to others, as an amiable, reasonable, interested, generally healthy, sexually normal, dependable, hopeful, fortunate human being. Which goes to show what a vexed thing even a fortunate human being is.

Surprisingly few clues are ever offered us as to what kind of people we are. Carlton Boyer said I had an excellent compositional sense. Ernie Rothermel said I had exceptionally large nerves, which gave a certain stylishness to my sufferings in his chair. Peggy Lutz once told me I had nice shoulders (maybe it was the only nice thing she could think to say). A woman seated behind me in the bleachers at a football game accidentally touched the hair on my head and exclaimed, "*Oh* – so soft!" At Harvard, playing the associational word game called "Botticelli," I was, unknown to me, the subject, and in asking for an identifying animal was told, by Manfred Karnovsky, who as a professor of biology would certainly have known, "A sloth – please don't misunderstand me – a nice, good-tempered sloth." The modifier "good-tempered" came up again when my second wife, in my startled hearing, told the producer of a TV show focused on me that I was the best-tempered person she had ever known. If I am good-tempered, it must be the daily venting of words that makes me so, because as a child I often felt irate and frantic, and have fought all my life sensations of being smothered and confined, misunderstood and put-upon.

We assume that only children are spoiled and pampered; but they also are made to share adult perspectives. Possibly the household that nurtured me was a distracted and greedy one – in severe Depression-shock – which asked me to grow up too early; at some point I acquired an almost unnatural willingness to make allowances for other people, a kind of ready comprehension and forgiveness that amounts to disdain, a good temper won by an inner remove. If I'm nice and good, you'll leave me alone to read my comic books. Have I ever loved a human being as purely as I loved Mickey Mouse or, a bit later in latency, Captain Marvel and Plastic Man?

Even toward myself, as my own life's careful manager and promoter, I feel a touch of disdain. Precociously conscious of the precious, inexplicable burden of selfhood, I have steered my unique little craft carefully, at the same time doubting that carefulness is the most sublime virtue. He that gains his life shall lose it.

In this interim of gaining and losing, it clears the air to disbelieve in death and to believe that the world was created to be praised. But I inherited a skeptical temperament. My father believed in science ("Water is the great solvent") and my mother in nature. She looked and still looks to the plants and the animals for orientation, and I have absorbed the belief that when in doubt we should behave, if not like monkeys, like "savages" – that our instincts and appetites are better guides, for a healthy life, than the advice of other human beings. People are fun, but not quite serious or trustworthy in the way that nature is. We feel safe, huddled within human institutions – churches, banks, madrigal groups – but these concoctions melt away at the basic moments. The self's responsibility, then, is to achieve rapport if not rapture with the giant, cosmic other: to appreciate, let's say, the walk back from the mailbox.